Some of the back cover quotations

My mom was always very quiet about what had happened to her in residential school - I remember the hushed tones between her and her sisters and cousins. And it took a while until I realized, for instance, that she had actually gone to two residential schools. Later, I realized too that my dad had also gone, and that in fact they had been at the same school for a year. That's where they met and fell in love. My mom spoke of abject loneliness and a deep anger at the injustice of being forbidden, at age ten, to leave school and go home for her father's funeral. My dad, who got very animated when he spoke of being taken, talked about "duking it out" with a Brother who tried to subjugate him as he shoveled coal into the school's huge furnace.

As an Honorary Witness of the Truth and Reconciliation Commission, I know that the stories of survival in this book are sacred. Though the words are uncomfortable and sad, they are stories we must all stop and hear. We must see beyond the horrors of adults' cruelty in residential schools to the resilience of our relatives - our cousins. They survived this depravity, they reconciled what came to pass, and they are here to push us further, enriching and strengthening us, in these words. They deserve nothing but respect.

Soon it will be up to us to remember and re-tell these stories. I take my role as a Witness and re-teller of this residential school story series. I hope you will too.

Dr. Evan *Tlesla II* Adams, Tla'amin Nation (Coast Salish)
Deputy Chief Medical Officer, Indigenous Services Canada
Actor, Thomas-Builds-the-Fire in *Smoke Signals*

These previously unwritten stories of lived, traumatized experiences are testament to the storytellers' courage and strength and resilience. When the rich Cree traditional and spiritual relationship with land and with family is harmed by separation, hatred, and fear - a harm resulting in anger and loss of values, identity, and self-worth - these storytellers find ways to heal. Through their stories, you learn about culture as treatment, about the power of forgiveness and love, and about peaceful co-existence in community as essential to healing, belief, and advancing true reconciliation.

> Chief Willie Littlechild, Ermineskin Cree Nation
> Former Truth and Reconciliation Commissioner
> Former residential school student athlete
> Order of Canada; Order of Sport
> Member of Sports Halls of Fame, Canada and North America

This is a difficult but necessary book. There's a power to truth and to the realities of the Indian Residential School system, but for those wanting to see strength and movement toward hope, this is the book for you. These stories hold that hope close to the heart. What shines through is a love of the land, a love of community, a love of the Cree language, a love of family – exactly what colonial forces like the IRS system tried to destroy but couldn't.

> Conor Kerr, Metis/Ukrainian author, *Avenue of Champions*
> Giller Prize longlist

To Vesna,

E nâtamukw miyeyimuwin

Residential School Recovery Stories of the James Bay Cree

Volume One

May these stories resonate—

Stories by James Bay Cree Storytellers

Written by Ruth DyckFehderau

Ruth DyckFehd

ᒥᔅᐋᓂᐱᔨᐊᐤ ᐊᐧᐋᐤᐱᕐᐦᒌᑕᕐᐳᐤ

CONSEIL CRI DE LA SANTÉ ET DES SERVICES SOCIAUX DE LA BAIE JAMES
CREE BOARD OF HEALTH AND SOCIAL SERVICES OF JAMES BAY

Funding for this publication was provided in part by Health Canada.

The opinions expressed in this publication are those of the storytellers and do not necessarily reflect the official views of Health Canada or of Cree Board of Health and Social Services of James Bay.

Some names and details in this book have been changed for the purpose of protecting identities. Any similarities between these changed names/details and real persons, living or dead, is not intended.

Printed and bound in Canada by Houghton Boston Printers, Saskatoon, Saskatchewan. Distributed by Wilfrid Laurier University Press: wlupress.wlu.ca

Cover artwork by Natasia Mukash of Whapmagoostui, QC.
Cover art based on photograph taken by David DyckFehderau of Edmonton, AB.
Cover and timeline designs by Cameron Mosimann of Edmonton, AB.
Illustrations done by Tristan Shecapio-Blacksmith, Jared Linton, Lexie Mîkun Saganash, Riley Bosum, and Nathaniel Bosum (James Bay Cree youth).
Main text set in Verdana font, chosen for its readability. Story title font created by Nicole Ritzer of Mistissini, QC, based on alphabets written by Payton Linton and Parker Linton.
Map adapted from official Cree Board of Health and Social Services map and from Atlas of Canada's *Distribution of Freshwater - Glaciers and Icefields* map (licensed under the Open Government Licence - Canada).
Printed on Forest Stewardship Council-certified paper, acid- and chlorine-free, with post-consumer recycled fibres.

resschoolrecovery.org | creehealth.org

Available in audiobook format.

Library and Archives Canada Cataloguing in Publication

Title: E nâtamukw miyeyimuwin : residential school recovery stories of the James Bay Cree / stories, James Bay Cree storytellers ; written, Ruth DyckFehderau.
Names: DyckFehderau, Ruth, author. | Cree Board of Health and Social Services of James Bay, publisher.
Description: Includes bibliographical references.
Identifiers: Canadiana 20220421234 | ISBN 9781989796238 (softcover)
Subjects: CSH: First Nations—Québec (Province)—Nord-du-Québec—Residential schools. | CSH: First Nations—Education—Québec (Province)—Nord-du-Québec. | CSH: First Nations—Québec (Province)—
Nord-du-Québec—Biography. | LCGFT: Autobiographies.
Classification: LCC E96.65.Q8 D93 2023 | DDC 371.829/973230714115—dc23

Storytellers

Johnny Neeposh

Diana Prince*

Mary Shecapio-Blacksmith

Marni Macbeane*

Shiikun*

Albert Johnny*

George Blacksmith

Harriet Snowe*

Rita Gilpin

Leslie Tomatuk

Alfred and Hattie Coonishish

George Shecapio

Lloyd Cheechoo

Juliette Rabbitskin

Matthew Loon

Wally Rabbitskin

Ally Lowell*

Silvester Stalone*

Thomas Chakapash

Names changed to protect identities.

Illustrators

Tristan Shecapio-Blacksmith

Jared Linton

Lexie Mîkun Saganash

Riley Bosum

Nathaniel Gordon Sam Bosum

This book has been designed to be user friendly for people with print disabilities, tired or low vision, and diabetes-related impairments. The shape is square-ish so that it lies flat on a table. The cover coating makes the book easier to grip for people who have lost sensation in their hands or who have lost fingers. The paper is bright but not reflective and the pages are mostly undecorated. The paragraphs have deep and even indents, the characters are kerned and modified as little as possible, and the Verdana font and generous spacing are recommended by the Canadian National Institute for the Blind in their Clear Print Guidelines.

Contents

For the storytellers of Eeyou Istchee
who remember

Listen. If you don't listen, you're like a tied-up dog, walking in circles, always seeing the same things, never knowing more than you know now.

- Tommy Neeposh

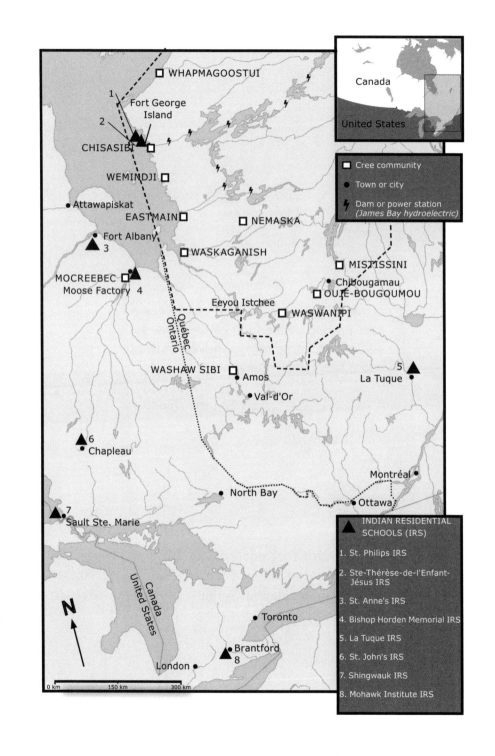

WHAPMAGOOSTUI

1

Fort George
Island

2

CHISASIBI

WEMINDJI

Attawapiskat

EASTMAIN

NEMASKA

Fort Albany
3

WASKAGANISH

MOCREEBEC
Moose Factory 4

MISTISSINI

Chibougamau

OUJÉ-BOUGOUMOU

Eeyou Istchee

WASWANIPI

Québec
Ontario

WASHAW SIBI

Amos

5
La Tuque

Val-d'Or

6
Chapleau

Montréal

North Bay

Ottawa

7
Sault Ste. Marie

Canada
United States

N

Toronto

Brantford
8

London

0 km   150 km   300 km

Canada

United States

Cree community

Town or city

Dam or power station
(James Bay hydroelectric)

INDIAN RESIDENTIAL
SCHOOLS (IRS)

1. St. Philips IRS

2. Ste-Thérèse-de-l'Enfant-
   Jésus IRS

3. St. Anne's IRS

4. Bishop Horden Memorial IRS

5. La Tuque IRS

6. St. John's IRS

7. Shingwauk IRS

8. Mohawk Institute IRS

Notes About This Book

THE CREE title of this book, *E nâtamukh miyeyimuwin,* is not easy to translate. A few times now, I have listened as James Bay Cree speakers and translators mulled over exactly how to say it in English.

"It sort of means *going forward to a good place of peace,*" they say. "Except that the Cree *going forward* is stronger, more energetic than *going.* It's almost *working.* And *place of peace* also means *comfort.* And *calm.* And *serene.* And *still.* And *home.* And *safe.* You know," they conclude, as their voices trail off, "it doesn't really translate..."

What you have in your hands is a book of stories telling how twenty James Bay Cree of Northern Québec experienced and are recovering from Canada's Indian Residential School genocide, how they are moving toward that *good place* that doesn't really translate. Each story was told to me by a James Bay Cree storyteller who was affected by Indian Residential Schools (IRS) either because she or he attended personally, or because a family member attended and brought those experiences home. In telling their own stories, they are also showing how their families and communities are *going forward to a good place of peace.*

My role in this community project is to gather and write the stories, but the material itself is owned and controlled by the formal health entity of the James Bay Cree, Cree Board of Health and Social Services of James Bay (CBHSSJB). Elsewhere, a book of stories like this one might fall under Arts or History or Literature or Humanities instead of Health. But in Eeyou Istchee, as in many Indigenous settings, medicine and story are one and the same.

Primarily this record is a James Bay Cree community project intended for Indigenous people to share, amongst themselves, ways of healing. It is meant to do the work that Talking Circles do: to make space for stories to be told and heard, and for information to be shared and processed. Talking Circles are inherently respectful, interactive, supportive forums, as we intend this book to be. A secondary intended audience is any non-Indigenous reader ready to know more about this profoundly influential chapter of Canadian history that was for so long concealed, a chapter in which Indian Residential Schools were used as genocidal practice, a chapter for which key parties have still not taken responsibility. As survivor Russell Moses said in 1965, when asked by Indian Affairs to write about his Brantford Mohawk IRS experiences, "[I]f I were to be honest, I must tell things as they were and really this is not my story but yours."

As writer, my own intention in this project is to honour the storytellers and their remarkable stories.

The James Bay Cree of Northern Québec call themselves Eeyou (*Cree of the Interior*) and Eenou (*Cree of the Coasts of Eastern James Bay and Southeastern Hudson Bay*). The urban Cree population in Québec is sizable, but most Québec Cree still live on the Northern territory of Eeyou Istchee (or *the People's Land*). Their traditional land region is large, nearly 450 000 km², approximately the size of Germany and Austria combined. They use the entire region as Elders and archaeologists say they have done for over

8000 years. To put that number into perspective, the famous pre-historic site Stonehenge was built about 5000 years ago.

Currently, Eeyou Istchee includes eleven Cree Nations (out of 634 First Nations in Canada), each with a distinct history and culture. They are (clockwise on the map, starting with the furthest south) the Cree Nation of Washaw Sibi, MoCreebec Cree Nation, the Cree Nation of Waskaganish, the Cree Nation of Eastmain, the Cree Nation of Wemindji, the Cree Nation of Chisasibi, Whapmagoostui First Nation, the Cree Nation of Nemaska, the Cree Nation of Mistissini, Oujé-Bougoumou Cree Nation, and the Cree First Nation of Waswanipi. Together, the Nations make a population of approximately 20 000. At time of writing, the Nations of MoCreebec and Washaw Sibi are not yet part of the James Bay and Northern Québec Agreement (JBNQA, the treaty affecting Eeyou Istchee) and, in fact, MoCreebec is located on traditional Eeyou Istchee lands that stretch into Northern Ontario. When we speak of Eeyou Istchee in this book, the community of MoCreebec is included but other Ontario lands are not.

Several Cree languages and dialects are spoken across Eeyou Istchee, but the James Bay Cree of Northern Québec are rigourously protecting, using, teaching, and publishing in two languages: Southern East Cree (Inland) and Northern East Cree (Coastal). The Cree half of our title, *E nâtamukh miyeyimuwin,* is the same in both languages. Unfortunately, because IRS focussed heavily on Indigenous language eradication, and because language recovery is difficult and costly, the other Eeyou Istchee languages and dialects are being used less and less.

Already as far back as the 1620s, there were mission schools in Canada for Indigenous children. But the Indian Residential School system as we know it began in 1831, when Mohawk Institute in Brantford, ON, began taking students, and it grew steadily and dramatically. While the Government of Canada authorized the IRS system, funded the Schools, and made some attempts to control them, for decades they were administered by Churches and often eluded Government control. The Church denominations involved in running Schools were Roman Catholic, Anglican, Methodist, United, Presbyterian, Non-Denominational, Mennonite, and Baptist. The conditions, rife with disease, neglect, and abuse, were so desperate that in 1913, discussing the last forty-five years of IRS, Duncan Campbell Scott, Deputy Superintendent of Indian Affairs, noted that "[F]ifty per cent of the children who passed through these schools did not live to benefit from the education which they had received therein." Nevertheless, just seven years later, in 1920, with the Schools failing in all education metrics, the Government Department of Indian Affairs bowed to considerable pressure from the Churches (who received funds per student) and made IRS attendance mandatory for all Indigenous children in Canada. In 1969, the Government ended the partnership with the Churches and took over the Schools, and immediately began the long process of shutting the system down and integrating Indigenous students into public schools. In the late 1980s, Canadian legal systems began responding to IRS abuse charges, and many non-Indigenous Canadians heard about the atrocities for the first time. Gradually, public awareness of the Schools and their abuses increased, Indigenous Nations took increasing control of Indigenous education, and the last School closed in 1997.

As of today, according to the IRS Settlement Official Court Website, 139 Schools have been deemed officially Indian Residential Schools. This number excludes many Schools, such as Schools in Newfoundland and Labrador, or Schools relying upon provincial or Church funding. The actual number of Schools, then, is closer to 200.

In the Residential School context, the word "Schools" is misleading. On paper, they were boarding schools meant to fulfill treaty obligations of providing Western education to Indigenous peoples of Canada. In reality, and on papers now archived, the Schools existed for other reasons: to control Indigenous Nations through controlling the children, thereby preventing uprisings while colonizers stole Indigenous lands; to provide missionary expansion opportunities and resource and employment streams to the Churches (Church denominations competitively built Schools and/or competed to control them); to eradicate Indigenous cultures and languages altogether; and, to assimilate Indigenous peoples into the colonizer culture not as equals but as a labourer-servant class. For most of IRS history, the Schools were primarily workhouses, "teaching" manual labour, light industry, domestic work, and religion. Many IRS "teachers" did not even speak the language they were "teaching." While individual student experiences varied throughout IRS history, and while some individual staff clearly tried to provide genuine education and ethical care, the Schools very quickly became places of disease, hunger, abuse, death, and, above all, fear.

Eeyou Istchee is remote. Not all communities have road access. And the Eeyou and Eenou are travellers, never in the same place for long. Even now, settled in communities with permanent addresses, most James Bay Cree spend months on the land, moving between camps with the seasons. As a result, the James Bay Cree of Northern Québec came to the Schools much later than many other Indigenous Nations partly because they were harder to reach. More than a century after the first IRS opened, airlines like Austin Airways began servicing Northern Québec, and soon after, James Bay Cree children were taken for the Schools. For some of the older storytellers, who noted that trauma piles up over generations, this late introduction was an important point of gratitude.

I am often asked why an outsider is writing these intimate Cree stories. It's a good question. This is the second major book project on which I have worked with CBHSSJB, the first being *The Sweet Bloods of Eeyou Istchee: Stories of Diabetes and the James Bay Cree* (2017), now in *Second Edition* and undergoing translation into Northern East Cree, Southern East Cree, Ojibwe, and French. Certainly anyone who has spent time in Eeyou Istchee knows there are many skilled and accomplished Cree writers who could do this work with more insight than any outsider.

Most CBHSSJB administrative decisions, by far, are made in the Cree language(s) and I don't speak Cree. There may well be reasons for my participation in this project about which I know nothing. What I do know is that for trauma stories, as quite a few stories in this book are, CBHSSJB sometimes hires outside writers because, as one of my supervisors said, "Our own have enough to carry." Indeed, some Eeyou Istchee trauma story projects have been stopped, paused, or prevented because of how participants were being affected. Deliberately assigning an outsider to write these stories, then, is an act of care, of allowing difficult stories to be recorded while putting some of the trauma recovery work on someone who has lived in Eeyou Istchee but who is not Indigenous.

That said, in Eeyou Istchee, Cree story traditions are thriving. IRS stories are mostly being passed on in traditional ways, in the Cree language, orally, from parent or grandparent to child. They are being passed on in Talking Circles around the territory and at Cree gatherings like the annual Fort George Residential School Gathering. They are being passed on from Elders to students in Cree classrooms and on the land. And they are being passed on in materials held at the Aanischaaukamikw Cree Cultural Institute and other Indigenous cultural centres. A quick internet search will show that they are also being passed on in films, documentaries, and other forms.

The stories in this compilation have been told to me by three main groups of James Bay Cree: people who want their stories in a book, as traditional Cree storytelling happens orally and rarely in print; people who want their stories shared outside of Eeyou Istchee to non-Indigenous readers; and people who want to share their stories but who wish to keep their identities hidden even from other Cree community members.

Storytellers who fall into this last group and choose to hide their identities here do so for various reasons. Some want to control when their children or grandchildren learn about their IRS history and prevent the kinds of night terrors that young children can have. Some mean to protect other IRS survivor family members who are struggling with the aftermath of their own experiences. Some storytellers hold community positions that prevent them from speaking freely about their experiences because doing so might cast another community member in a harsh light. Some storytellers don't want to be found and subsequently hounded on social media. And some don't reveal their identities simply because they are private people.

Although I didn't know it at the time, our previous book, *The Sweet Bloods of Eeyou Istchee: Stories of Diabetes and the James Bay Cree*, was something of a pilot project for this book, first in a series. In that project, we determined approximately what length a story in a book like this should be. We determined that this format – creative nonfiction in a short-story structure with third-person narration – resonated with storytellers more than, say, word-for-word interviews or news journalism. And we learned that accessible design for the printed book was vital if we wanted those James Bay Cree readers who struggle to see print and to read conventionally designed books to be able to read it.

For this project, when I enter a community, we advertise the project in public places (radio shows, bulletin boards, etc.) and I collect information about supports available in that community to IRS survivors: Elders, counsellors and psychologists, Government programs, traditional healing, back-to-the-land programs, twenty-four-hour call-in lines, and so forth. The James Bay Cree have been working on Residential School recovery for a long time and every community has designed its own supports. Then, one way or another, storytellers let me know they want to participate. We do not aim for a representative cross-section of any demographic. I meet with anyone who wants to tell their story.

These aren't interviews as much as informal conversations. If the storyteller agrees, I will record the conversation. If not, I will take notes. And if they prefer me not to take notes, I listen as carefully as I can and madly scribble all I remember immediately after. The conversation takes its natural course and I don't try to direct it. In particular, I don't press for more detail or information surrounding traumatic events. The storytellers say what they feel they can say. In some cases, if they are not comfortable in the English language, we use sketches to aid in communication. Sometimes they teach me a Cree word or two.

Hearing a story can take as little as forty-five minutes or as much as several days until the storyteller seems finished. Storytellers always have the option of speaking through a translator or with a support person present, though no one has yet taken either option. When we part ways, the storytellers have a list of emotional supports available in their community. Inevitably they know more about them than I do.

After hearing the story, I go to my home to write it up. I try to craft it in a way that resonates with the storyteller's account, with the teller her or himself, and with the emotions that filled the room when I heard it.

With a draft in hand, I return to the community. I sit down again with the storyteller – in a territory as large as Eeyou Istchee, reconnecting with storytellers months later can be a significant challenge – and we review the story together, line by line. At this point, storytellers often add, remove, or adjust details. We repeat this process as often as necessary until the storyteller is satisfied with the story. At each stage, I delete the notes and recordings and drafts of the previous stage so that the approved story is the only remaining record and any private details that came up in conversation are again unrecorded.

Even though we go to lengths to ensure the stories are accurate to what the storytellers expressed, a document the size of a book will have errors in it. And, since I am not Cree, there are inevitably nuances and subtleties that have not translated, that I am unable to put on the page.

I heard some things many times. First, storytellers spoke often of healing – but they spoke just as often of addressing injustices. Healing is important, they said, and often a sign of substantial inner strength, but that someone has healed, or alternately, that someone has forgiven, does not mean that justice is done or that reconciliation has in any way been accomplished. Second, they expressed frequent concern about their stories spilling over into the stories of other people. Occasionally, then, you as reader might come across a paragraph with a more distant tone, or a certain amount of vagueness, because the storyteller asked for details to be removed in order to respect someone else's story. We have also sometimes been deliberately vague about which community is at the centre of a story. And third, I heard from nearly all storytellers that they were participating in this project because they thought it might help someone else.

A few other relevant notes.

Because White culture, Government, Churches, and Residential Schools function as proper nouns for most storytellers, we have capitalized them here.

The "Stories Heard Along the Way" are just that – stories I or another participant heard in hockey arenas and airplanes and tents and conference rooms and kitchens across Eeyou Istchee in the years this project has been underway. We did not confirm them for accuracy. And the "Records" pages present material from existing records that reveals discussions and exchanges, often in Government settings, relevant to these stories.

If a storyteller passed away after telling me her or his story but before we were able to print it, we approached the family for permission to print, even though the storyteller had already approved the final version.

We intend another two or three books after this one. And we hope to release one every few years until there are a total of three or four volumes.

It's difficult to communicate the magnitude of what each story is. For most storytellers, the act of telling came at significant personal cost. We made the process as gentle and as respectful as we could, but for no one, not one single storyteller, did telling the story appear to be easy. In fact, for several storytellers, telling their story here was the first time they had *ever* spoken of their IRS experiences.

And take heart. Though there is brutality in the pages that follow – the entire book comes with a trigger warning – there is also laughter and joy. These stories come to you from the *good places of peace* these storytellers have worked hard to reach.

To them, I have more gratitude than I can say.

Ruth DyckFehderau
Writer
August 2022

For a while, Johnny watched from a safe distance.

Artist: Jared Linton

Johnny Neeposh

JOHNNY spends quite a bit of time out on the redirected Rupert River where his land used to be. He sits in his boat on the water and thinks about his grandmother, his mother, about how they lived on this land that's now under water. He thinks about things that happened to him when he was a young boy and what they meant. And about his father. He thinks often about his father. Memories come easily these days.

"Stop!"

Four-year-old Johnny stopped instantly. He looked down at his feet. His dad's voice had a warning tone but Johnny was standing on the thick ice of the river. Everything looked fine. Confused, he looked over at his father.

"Use your ice chisel to test the ice in front of you."

Johnny pulled his chisel out of his leather sack, then he squatted down and raised his arm high. It was the dead of winter, the ice was hard, and he was little. He would need all of his strength to make a dent. He rammed the chisel down – and it burst right through! His glove was soaked. Another step and he would have gone under the ice.

He sucked in a lungful of cold air and stepped gingerly backwards onto thicker ice. Then he looked at his dad again.

"There and there, about four feet across." His dad gestured along the ice. "In the wintertime, that's where the currents run. They don't run straight. They zig-zag like a creek down the river. Even at thirty below, the ice is thin. It's thick over here though."

Later, back in their cabin, Johnny lay safe in his bed beside his sister and looking up at the baby moss roof. How was it that his father knew exactly where – on that wide, snow-covered river that looked the same all the way across – were the four feet of thin ice? His lungs chilled again when he thought how close he had come.

His father's lessons were always like that. Practical, straight-forward, but with something to make you think for a long time.

A few months later, at the end of summer, Johnny and his family were at McLeod Point on Lake Mistassini. Other families were there too. For a few days now, ever since the Indian Agent and Royal Canadian Mounted Police had visited, the camp had been quiet, somber. Like everyone was waiting for something bad to happen.

"It's here," someone said.

A black machine, the strangest thing Johnny had ever seen, glided out of the clouds, buzzing like an insect, and landed on the water. The side opened. RCMP men with sticks and guns stepped out.

"That's your airplane, Johnny," his dad said. "You're going with those men."

Johnny looked at his dad. "I'm – what?"

"It'll be okay. All these boys are going. You're going to School."

His voice seemed less certain than usual, but Johnny didn't question him. Instead, he obediently followed the other Cree boys down to the shore and into the belly of the black plane. He sat where the men told him to sit.

The airplane was a World War II bomber, the older boys said, and they pointed to where the bomb workings used to be. The thin metal on which they sat cross-legged was actually the bomb bay door. When the plane took off, Johnny felt the cold air currents

Johnny Neeposh

right through the door and through his pants. The door was made to open and drop things out. Johnny hugged his knees to his chest and hoped the hinges would hold until the plane landed on Moose River, that he wouldn't burst right through.

Up until then, Johnny's dad had always been right – but Moose Factory Bishop Horden Memorial Indian Residential School was not okay at all. Oh, the classroom stuff was fine. The lessons weren't as practical as his dad's lessons on the land, but they were interesting. It was the other stuff that was not okay. Even now, it's hard to believe how not okay it all was.

On one of the first days there, Johnny approached one of the adults, a supervisor.

"Please sir, I'm hungry," he said. "May I have some bannock?"

He didn't know much English yet, so the sentence had some Cree words.

The supervisor reached around – and gently grabbed Johnny's collar. Then he half-pulled half-carried him around the corner and down the hall to a closet where he pushed him in, along with a bucket for a toilet and nothing to eat or drink, and locked the door. *Click.*

Two days later, he opened it again. Johnny was so dehydrated that he barely felt his body fall to the floor. The supervisor picked him up and set him on his feet.

"Don't you dare tell anyone about this," he whispered.

Another day, another Cree word, and another supervisor lashed a thick leather strap across his open hand. The impact broke Johnny's little finger. He wasn't allowed to have it set, and it healed permanently broken.

Other days he was made to scrub a toilet or a floor with a toothbrush and then to brush his teeth with that same toothbrush.

Once, Johnny was eating supper, and he saw a supervisor pull a leather strap from inside his priest's robe, silently approach a boy from behind, raise it high and, with all his strength, lash it down, across that boy's back. No warning. The air went right out of Johnny. What had the boy done wrong?

After the supervisor had moved on to the next table, the boy beside Johnny leaned over and whispered, "He was eating too slowly."

Johnny came to expect the violence. It might happen because he broke a rule he didn't know about or he said a Cree word – but just as often it happened because a teacher didn't like him. A couple of the teachers really didn't like Johnny.

Once, back home, when Johnny was very young, his dad had spanked him. Johnny had caught a good-sized frog and his sister was standing right there and so he threw it at her. *Splat.* It had seemed like a fine idea – but his father saw, put him over his knee, and swatted him once.

"Enough!" Johnny's mom said, and his dad's hand stopped mid-air.

Later, Johnny couldn't sit. His mom lowered his pants and looked at his bum. Johnny twisted his head around to see. There was his dad's handprint right across it. She called his father over then.

"Look what you did," she said.

His dad was horrified. "How is that possible? It was a light swat!" he said. "Frustrated people hit harder than they think," she said, "and that's why we never hit kids."

He never hit Johnny again.

But the priests at Bishop Horden Memorial Indian Residential School thought differently. They weren't horrified at what their punishments did. Instead they smiled, as if the scars should be there.

Johnny lived for the summers. In June, the plane flew the Schoolboys home again. His dad picked Johnny up at the plane and first thing they all did was paddle up the lake and get right down to catching fish. His dad showed him how to catch and clean a fish,

JOhnnY NeerOSh

and his mom showed him how to smoke it. They hunted game, big and small. With each animal, his dad showed him how to butcher. A muskrat had to be cut up differently than a beaver and a caribou had to be cut up differently yet again. His dad knew anatomy, how the muscles and tendons and ligaments worked. He showed Johnny how they connected to one another and made him name the organs and joints as he worked. Some glands, like those that helped an animal fight infection, had to be cut out right away, within minutes of death, or all the meat would spoil.

And then there were snares. Johnny *hated* the snares. A rabbit caught in a snare could chew through the rope and escape so Johnny's task was to make the rope smell so awful that the rabbit wouldn't go near it, no matter what. The way to do that was to smear the rope, cover it completely, with dog poo. It was poo. It was *disgusting.* Johnny pushed his tongue out and curled his nose. His dad laughed at him then, and picked up a handful of poo himself and helped Johnny to smear it. Even later, when Johnny ate his mother's wonderful rabbit and dumplings, he didn't think it was worth the trouble.

Out there on the land, Johnny and his dad often sat on shore, leaning against a tree, looking out on the sparkling lake. Johnny told him everything about School, holding nothing back. His dad listened. Sometimes he asked questions. Often he was completely silent, his eyes shiny.

"Our language is our lifeblood," he whispered. "Why do they want to take it?"

Then he talked about respect. Every person needed it, even if that person locked you in a closet for speaking Cree. Even if that person didn't respect you. Respect was why the family sometimes attended Church, his father said. He believed the Old Ways himself but he went to Church and sometimes even walked up for altar calls so that the Pentecostals could feel better about themselves, feel respected.

Often he talked about the Chain of the Nation, the ways each generation linked to the next. "If we let it break," he said, "we lose everything." And under reddened cheeks he admitted that if Johnny didn't attend School, the temple of disrespect, the Indian Agent would starve them. Flour, sugar, rice, oats, even the powdered eggs Johnny loved, they'd all be taken away. Then his brothers and sisters would have only hunted meat to eat, and, since the Agent controlled ammunition, they would soon not even have that. Every spring, they heard about another such family found dead in their tents, starved to death over the long winter. He blamed himself, he said, that he had not yet found a better way.

They talked often. With each conversation, Johnny healed a little more.

And saw that his father was also trapped by the White people.

And then, in August, it was back to the black bomber plane, back to School where things kept getting worse.

One day, early in term, Johnny and a friend tried to run away. They didn't get far before they were caught and brought back.

Every day after that, a priest forced Johnny's feet into a special pair of shoes that were much shorter than his feet and had extra laces down the side. First curling the toes under, the priest carefully wrapped the shoes around Johnny's feet and laced them as tightly as he could. He did the same to Johnny's friend. Then he made the boys stand by the wall in the special shoes for hours and hours. Each day, the priest pushed the toes further under and laced the shoes tighter, and each day Johnny stood there beside his friend as their feet grew more misshapen. At first Johnny's feet hurt more than anything had ever hurt before but, after some time, they went numb and he felt nothing in his feet at all. In front of the priest he didn't cry about it. But he couldn't wait to get home.

In June, just before it was time to leave, a supervisor brought Johnny a paper. If Johnny didn't sign it, he said, he couldn't board

JOhnnY NeepOSh

the plane to go home. Johnny recognized the paper. Some of his friends had signed the same one before a School trip and he had never seen them again. He was desperate to see his parents so he took the pen and signed. Then he clambered onto the black plane – his feet were now too broken to walk up the ramp – and went home.

At home, his parents met the plane. Johnny had never been so happy to see them and couldn't stop laughing. But his father's face, as he watched Johnny hobble down the ramp, leaning on another boy for support, was stone. He walked forward and picked him up, hugged him close, and carried him out to the canoe where his mom sat quietly with wet cheeks.

Off they all paddled, up the lake to catch fish. The trees smelled wonderful. The lake was clear. Fish were jumping and birds flew free. Johnny was home.

Out there, under their tree at the side of the lake, Johnny's father examined his feet. He felt along the bones and ligaments, he twisted the feet this way and that, he pressed up into the arch and under the toes that now grew permanently under the main foot in the direction of the heel. His face was unreadable.

"We can fix this," he finally said. "For now, wear moccasins and begin stretching your feet back. It will hurt. In wintertime, we'll use snowshoes to fix them the rest of the way."

Moccasins made sense – Johnny couldn't wear regular shoes anymore at all. But how was he going to use snowshoes in wintertime? At School? In class? He wondered, but he didn't ask.

Johnny's dad asked more questions then, about the special shoes, about standing for hours, day after day, week after week, about how long it took for the feet to go numb.

"This was very dangerous," he said. "When your feet went numb, the blood circulation to them stopped. In that situation, things can happen in the veins that can kill you. You could have died. Now tell me more about this paper you signed."

Johnny talked about the paper and the kids who didn't come back.

"The Elders said something like this was coming," he said. And then he was quiet.

Things were different that summer. At age twelve, Johnny had to learn to walk again, as his feet gradually and painfully took their shape once more. But even so, his parents seemed to be teaching him more than ever how to live on the land by himself, without any help. Here was a wolverine footprint. There was the scat of a skunk. This was how you made a medicine from a certain weasel part and this was what you drank if you were bleeding badly and needed the wound to clot quickly. The flesh of that animal would draw the heat from a burn and the sap from this tree applied to an axe wound could save the limb. After you killed a bear, you had to do this with the skull. That plant could be made into tea, that one should never be touched, and these roots could be eaten raw.

It was so much information, much more than ever before. Sometimes Johnny got bored or overwhelmed by pain in his feet and his mind wandered.

His father was strict. "Listen," he said. "If you don't listen, you'll be like a tied-up dog, walking in circles, always seeing the same things, never knowing more than you know now."

By the end of summer, Johnny's feet had stretched out enough to walk again and, if he was careful, run a little. The family packed up the canoe and paddled out to meet the black plane.

At their campsite, when the plane was still a faraway dot in the sky, coming in to land, Johnny's dad reached into his jacket, pulled out matches and Johnny's slingshot, and handed them over.

"Run," he said. "Into the woods. Hide. Don't come out, no matter what, until you see that airplane fly away. You know enough to live on your own for a few days."

"But – "

Johnny Neeposh

"Run! Don't let them see you!!"

Johnny took his slingshot and matches and ran.

From the woods, he heard the rage of the RCMP men. They shouted – Where was Johnny? Why wasn't he here? Someone would have to be punished!

"He's gone," his mom said. "We don't know where. He left a while ago."

They stomped around, they waved their guns and pushed people, they poked into every tent, they even searched the out-skirts of the woods. For a while, Johnny watched from a safe dis-tance and then he moved silently further into the woods and began hunting for dinner.

Now all the extra lessons made sense. Johnny knew exactly what to do. He wasn't afraid at all.

Hours later, after supper, getting close to dark, the black dot buzzed once more into the sky. Johnny collected his things and walked out of the woods to meet his parents.

"No more School!" His father laughed when he saw him. "Now you come on the land and learn our ways."

The family lost the winter ration. The Chief asked at every tent for what people could share. They were all poor, but every-one could see how badly Johnny was being hurt in School and they shared what they could to make it stop. Some ammunition, a pair of socks, an extra pair of boots, some precious powdered eggs. The Hudson Bay minder and a French trader helped out too. Johnny's family went into the bush that year with much less than usual. His father was a skilled hunter, Johnny was becoming one, and they had what others had given them. Still, it was a hard winter.

The next year, Johnny's sister had to go to School. They got the ration again.

Years later, Johnny would learn about the paper he had signed. The White people were trafficking Cree children, taking them from hospitals and Schools and sending them South to be adopted into White families. The paper with Johnny's signature was meant to place him in a White family. As if he didn't already have a family who loved and needed him. This tactic, which continued into the 1980s, would be called The Sixties Scoop.

For the next eight years, under his father's teachings, Johnny studied the ways of his people. Mostly, his dad taught survival skills. But he also taught Cree history. How people once boiled water by firing rocks white hot and dropping them one by one into a birch bark pot full of water, how people buried the last dry bones of a carcass at the end of a portage so that the next person there could dig them up and grind them into a powder and boil that powder into a nutritious broth, how they carved wooden dishes to eat from, how an especially wide tree often marked an ancient campsite because the nutrients from long-ago cooking fires made it grow wide, how the Old Ones had thrived in the harshest conditions, always keeping the Nation Chain going.

Sometimes, his father talked about White people. "Something is coming, Johnny, something even worse," he said. "The Elders say it too. The White people are cooking something up."

In any one of those eight years on the land, Johnny learned more than he had in all six years of School. But his dad could do some things that Johnny never managed to perfect. When his dad built something from wood, like a snow shovel or a snowshoe, he measured it with his thumb or his fingers, then held it up to his eye. Johnny sometimes asked him how long it was. "Oh, about five-foot-nine-and-a-half inches," he'd say. Or "Four-foot-eleven or thereabouts." Doubting someone was disrespectful, so Johnny said nothing in the moment. Later, when his dad was gone, Johnny got out the tape measure. Every time it was exactly the length his father had said. To this day, Johnny can't do that. He uses a tape measure.

Johnny Neeposh

One day, when Johnny was twenty years old, he and his father were out checking muskrat traps and stopped by the shore for lunch, as they usually did. Johnny built a small fire and over the flame his father cooked thin strips of smoked beaver on birch bark.

"I've decided – " his father said. And paused.

"Oh no," Johnny said. "Am I gonna have to get married?"

His dad looked at him, eyebrows high, then he threw his head back and laughed.

"Married!? Why do you think that?"

"Other parents are arranging marriages…" His voice trailed off.

"You don't have to marry," his dad said, still laughing. "But I've decided to give you this."

He handed Johnny the stick he had been poking in the dirt. Just a stick. Nothing special about it.

"You're ready to live on your own. Now that you know what you know, that stick is all you need to survive."

His eyes were a little wet.

Johnny took the stick and went to live on his own.

Quite often, Johnny and his dad met at their place under the tree by the lake and talked about what the White people were cooking up: the Québec Government was building a highway up the coast and moving their great machines onto Cree and Inuit land, preparing to flood an area about half the size of James Bay for a dam to sell electricity to the United States. "There are no people in this region," they said to Canadians, though tens of thousands of Cree and Inuit had lived there for millennia. The Cree began to fight for their land in the courts but, as they decided amongst themselves how best to proceed, deep rifts in the communities began to open.

Then the archaeologists assessed the area to be flooded. Underneath, they found Cree cultural objects five or six thousand years old, sometimes older – and promptly sent them South to be displayed in White museums. Even Cree history they claimed for themselves. "You don't know how to look after these things," they said to the Cree. "We'll do it for you."

Together, Johnny and his father marvelled at a people who freely tortured and trafficked children, who thought nothing of killing off families to access a child's mind, who believed they could better care for objects that the Cree had safeguarded for thousands of years. And who, all the while, thought themselves generous, helpful, faith-guided rescuers.

Back in Mistissini town, many Cree youth who had grown up in the Residential Schools, never on the land, began to lose their way, lose themselves. "This is what the Elders warned about," his father said. Keeping the Chain of the Nation going seemed a worn-out, impossible refrain. Those were difficult years.

Eventually Johnny married, had children of his own. He took his sons out on the land and taught them the ways of their people. To support his family in changing times, he worked as a guide for the archaeologists and took the opportunity to learn what he could about the White ways.

He learned enough to negotiate a museum to be built in Oujé-Bougoumou, on Cree land. It would be better if the Cree objects stayed safe in the ground, but now the White people were here, stealing them. If the Cree had their own climate-controlled museum, then even the White people could find no reason to take them. And Cree youth could see and study them. It was a start.

The summer of 2004 was nearing the end, the leaves just beginning to change. One day Johnny received a letter in the mail. Hydro-Québec was building the hydroelectric dam, and they wanted to redirect the Rupert River right over Johnny's family land and submerge nearly half of it. The land on which he had learned to fish, to hunt, to survive. The land that had healed his broken feet, and, more than that, his spirit. The land where he and his

JOhnnY NeepOSh

father had sat under a tree overlooking a lake and talked about so many things.

The letter also said that the Cree negotiators (now deft in White tactics) had organized a vote, and Hydro-Québec had to obey it. If the Cree voted no, then the Rupert could not be redirected. If they voted yes and the dam was built, the Cree would be compensated. Clinics, recreation centres, Cree-run schools, the list was long.

But – Johnny's land. His life and identity. Once again, the White people had struck him in the most intimate way.

Of course Johnny would vote against the dam. The land had looked after him, had healed him when the White people had tried to break him. Now he would protect it.

Johnny drove over to his father's place. This time, they didn't sit at their spot under the tree but at the kitchen table in his father's green Mistissini house. A photo of their tree by the lake was stuck to the fridge with a magnet, and an old canoe paddle rested by the door. His father put some smoked beaver strips on to fry, poured out hot tea, and scooped some sugar into his cup.

Out loud, Johnny translated the letter into Cree.

His father listened carefully.

For the longest time, he said nothing at all.

"That land is everything to me, son," he finally said. "Everything. But one way or another, a river changes its path over time. The White people are here and they have no conscience. Our youth are losing their way. Half the time I don't know what to say to them. They're the next link in the Chain. The decision here has to be for them. How do we keep the Nation Chain going?"

Quietly, Johnny sipped his tea. He didn't like where this conversation was going.

In the end, Johnny voted to surrender the family land, that which had sustained him, to the redirected river. His community got a clinic, a rec centre, schools, paved roads. Things that these new youth, the ones who had never lived on the land, valued and understood.

Because of how they voted, Johnny's family became targets in their community. Twice his father's house was broken into and utterly ransacked, everything broken. Johnny's brothers got death threats. His father's health became fragile from harassment.

Johnny wasn't surprised. These were his people, he understood their reaction. The land was precious to everyone, even those who hadn't lived on it, and redirecting a river for a dam has a certain violence to it.

His father agreed. "Don't worry about it, son," he said. "Angry people hit harder than they think. The Schools did terrible things to them and they haven't had time on the land to heal. It will pass. Like the animals, like the river, we will adapt."

Not long ago, in 2008, the White people finally admitted what had long been obvious to the Cree – that the Indian Residential Schools were invented for cultural genocide. And now times had changed, this part of history made the White people look bad, and they wanted to smooth things over with money.

Anyone who had attended a Residential School, they said, would receive a set amount of compensation for each year they had attended. People who talked about further abuses got a little more. But when Johnny said he had attended for six years, the Government representatives looked at their papers and said that he had attended for only five. They would pay for five. In this way, they saved themselves a little money.

Ah, it didn't matter. The money Johnny did receive he just handed over to his daughter. She needed a car to get to work and he wanted nothing to do with that money. He sure didn't want to talk about the abuses he had endured to make a little more. Those Schools destroyed lives. No amount of money can compensate a life.

About four hours' drive from Mistissini, in the bush out towards Nemaska, stands a cabin. Inside are two beds and a stove. Anyone can use it. Johnny is the one who uses it most. He spends

JOhnnY NeeposH

most of his time there. He'll gas up his truck, take some groceries to tide him over until he has a chance to go hunting. One big animal, say a caribou, will feed one man – even a tall man like Johnny – for a long time. In the warmer months, he gets into his boat and heads over to the redirected Rupert River, over the land that was once his and is now submerged. He sits there and thinks, remembers. Memories come easily these days.

What a life he has had. Every day he sees his permanently broken finger, every day he pulls his socks onto feet that still have something of a bend to them, every day he recalls the injuries. He taught his sons the ways of the land that his father taught him. That was a very great privilege. But he was never able to pass on the stick. Both boys died, in car accidents five years apart, before he could do so. His father is gone now, too. Grief is heavy, sticks around a long time. The losses have been so personal.

In Eeyou Istchee, some things have healed. The clinics and recreation centres make a difference, kids stay with their families through the school years, and Cree language is taught in the schools. Despite the colossal efforts of the Residential School staff, nearly everyone in Eeyou Istchee speaks Cree. And youth are going out on the land again. Not many get the chance to live there for eight years at a stretch, but they stay there for weeks or months and make relevant for a new generation the ancient Cree knowledge of the land.

The culture is changing. It's not what it was, but the next link in the Chain is secure. Now it's Johnny's responsibility, as grandfather to about thirty people, to pass on the knowledge and the language, the strength and tenacity, to the children. Even if they don't use it right away, they'll have it for when they need it. It's the only way to keep the Nation Chain going.

Even rivers adapt.

Stories Heard Along the Way: Airplanes

A seaplane landed in a coastal community at high tide one day and the pilot went in to the community for some days off. A few hours later, another community radioed: someone needed an urgent med-evac. The pilot ran out to his plane on the shore, but by then the tide had gone out. Way out. The plane sat on dry land. A Cree person saw the problem, hollered out, and a crowd quickly gathered. The pilot climbed into his plane, the people organized themselves around the pontoons, they picked up the plane, and they carried it out to sea where it took off and transported the patient to hospital.

Up on Hudson Bay, a group of seal hunters floated away on an ice floe while neighbours looked on from shore. When a bush pilot delivered goods a few hours later, the neighbours asked him to fly north and pick up the hunters. A strong northerly wind was blowing everything south and the pilot was sure that he should fly south instead of north, but he did as he was told. Straightaway, he found the missing hunters and brought them home. His own calculations had accounted for the north wind but not for the strong current that carried the ice floe right into the wind.

In the 1940s, official James and Hudson Bay maps were rough and inaccurate, but Cree trapper memories were detailed and reliable. The maps drawn by trappers of their own hunting regions were so accurate that pilots compiled them into maps of the larger inland region and used them instead of official maps.

In the mid-1960s, looking to raise funds, the Chief and Council of a new community flew in a planeload of beer and stashed it in the one-room jail. Then they sold jail-tour tickets to locals. Each tour came with a complimentary can of beer to refresh the participant on the lengthy tour. What the locals were not doing was buying beer, and what the Council was not doing was selling beer, because, after all, the Cree were not supposed to drink. One winter, they flew in their usual planeload of beer, stashed it in the jailhouse – and the furnace went out. Every can burst and froze. That year, the jail-tour came with complimentary beersicles. Some of the cans made their way into the river and made for the Cree version of beer-battered fish.

←

Pilots use the acronym "Roger" (for *Received the Order Given. Expect Results*) to let air traffic controllers know that they understand. In the late 1980s, a young Cree woman wanted to get to a hospital in plenty of time to give birth. The drive was 600 kilometres long, so she took instead the short one-hour AirCreebec flight. Up in the air, the baby, who already knew that he liked airplanes much more than hospitals, was born healthy and hollering. Meanwhile, the pilot was on the radio, arranging ground support. He ended his conversation with the customary "Roger." The mom heard him and named her son Roger. Roger's preferences and urgency so impressed AirCreebec administrators that they gave him a lifetime pass.

The bear fell.
"Alfred! You got it! You're amazing!!" Hattie shouted.

Artist: Tristan Shecapio-Blacksmith

Alfred and HaTTIE COOhish ish

Alfred and Hattie Coonishish

"HEY ALFRED."

"What?"

"You know the geese in the park?"

"Yeah."

"Their wings are clipped."

"Why?"

"I dunno. Someone clipped them."

"But – then they can't fly."

"Right!"

"Ohh! *They can't fly!*"

"Right."

Up in their dorm room, after lights out, Alfred and four of his friends whispered back and forth until they had a solid plan.

The next Saturday, they walked down to the park and put the plan into action. Carefully, so as not to be seen, they found a big goose and herded it away from the others. The five of them surrounded it, four tried to distract it and the fifth reached for the neck. Even with clipped wings, a Canada goose is a big bird, strong as anything. It can really hurt a person and the boys were weak with hunger. The goose hissed and lunged at them, bit them and beat them with its wings. Every boy was bruised and battered. But they managed. Then they snuck into the bush, lit a fire, and cooked it. That night they had real meat in their bellies and goose grease on their chins. What a day.

That was the main thing about Indian Residential School. Sure, classrooms and language battles and missing your parents and abuse and bullying and all the things you expect if you know a little bit of Canadian history. But those were things that happened some of the time. Or most of the time.

Hunger, though, hunger happened all the time. At Shingwauk Indian Residential School in Sault Ste. Marie and at Bishop Horden Memorial Indian Residential School in Moose Factory, the Schools that Hattie and Alfred both attended, you were hungry every minute of every day and of every night. Hattie went to Brantford Mohawk for a year too but it wasn't much different. In Residential Schools of the '50s and '60s, there wasn't nearly enough food to go 'round.

Whether you were hungry or not, the people in robes made you stand and pray, head bowed, hands behind your back, and give thanks for what you knew was not enough. Once, during prayer, Alfred heard a crash. When he opened his eyes, his friend was on the ground. He had fainted from hunger while giving thanks for food.

And so, Alfred and his friends provided for themselves.

In fall or spring, they walked around the Sault Ste. Marie golf course and picked up golf balls. They wiped the dirt off on their pants or with a rag and dropped them into clean bags. Then they went to the rich part of town and knocked on the doors of the fanciest houses.

"Would you like to buy some golf balls?" they asked.

"That would be lovely," the rich people said, and they picked out the balls they wanted.

In wintertime, nobody golfed but the fancy houses had long driveways and lots of snow. They knocked on doors then too.

"Can we shovel your driveway for some dollars?" they'd ask.

Alfred and Hattie COOhishish

"That would be lovely," the rich people said. "The shovel's around the back."

The boys took their earnings then and went to the grocery store. They didn't buy chips or candy. Chips and candy tasted wonderful, but they don't satisfy hunger. Instead, they bought loaves of brown bread and jars of jam and peanut butter. They snuck the grocery bags up into the dorm rooms and stored them under their beds.

Late at night, after lights out, they opened up their grocery bags and ate jam and peanut butter sandwiches and prayed that the priests wouldn't notice crumbs in the bedclothes.

Sometimes there was no way for a six- or seven-year-old to earn a bit of money for food, and a goose supper was out of the question. Instead they stole turnips and apples from neighbourhood gardens, shook the dirt off the skins, and ate them raw.

Several years later, it was Hattie's turn to go. She didn't know who Alfred was. But she knew hunger.

Little girls couldn't easily earn money in Sault Ste. Marie. And their uniforms and choppy haircuts made them too obvious to surround geese in a park without being noticed.

Instead they stole. They snuck down to the School kitchens at night. Brown sugar and peanut butter by the handful. Apples, oranges, crackers, bread, whatever they could find. They got pretty good at it.

Pretty good, but not perfect. And for girls who were caught stealing – bad things happened. Some of the older girls had been punished so many times that they didn't want to take the risk anymore. Then they grabbed Hattie and her friend by the arms, pressing in bruises with their fingers.

"Here's what you're gonna do," they said. "You're gonna sneak down into the kitchen and you're gonna steal food, and you're going to bring all of it back to us. If you eat any of it, even one bite, we'll know and then we'll beat you up."

Threat was all over their faces. What could Hattie and her friend do but obey?

They waited until all the lights were out, and then they tiptoed downstairs as quickly as they could. Hattie grabbed some bread and her friend scooped blueberry jam into a plastic bag. They ran upstairs and gave it to the bullies and jumped into bed. They didn't eat a single bite. It was so dark and they ran so quickly that they didn't notice their plastic bag, like something out of a fairy tale, was leaking a purple trail of jam.

"Ugghhh!"

The supervisor's voice. Downstairs in the dark, he was making rounds and had stepped in something. The downstairs corridor lights flipped on and shone a glow into the girls' dark bedroom. Then, clunk, clunk, step after heavy step as he followed the jam trail up the stairs, and into the girls' dorm room.

Everybody's heads ducked under the covers.

The lights in their dorm room snapped on.

Studiously, every girl in the room pretended to be too fast asleep to notice.

Hattie held her breath. Surely the supervisor could hear her heart. Her punishment was going to be awful.

But he was following a jam trail. It didn't go to Hattie's bed. It went to the beds of the bullies – who were still finishing their nightlunch under the covers. Caught purple-handed.

They were so badly strapped that Hattie almost felt sorry for them. She was hungry and her stomach was singing opera, but she had stolen and wasn't punished at all. What a day.

Eventually, the School people put locks on the cupboards. Then the bullies ordered Hattie and her friends to break the locks. They tried, but the locks were stronger than the girls. So the bullies, hungry as they were, beat them up.

When Hattie was older, she could babysit for food. The teachers with kids hired their babysitters from the Residential

Alfred and Hattie Coonishish

School. They didn't pay in money, they paid in fruit. An apple or an orange or a banana. It made a big difference. You could sleep right through the night if you had an apple or orange or banana in your stomach. Everybody wanted to babysit.

Indian Residential School was preparing the pupils for work in the White world, the teachers said. But when Alfred and Hattie think back on it, mainly they think back on hunger.

In Moose Factory Bishop Horden Memorial, another School they went to, it was hard to sleep. Kids cried all night long. From hunger, of course, because their bellies hurt. And because they longed for love and fairness and were in a place where neither could be found. Others cried because they had been beaten that day and were in pain. And when Alfred and Hattie were older, they heard about some of the other things that had been happening in the dark in the beds of their friends. Then they understood the crying even more.

There was one kid in Moose Factory who was especially bullied by other kids. He was younger than Alfred, but Alfred felt sorry for him and looked out for him as much as he could. When he saw the older kids coming for this kid, fists balled and drawn, he got in the way. Sometimes that meant that Alfred got a fist in the face himself, but looking out for underdogs was important. Everyone's an underdog some of the time.

One night, Alfred was awake in the night, as usual, when he heard footsteps of many people. The safest thing to do was to hide under the covers and pretend to be asleep – but Alfred kept his eyes ever so slightly open so that he could see.

It was a group of adults. About seven or ten of them. They were all dressed the same, from head to toe in plain white robes, and their heads were bowed. He couldn't see their faces.

They went directly to where the bullied kid lay, fast asleep, and they formed a circle around the bed.

Alfred's ears were under the covers so he heard some whispers but not much more. And their big white gowns were in the way, so he couldn't see a whole lot of anything either. After a while they left, heads still bowed. What exactly they did, Alfred never found out.

But whatever it was, two days later that kid – a healthy kid, not sick in any way – was dead.

So maybe it was better not to sleep. Sure, you could hardly make it through class the next day, but at least you'd be alive.

Now that he's older, Alfred thinks back to the kid often. He never did find out the cause of death. Or why that kid was the one who had to die.

One summer, when Alfred was about ten years old, he made a plan to get away from it all. White people liked papers. Documents, they called them. They *believed* papers. So Alfred got himself a paper that said he had been contracted to bring ten beaver pelts to the Hudson's Bay Post in Mistissini. To fulfill it, he would go with his parents into the bush – and not go to School.

In August, the big Canso plane came and landed on the water to pick up the kids for Residential School. Alfred went to the shore with his father. Confidently, he approached the closest RCMP officer and showed him the document.

The officer read it. He smiled at Alfred.

"I'm sorry Alfred," he said politely, "but School is more important. Here. We'll give the paper to your father so that the money stays in the family."

He passed the paper to Alfred's dad. Then he picked up Alfred by the waist and swung him into the big canoe ferrying kids out to the plane.

That night, in bed in the dorm, knowing he'd be in School for ten hungry months, that was a hard night. He had been sure that his paper would work.

Alfred and Hattie Coonishish

Hattie brought an important paper with her too. Her mother had written a letter to her friend Jean, who was a lady supervisor at Hattie's School. Hattie's hair, the letter said, was not to be cut.

All of the other girls had their hair chopped off in three or four crooked swipes and it looked terrible. But Hattie's hair grew as long and glossy as the poor diet would allow. Every morning, Jean brushed and braided Hattie's hair while the other girls looked on. It made Hattie feel a little better on those rare days when they all went to the Moosonee village, a long single-file row of brown kids in strange uniforms and sloppy haircuts. Hattie could feel the stares of the village people, the disdain. At least her hair was long and tidy.

One day, in Hattie's second year, Jean went to the movies for a few hours and left a senior girl in charge of the dorm.

The moment the door clicked shut, the senior girl went to a cupboard and grabbed a pair of scissors. Then she turned and looked right at Hattie.

"Haircuts!!" she said. "Hattie's first!"

She grabbed Hattie by the braids and pulled her down into a chair. And five seconds later, Hattie's thick braids lay on the floor. She kept cutting and made sure that Hattie's hair was extra short and extra sloppy. She even chopped crooked bangs across the forehead.

Hattie was horrified. She went straight to bed and covered her ugly head with blankets. She cried all night long.

The next morning, Jean woke all the girls.

Hattie stayed in bed, under the covers.

Jean tugged at Hattie's blanket. "It's time to get up," she said.

"I don't wanna get up," Hattie said from under the blankets.

Gently, Jean tugged at her blankets to look at Hattie's face. And saw her hair.

"Hattie! Who did this to you??"

Hattie blurted out everything. She felt so ashamed.

Jean went and found the other girl. She was punished. But Hattie could see on the other girl's face that, even with punishment, she wasn't sorry at all. She was glad.

Sometimes Hattie sees that girl around town in Mistissini. She's an older woman now with a lifetime behind her. She wears her hair very short. They never talked about what happened. Sometimes Hattie wonders if she has forgotten.

Every June, when Alfred stepped off the plane at Lake Mistassini, he knew that that night's supper would be enough. That that night's sleep would be safe. That his parents would fill him up with as much love and food as they could before being forced to send him back.

But what to do about speaking Cree? In School, even more important than speaking English was not speaking Cree. If you spoke Cree you were punished. You were strapped, or you'd miss a meal or two, or your mouth was washed out with soap. When Alfred got home for the summer, then, he was afraid to speak Cree. Something terrible would happen if he did.

"Here, sit," his mom said to Alfred in Cree. "Eat something. You're too skinny."

He sat and ate.

"Tell me about your friends in the dorm this year," she said, in Cree.

He answered her in English, but she couldn't understand, so then he translated it into Cree.

"Tell me about math class," she said to Alfred in Cree, and brought him a cup of tea.

Again, he answered her in English, and then translated.

"Now tell me about your teachers," she said to Alfred in Cree.

And he answered her in Cree.

Just a little patience and gentleness, that's all it took, and all the Cree came flooding back.

Alfred and Hattie COOhishish

"We teach you," the teachers said, "so that when you graduate from Indian Residential School, you'll be prepared for the sorts of jobs that White people hold. Indian bush education doesn't have much use in the real world."

Alfred was a good student. He finished Indian Residential School for the Elementary years and then attended Boarding School for the Secondary years. Then he did what his teachers had prepared him for. He stayed in Sault Ste. Marie and applied for work.

First, he applied to work in the steel plant. He got a temporary contract.

He asked the supervisor about a permanent position, like the ones White people had. Those positions, he learned, were not for Cree people. Alfred was laid off with seasonal changes.

Then, at Kentucky Fried Chicken, he found work as a cook. It was more regular and year 'round. But it did not pay well. And the food was boiled in big vats of oil. Alfred knew hunger and he also knew, from his childhood on the land, what good food should do for the body. He didn't want to be a man who served bad food to people.

He looked around for something else, anything really, that a Cree guy could do that had some meaning to it and that let him pay the bills. But for all of his schooling and classroom skills and English language fluency, the White world didn't have a real place for him.

What, then, had been the purpose of those Schools?

He longed for his own people, his own language, his own way of life.

He had been away for years.

It was time to move home.

When Alfred had left on the Canso plane as a child, "home" was mobile. His family had gathered on the side of Lake Mistassini for the summers, and then moved into the bush for fall, winter, and spring.

When he returned home again, after so many years, it was unrecognizable.

The White people had been there too. Houses, they said, were better than mobile teepees and cabins. Cree people should live in the same place, all year 'round. Like White people did. Houses were going up in rows on the lakeside. People were moving from the bush and settling in them. The Hudson Bay post had expanded the store section and now had some offices too. A road was being built right to the new town. And a school and a fire house and electricity and plumbing and everything. The town was going to be called Mistassini. Eventually it became Mistissini.

First of all, Alfred needed work. He walked to all the Cree businesses in Mistissini, looking for work. But Indian Residential School was fresh in people's memories. "Overqualified," people said when he applied. What they meant was that they couldn't trust someone who had made it all the way through to the end of White high school. There was no place for him.

Finally, he found a position working Monday to Friday in the Mistissini office of the Hudson Bay Company.

On Saturday nights, he went to Church. The Roman Catholic priest had somehow managed to transport a film projector all the way up to Mistissini. On Saturdays, in the Church basement, he projected movies against a portable screen. Disney movies, Westerns, pretty much anything black and white. He screened each movie a few times and he charged fifty cents a person.

Alfred attended faithfully.

Hattie, after School, had not even tried to find work in the White world. She moved on the land to be with her family and to learn as a teenager what she should have learned as a child. After some years, her parents moved to town and Hattie came along and found work as a clerk at the Hudson's Bay Company.

There she met Alfred. He worked in the office.

They went on a date to the Church and watched that week's movie.

Alfred and Hattie Coonishish

A few years later, they were married. Eventually, they had five kids.

Whenever they could, Hattie and Alfred went to the bush, inland to Alfred's father's hunting grounds. Missing a solid bush education, Alfred tried to figure out again how to use and clean and load a gun, how to find the animals, how to find food.

He and Hattie were out walking the trapline one day and noticed something in the bushes. He looked up and there was a bear. Looking right at him!

Alfred raised the rifle and shot.

The bear fell.

"Alfred! You got it! You're amazing!!" Hattie shouted.

And then her face fell.

"What do we do now?" she said. "There's something we have to do right away or the meat goes bad. I don't remember!"

Alfred just looked at her. He felt stunned. Maybe more stunned than the bear.

Hattie ran back to the cabin and got on the radio to call her uncle. He was out on the trapline.

"Alfred shot a bear!" she shouted into the radio! "He got it with one bullet! What do we do now?"

The voice on the other end crackled a bit, then cleared up.

"That's good news," her uncle said. "Now do you have a sharp knife?"

And he walked them through it.

The bear fed them for a long time. It was good to be Cree.

Alfred looked for better-paying work. For a while, he was the employment officer at the band office trying to help people find work in a place that didn't have much.

Then they moved their family to Chibougamau so he could work in the mines. But the mines destroyed the land that he had moved home for. And they were underground, damp, unventilated, deeply unhealthy, and extremely dangerous. People died down there. Mine work was for people with expendable lives. Maybe not so different from Indian Residential School then.

Alfred's family depended on him. Hattie was working hard at home with five little kids. His life was not expendable.

It was like that for years. Always looking for the work that Indian Residential School was supposed to prepare him for and never really finding it.

Eventually, after the kids were grown, Alfred and Hattie moved to Montréal for more schooling. They didn't really want to re-enter that kind of education, but how else could they work in this White world?

Alfred studied Administration at Concordia University. It took just one week for him to understand that everyone else in the program had had a much better education than he had, and that he was far behind. With a great deal of work, he caught up, but it was extremely difficult. And now he knew for certain: Indian Residential School had prepared him for nothing but hunger, sleeplessness, and poverty.

What, then, had it been for?

The family moved back to Mistissini. Hattie worked first with Elders for the Cree Health Board, and then with Students with Special Needs for the Cree School Board.

Alfred worked for the School Board. He worked hard to get Cree language study into the Eeyou Istchee schools, and he was part of the committee that interviewed teachers. Once, he was flipping through a pile of applications of people who were to be interviewed and he came across a familiar name. He pulled the application out of the pile and read it more closely. The applicant was a certified, experienced teacher – who had taught at Bishop Horden Memorial Indian Residential School. Memories of violence washed over Alfred.

Alfred and Hattie Coonishish

Ear twisting, dragging kids down corridors by their hair, head bashing, so many vicious strappings. Alfred's breath lurched.

He took out his pen and wrote across the top of the form: *Application Rejected*. This man would abuse no Cree children on Alfred's watch. He didn't even want to run into him in Meechum.

Alfred and Hattie look out of their kitchen window over Lake Mistassini. The sun is out, glinting off of snowdrifts. It's a good life now, though the walls of their living room are covered in tributes to those whom they've lost. A grandson, a son, and three close childhood friends. The last Indian Residential School closed in 1997, but the aftermath is everywhere.

They are Elders now. Every year, they go on the land for moose and goose hunts, and still work on re-learning the skills they had as young children, before they were taken, and those they should have learned as teenagers. Every time they're out on the land, it's harder to come home.

In 2008, the Government of Canada finally revealed that the Schools had existed not to provide a proper education at all, but to commit cultural genocide. A Truth and Reconciliation Commission was organized. Because of the title, Alfred and Hattie thought that now there might be some truth, some reconciliation. But when Alfred said he'd attended for thirteen years, the Government people said their documents claimed he had attended for just ten, and that's all they would compensate for. The last few years at the Boarding School didn't count, they said.

Alfred chuckled to himself when he heard that and thought back to a paper that contracted him for ten beaver pelts. So many things had changed. And some things had not changed at all.

Records: Teachers

For most of IRS history, Churches were responsible for teacher hiring.

December 1886. Many Residential School teachers are "illiterate persons, ignorant of the first elements of teaching and powerless to impart any ideas..." *School Inspector Macrae*

July 1897. The teachers are "not as a rule well fitted to the work." *Indian Affairs Official M. Benson*

July 1909. Recruiting trained principals requires higher salaries than the Department is "disposed to entertain." *Indian Affairs Superintendent A. Vowell*

October 1916. A new principal and his wife "are said to be very nice people but without the faintest idea of managing an institution of this sort." *Deputy Superintendent General D.C. Scott*

October 1920. Inspector Ditchburn opposes Churches "sending persons to teach Indians just because they want a position."

October 1922. "The teachers who are about the poorest of their class are in charge, and the waste of time is painful to witness." *Inspector Hutchinson*

April 1932. Superintendent R.T. Ferrier notes the "proneness of Church officials to assign to Indian work Reverend gentlemen and instructors who have not been too successful in other fields of activity."

February 1943. "Missionary zeal in a teacher is important, but it is not enough. It should be reinforced by other desirable personality qualifications, and by knowledge and skill [which] these teachers appear to lack." *Inspector H. McArthur*

September 1944. A School "is not being operated, it is just running." *Inspector A. Hamilton*

1948. "[O]ver 40 Per cent of the teaching staff had no professional training. Indeed some had not even graduated from high school." *Indian Affairs Department study*

June 1950. Residential Schools have, "up to the moment, been rather ineffective largely because teachers were not qualified, no curriculum was laid down, no standards were set up, and there was little supervision, guidance or inspection by an independent authority." *Education Sub-Committee, Northwest Territories*

1954. Teacher hiring moves from Church to Government control.
1957. Number of unqualified teachers in the Schools is halved.
1962. Less than 10% are unqualified.

1969. Integration into the public school system is mandated and Church partnerships ended.

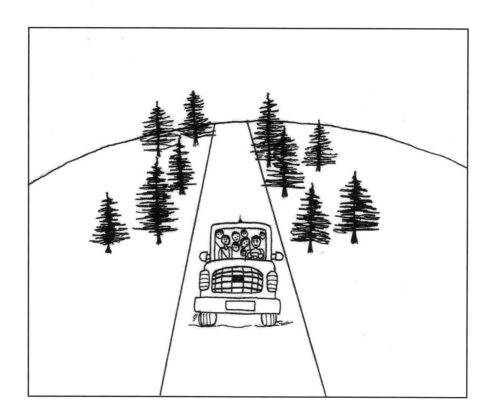

They all drove away from the riverside camp.

Artist: Jared Linton

Diana Prince

Diana Prince*

*Names and details have been changed to protect identities.

IN THE ONE store that Chibougamau had in the 1970s stood a teetering rotating comic book display. On Saturdays, while her parents were shopping for groceries, Diana paged through the comics. Sometimes, if she had some coins, she bought one. Of all the superheroes, Diana liked *Wonder Woman* best. Like Diana, Wonder Woman was Native, though she came from a different river basin. She was always protecting people, either by fighting Bad Guys or by mediating and peacebuilding. She wore gauntlets that made her ten times stronger and she could force people to tell the truth. She could do *anything*.

One day, when Diana was about six, her mom said, "Put on your coat, Diana. We're going to visit someone."

Cool! Diana thought. *Visiting people is fun.*

They went to the basement of an apartment building and into a two-room apartment. Another family was visiting there too, and they had a boy and girl. The adults talked and Diana played with the kids.

After a while, she went to the bathroom. When she came out, her parents were gone.

They had left without her.

The mom of the strange family said to her, "Diana, you're coming with us. I'm your real mother. This is your brother and sister."

Diana began to scream.

"Shhh, shhh, Diana! I'm your mom, really I am. I'll take good care of you," the strange lady said.

Diana couldn't do anything but go with the strange family.

Everything was wrong. They lived in the wrong house on the wrong street in the wrong part of town. She was scared to go to the bathroom, scared to go to bed, scared to go to sleep. She cried for a week.

Eventually she stopped. Crying didn't change anything anyways.

When she was older, the strange lady, who really was her mom, told her that when Diana was a baby something had been going around. Kids in the bush weren't always surviving the hard winters. So they had placed Diana with another family until she was bigger and stronger.

The main thing Diana remembers about the family of her first six years is the love.

There sure was a lot to get used to. This new family lived in town only for the summer. Fall and winter and spring they spent out on the land. And they were *strange.* Always, the dad was drinking. He smelled bad and said things that didn't make sense. He punched and bit and dragged the mom across the cabin floor by her hair. Then, maybe to soften the pain of her bruises, the mom started drinking too. Whenever the ruckus started, the oldest brother took Diana and her sister outside to keep them safe. Diana never got hit, she doesn't think, but still, she had to be careful. And even though she wasn't yet sure about this new mom, she didn't like to see her beat up. It made for bad dreams.

Diana Prince

One summer, around '75, a social worker dropped by their house in town.

"These kids can't go on the land with you," she said to Diana's new mom. "They have to go to school. If you don't figure it out, we'll take them away from you."

The nearest school that would take Cree kids was in Mistissini. Diana took a bus to stay at a boarding home in Mistissini while her new parents went back out on the land. On the bus ride, the other Cree kids cried, sad to leave their parents.

Diana didn't cry at all.

The other kids cried in their boarding homes too.

Diana liked her boarding home. Nobody punched or bit or dragged anybody. Lots of girls lived there and they treated Diana like a sister. It felt like a *real* family.

For three or four years, throughout her school days, Diana stayed in the boarding home and went to her parents' place only for holidays. And every year, there was another brother or sister. Until Diana had twelve siblings.

The main thing Diana remembers about her boarding home family is the love.

Eventually Diana's new parents moved the whole family out to a riverside camp. They lived in a log cabin by a river, and both sets of grandparents lived close by. Diana spent weekdays in Mistissini and weekends at the riverside camp with her family.

Diana, now ten years old, hated camp life. The cabin was dark and just two rooms. They slept four kids to a bed. Her parents were always out working or busy with something, and her mom expected Diana to run the house. Babysitting, cooking, cleaning, laundry, everything. There were so many kids. And they all needed to be fed and entertained and bathed and diaper-changed and nose-wiped and every other messy, sticky, smelly thing that little kids need. Diana felt like a slave.

And that wasn't even the worst.

The worst was that, back when Diana's mom had been in Residential School, she had learned one important thing: on Sundays, she should go to Church. Every Sunday at the riverside camp, then, she dressed in clean clothes, left her husband and the kids behind in the log cabin with Diana to look after them, and went to a nearby Church.

The second she was out the door, Diana's dad clicked the lock shut behind her, took Diana into the bedroom, and locked that door too.

Then he raped her.

He was huge. Diana was ten years old. Nothing had ever hurt that much.

It happened every single Sunday that whole long year she was ten.

And every single Sunday the whole incredibly long year she was eleven.

And every single Sunday the whole incredibly, unbelievably long year she was twelve.

Sure are a lot of Sundays in a year.

Always, he warned her: "If you ever tell anyone, Social Services will send your mom away for a long time." Or "If you ever tell anyone, I'm gonna beat your brothers and sisters worse than anything you've ever seen."

In the nights, Diana cried herself to sleep. In the days, she vomited.

When she heard the click of a lock, any lock, she felt sick.

And what she couldn't figure out was – all these kids she was looking after, how could she keep them safe when she couldn't even keep herself safe?

And always, always, always, she felt filthy. Inhuman. Like it was all somehow her fault and she should be punished.

Diana Prince

So she picked up whatever sharp thing she could find and slashed at her own skin.

She wanted someone to notice. To ask her what was wrong and to force her to tell the truth. To fight for her and keep her safe.

Since that wasn't gonna happen, she wanted the next best thing: for it all to end quickly, in some gory and violent way. Like walking out onto the highway and waiting for the world's most enormous truck to mash her into the pavement.

Something about her mom in those days made Diana think she knew what was going on but maybe didn't know what to do.

Diana wanted to talk to her about it. She never did.

One day, when Diana was twelve and her older sister was thirteen, they were washing dishes and were alone in the kitchen.

"Hey Lila," Diana said, passing her a plate to dry.

"Yeah?" Lila took it and methodically swiped a damp towel over it.

"You know how Mom goes to Church every Sunday?"

"Yeah." Another plate, another swipe of the towel.

"You know how Dad pushes me into the bedroom then, and locks the door?"

"Yeah."

Diana looked down into the dishwater to say it: "He rapes me. Every Sunday."

"What?"

"You heard me."

Diana passed her another plate but her sister didn't take it. She just stood there, wet towel in hand, and looked and looked and looked at her. Diana finally turned to face her and could tell, just by the looking, that her sister didn't know what to do either.

And now Diana had told someone.

What if her dad found out?

The next day her grandma, who lived in the same camp, came to their cabin. Diana was on her bed reading comics.

Her grandma came into the bedroom and sat beside Diana on the bed.

For a long time she just sat and looked at the wall. She didn't say anything.

Finally she spoke.

"Your sister says your dad is, um, doing things to you. Is that true?"

Diana looked up at her. Her heart was running a race with itself. Her chest was gonna break open.

"Yes," she said.

Her grandmother's face went stiff, like she had to never again show what she was thinking. Diana expected her grandma to hug her, but now she can't remember if she did. She doesn't remember what happened the rest of that whole day.

The next weeks went normally. Her dad worked in construction and beat her mom, Diana looked after kids that weren't her own, people dropped in and visited, her mom worked all week and went to Church on Sundays. When Diana's dad locked her in the bedroom and raped her again.

On an especially windy summer day, just as Diana was wiping another kid's nose, there was a knock on the rickety door.

The outer plywood door was already open to air out the diaper smell and their parents were both gone. Diana was in charge. With the snotty hanky in her hand, Diana opened the inner screen door carefully so that the wind wouldn't rip it off the hinges.

It was a social worker. In the wind her hair was whipping all over the place. She had brought the police. Their hair didn't move at all.

"Diana, you're not safe here," the social worker said. "You're coming with us."

Wow. *Wow!* Her grandmother must have called them.

Diana Prince

Except –

"What about all these kids? I'm supposed to look after them."

"They're coming too. Bring whatever you want. You are never coming back here."

Diana gathered a few clothes and comic books, called her brothers and sisters, and sent them to the police car. She went to the bedroom to pick up the baby.

When Diana came out with the baby, she saw her granddad come running from across the camp. There was dust in the air and the wind was blowing his shirt around. He looked angry even before he said anything.

"Don't you dare take those children!" he hollered. "They don't belong to you!"

He reached for a kid not yet in the car – and the social worker stepped between.

"Mr. Prince," she said politely, "we have no choice. The children are not safe here so they're going into Cree Youth Protection. But they still belong to your family. You are still their grandfather. And their mom can visit them at this address."

She handed him a piece of paper. And then she folded herself into the front seat, took two kids on her lap, and they all drove away from the riverside camp.

The social worker was right. Diana never ever went back.

That was the best day of her life.

Diana and her siblings stayed in a women's shelter. It felt like a palace. Diana had her own bedroom. The police and social worker sometimes visited. And her mom visited too. Her dad wasn't allowed.

Diana liked the shelter. Nobody ever raped her there.

But her mom. Her mom did not like it at all.

She cried and cried and begged Diana not to press charges against her dad. Not to tell anyone what had happened, not to talk about it at all. Diana felt sorry for her then. Her dad was probably making her beg and she had no choice but to go home to him where he'd probably drag her across the floor by her hair for not bringing the kids.

Diana didn't press charges. Even though she really wanted to. Sometimes enabling abuse just looks like taking care of your mom.

Then her mom cried and cried some more and begged the social worker not to press charges. The social worker did anyways.

After a while, Diana moved out of the shelter and in with a family in Chibougamau. She attended school in town and found part-time work cleaning houses and offices. What she remembers most about the Chibougamau family is all the love. One of the girls is still a close friend.

One day she was cleaning the house of a Cree lady she had known for a long time. The lady invited her to sit at the kitchen table. She poured them both some tea.

"Diana," she said, "Remember, back when you lived by the river, my husband and I visited your parents?"

"Yep," said Diana, scooping sugar into her tea.

"I felt something awful there," she said. "You looked so strange. Like something was terribly wrong and you needed help but couldn't ask."

Diana stopped breathing.

"So I called Cree Youth Protection. That's why they took you away from there. Are you okay now?"

Diana nodded silently and began again to breathe.

Someone *had* noticed. And had done something to help.

Others had noticed too. In the sideways glances, in the ways people stopped talking the instant Diana looked their way, in the stares that drilled into her back, Diana saw that every Cree in a

Diana Prince

hundred miles knew what had gone down. For ever and ever, she was gonna be the girl whose mom went to Church while her dad raped her.

She wanted to leave. And if she couldn't leave, then she wanted to die, to be mashed into the pavement. Surely there were some big trucks around.

Again, the same lady helped. She called some people and made arrangements, and then she and her husband drove Diana over a thousand kilometres, all the way down to London, Ontario. In London, they left Diana with a family they knew.

Diana went to college. The family drove her to class every day. They made sure she had a safe place and a hot supper to come back to. She had her own room and time to study. She didn't have to look after any kids. They introduced her to a counsellor who introduced her to a psychologist.

And that's how it was that, in London, over a thousand kilometres away from the riverside camp, away from the land, away from her family, with time and space to herself, Diana could think about all the things that had happened to her and about what she wanted to happen. The main thing she remembers about the London family is the love.

Every week Diana met with the psychologist. The only way out of all the hurt, she learned, was through talking about what had hurt her.

Diana talked about the basement apartment where she lost her first family. About watching her second mom be beaten and dragged across the floor. About Church and the Sunday rapes. About shame and filth and cutting herself and wanting to die. About how much she hated her dad. Every ugly, painful detail.

Half the time, Diana vomited just to be talking about it.

Not even once did the psychologist complain about the vomit, or say it was Diana's fault, or ask her to stop talking.

Instead, she said that Diana had to be ten times as strong as most people to survive all that.

Once or twice a year, Diana took the bus North to visit her family with all the kids. Now that those kids didn't need her to change their diapers or wipe their noses, she didn't mind seeing them. She didn't even mind seeing her mom.

But her dad. He wasn't a dad. He was a great big bully. A Bad Guy.

Each time she returned to London, her psychologist asked Diana if she could ever forgive him.

"Nope," Diana said, every time.

Until the day, after living in London for five years and talking to the psychologist every week, she said, "Maybe. One day."

Diana's degree was almost finished and she was moving back to Eeyou Istchee, back to her home community.

Her small home community. Where you could stand on one end of town and see the other end. Where everyone knew every-thing. Where family was unavoidable.

If she was ever gonna forgive her dad, now was the time. Either that or hate him, and hating someone who lived in the same small community took too much energy.

"Okay," she said to her psychologist. "I'm ready to forgive him now. Or at least try."

"Alright," the psychologist said. "First, you should write a letter. A long and detailed letter about all the ways he's hurt you. He might be able to hear it better if he's read it once already. And forgiveness is easier if he hears and acknowledges what happened."

A letter was easy. Diana took up her pen.

"Dear Big Bad Guy," the letter started. There was no way she could call him "Dad." *"You ruined my life. For years, I just wanted a big truck to run me down."*

Diana Prince

She wrote about all the times he had dragged her mom by the hair, all the drinking, all the violence, all the rapes, all the ways he had made her life so awful that she had wished, for years and years, that she could just *die.*

She folded the letter into an envelope, pasted on a stamp, and sent it.

She never got an answer, but that was okay. She didn't expect one. Just having written it down felt good.

"Are you ready to face him, do you think?" the psychologist asked. "What are you gonna say?"

Diana thought about it. The therapist was right. She was going to have to prepare what to say ahead of time, because once she laid eyes on him, she was gonna be sick. Just thinking about seeing him made her wanna puke.

So she stood in front of a mirror, imagined looking at him, and practised saying what she needed to say. She practised until she was absolutely sure she could say it to his face.

Then she went home.

Her first morning home was a Sunday. She woke up and looked at a waterspot on the ceiling. She heard her mom put on her coat and go out to Church.

All those Sundays in this guy's house. He had pressed so much heaviness onto her. She just wanted to be out from under it.

Today's the day, she thought. *I'm gonna say it.*

She got dressed and went to the kitchen.

Outside the kitchen window, the last of the spring snow was melting and everything was sloppy and brown. Two of her brothers were watching TV on the couch. Her dad sat at the table, drinking coffee. A small plate at his elbow still had a few crumbs in it. Toast, probably. Everything looked ordinary and innocent. Like he could never be a Big Bad Guy.

But today was the day. Diana took a chair opposite him.

"Dad" – she had never called him that before – "I need to talk to you."

Something in her voice. Like in a comic, her brothers' heads whipped together in her direction. Quick as they could, they both scrambled for the remote, toppling over each other to switch the TV off and get out of there.

"Okay," he said.

Diana closed her eyes. She could feel everything in her stomach pushing at her throat, wanting to explode all over the kitchen table.

She took an enormous breath and pushed it back down into her gut. Really, she wasn't here. She was standing in front of her own mirror back in London.

"You ruined my life," she started.

And then, instead of vomit, all the words, the ugly burning stories, tumbled out of her mouth.

He listened to her.

Sometimes he sipped at his coffee.

Never once did he interrupt.

When she started in on all the rapes, tears began to soak his face. He didn't wipe them away.

It was such a long list. It seemed to go on forever.

And then Diana was done.

The kitchen was silent. A radiator crackled as it came on again. That was when she noticed that her heart was running a race with itself.

He reached back for a kitchen towel to wipe his face.

And then the most amazing thing happened:

"I'm sorry," he said. "I did all those things to you. I hurt you terribly. I'm so sorry for what I did to you. For how badly I hurt you."

Diana Prince

He didn't blame her.
He didn't say it wasn't so bad.
He owned it all. Every last ugly bit.
What a big man.

Forgiveness isn't an instant thing. Over the next years, Diana had to make choices that a person who loved him would make, even before she felt any love. She started by forcing herself to call him "Dad," even when she didn't want to. And by letting him hug her even when it made her wanna vomit.

Also, she studied history. Family history.

She learned that, when her mom was a kid, she had been sexually abused by people who had been abused at Indian Residential School. Then she started having kids when she was still a young teenager herself. She had never really had the chance to heal. No wonder, then, that she couldn't look after Diana.

She learned that her dad had been sexually abused in Residential School, and then again at home by siblings who had been abused at Residential School.

Rape and abuse had been living in the family for generations, ever since Cree kids began going to Residential School.

One day, Diana realized that she didn't have to choose like a person who loved him anymore. He had really become her dad, she really did love him, she really had forgiven him. She was still sometimes triggered, of course; memories don't just disappear. But mostly, she felt sorry for him. He was in so much pain.

And Diana felt *so much* better.

It's still a small community. You can stand on one end and see the other. When Diana goes into the store, she can feel eyes drilling into her back, the whispers and glances. So many stories. Some of them are even true.

She tells her own story. And when she does, people in her community shush her. Don't talk about that, they say. Just carry it in yourself and let it be.

Not talking about it. That was how Cree people dealt with hard things in the days before Residential School and the specific kinds of abuse it brought. In the old days, when everyone lived on the land, far apart from each other except for a few weeks in summer, if they didn't open old wounds, they might eventually heal over.

But not talking about *these* kinds of abuses just leads to more abuse, more pain, more generations of trauma.

So Diana talks. Especially, she talks to her kids. Better they hear it from her than from the community stories. They don't know who her abuser was – she wants them to feel comfortable around their grandpa – but they know that, when Diana was a girl, she was often raped. They know, too, what someone who's being abused might look like, what to do if they see it, and how to protect themselves.

Wonder Woman is in the movies now. When Diana sees her on a poster or screen, she smiles at her, one strong Native river-basin truth-telling girl to another.

Diana Prince

Stories Heard Along the Way: Sport

A Hudson Bay manager in Fort Albany had a friend ship some cricket bats to his post. He then taught cricket to the Cree kids who lived there. They didn't have the usual cricket uniforms or padding, so they wore long socks and stuffed them with grass, and they used tennis balls instead of the hard India rubber balls that have broken so many British noses. The Cree kids didn't really take to all the rules of cricket and replaced them with rules of their own. They played Cree cricket even in the snow.

When the Province of Québec was building the La Grande-1 hydroelectric dam, the workers didn't always get along with one another. Sometimes union disputes were so bad that people went after each other with baseball bats and hockey sticks. One guy really needed to prove he was right, so he climbed onto the bulldozer and drove it into a generator. The whole camp was then without power for several days. Whether or not he was right, however, has not yet been determined.

Hockey players in La Tuque were famous. Much of their equipment was broken and there wasn't nearly enough of it. They had to share and sometimes had to make their own equipment out of scraps. Still, the hockey team was well known in the area as being the best team by far. At the School, the hockey players were sometimes given privileges that other students didn't get.

There, on a pumpkin-coloured melamine plate, sat a sandwich. The filling spilled out the sides. It was wondrous, like it had a halo or something. It glowed.

Artist: Tristan Shecapio-Blacksmith

George Shecapio

George Shecapio

ANY HALF-DECENT cook can tell you wonderful things to do with spinach. You can stir it into a pan of raw eggs and bake it into a quiche. You can sauté it with a chopped tomato and an onion and serve it alongside roasted chicken. You can mix it raw with mushrooms and cranberries and walnuts and toss it in a raspberry vinaigrette. You can even bake it into brownies.

But the cooks at La Tuque Indian Residential School.

What they did to the spinach.

They boiled it and boiled it, and, when that was done, they boiled it some more. By the time they had finished with it, it looked like seaweed that had been chewed and regurgitated and chewed again. It smelled like sewage. Some kids just couldn't swallow it, gagged a few times too often, and were punished. George Shecapio always managed to force it down. Somehow.

Thank goodness for the baked beans. They were served at Friday suppers and Julia Child herself might have baked them. The softness of the white bean, the bacon chunks with just the right chewiness, the thick sauce, sweet and savoury all at once. Of course no one ever got enough, but every morsel George got, he appreciated. He decided then that, when he grew up, he would bake his own beans.

He would eat until he wasn't hungry anymore.

Breakfast at La Tuque in the mid-1960s, George's years, was a half cup of oatmeal (into which you could stir a teaspoon of peanut butter) and a half slice of toast. Sometimes, on a rare occasion, a whole slice. Occasionally it was Corn Flakes in place of oatmeal, and every couple of weeks there'd be a boiled egg instead. What a treat. George always wanted a second egg, but he could have only one, so he peeled it carefully, sprinkled it with salt and a bit of pepper and ate it as slowly as he could. Wednesday's lunch was a half cup of Jell-O (orange or strawberry) along with a single square social tea biscuit cookie, just about two inches across and less than a quarter inch thick. On Fridays, lunch was fish. It'd taste okay, but it came with all these tiny bones and you had only fifteen minutes to eat, so you'd spend all your time trying to pick tiny bits of meat from the bones, and when the fifteen minutes were up, half the fish was still on the plate and you'd be hungry. You never saw grilled meat of any kind but sometimes, on Mondays, there was stew for supper with vegetables and gravy and a few actual pieces of beef. Tuesday night was shepherd's pie, and Thursday – well, on Thursdays they could serve almost anything and you'd eat it. If you really couldn't swallow something, say, regurgitated-seaweed-spinach, you wouldn't get supper the next day at all, and Friday night was Julia Child's baked beans, so it was worth the effort to eat everything they served you on Thursdays, no matter how vile. George ate his Friday one-third-cup of baked beans one bean at a time, making it last as long as he could. It'd come with a slice of bread (sometimes two!) and a glass of milk. If the cooks had baked a few extra beans, then they called it out and everyone scrambled back into line, oldest first. The little guys had to stand at the back of the line and by the time George and his friends got up to the counter, longing for more baked beans, the cook shrugged his shoulders. "No more," he said.

Sometimes hope was downright cruel.

George Shecario

By the time bedtime rolled around, George was hungry. Starving. Much too hungry to sleep and besides it was only 7:30 PM and the sun was still high in the sky. So he lay in bed and discussed the day's events with his colleague the next bed over who was equally hungry. And then, after a couple of hours, the older boys (who could stay up until 9:30 PM) sometimes got a bedtime snack of half a PB&J sandwich.

From where he lay, George could smell the sandwiches. That sweet sharp strawberry jelly cutting through creamy peanut butter. He could almost feel it sticking to the roof of his mouth. And, at moments like that, he wanted one of those half-sandwiches more than he had ever wanted pretty much anything.

Even now, when he needs a snack out on the land, he reaches for PB&J. It'll never go out of style.

One night, George and his friend were assigned to go take the week's used bedsheets to the laundromat. The lucky thing about this chore was that the path to the laundry passed by the kitchen.

The kitchen where the PB&J sandwiches were kept.

One of the older boys was sitting at a desk in the dorm, doing his homework. Slyly, so as not to let on, George approached him.

"Hey Julius," he said. "Those sandwiches you guys get at night. What do they do with the extras? Where do they put them?"

"Why?"

"Just wondering. If they feed the ravens or anything."

"No ravens. They put 'em in the bottom cupboard on the right-hand side of the kitchen."

George and his friend delivered the bedsheets as quickly as they could, and then, straight to the kitchen. In their sock feet, they slid to a stop just outside, then listened carefully. The kitchen was silent.

They opened the door and closed it behind them, slid dir-ectly to the bottom cupboard on the right-hand side of the kitchen, and opened it. There, on a pumpkin-coloured melamine plate, sat a whole stack of PB&J sandwiches. The filling spilled out the sides. It was wondrous, like it had a halo or something. It *glowed*.

George and his friend grabbed two sandwiches each for themselves, and one for each of their roommates with which to purchase their silence. They left a few there on the plate.

A couple minutes later, back in their dorm room, four boys sat quietly concentrating on the wealth of an evening sandwich. All the better for having been stolen.

That night, George fell asleep contented and fed, dreaming of glowing sandwiches. That was really something.

The walls in the La Tuque Indian Residential School dormitory didn't quite reach the ceiling. The space near the ceiling, where the plywood stopped, allowed for the telling of stories late at night. George and his friends in the next room could talk to one another. Unfortunately, conversation after lights out was expressly forbidden. Nevertheless, the need for George and his colleagues to discuss the day's events was sometimes so great that the rule was disregarded.

Once, when George was caught talking after lights out, he had to wash the stairs. He didn't have to do it with a toothbrush, though. He could use a mop. Some boys were made to wash floors with their own toothbrush. Or sometimes a boy was strapped and the welts stuck around for days. George got walloped on the butt with a Size Three Dash running shoe a couple of times. He'll drop his drawers and show you the imprint if you ask, though nowadays it's more like a Size Twelve. But he never saw the strap. Come to think of it, when it came to punishments at La Tuque Indian Residential School, George Shecapio got off pretty light.

In 1963, George's second year, La Tuque Indian Residential School was inaugurated and it was a pretty big deal. So big that Federal Deputy Minister of Indian Affairs Mr. Jean Chrétien came to visit. George and the other kids didn't really understand what was

George Shecapio

going on, but obviously the White folks cared about it. One of the older boys approached Federal Deputy Minister of Indian Affairs Mr. Jean Chrétien with a letter. The letter, he told everyone later, asked Mr. Chrétien to please do something about the food. For a while, then, everyone hoped it would get better, that there would finally be enough.

And maybe it did.

George was surprised to be at School at all. That first September, the silver single-engine Otter float plane landed and the Abitibi Indian Agent picked George up from the dock so casually and with such pleasure, swinging him up into the plane without even nodding to George's parents, that George thought he'd be gone for the day. A nice short trip to the James Bay coast, see the land from the air with fourteen other boys, and be home for supper.

He ended up staying at that School month after month, like everyone else. The classroom learning was fine, he liked it actually, but all the knowledge in the world wasn't going to make up for the hunger, the regurgitated seaweed spinach, the nonsense rules, the extreme punishments, the unspeakable things that happened there every day. It always felt a bit like the people at the School were after something no one was talking about – like they wanted to erase you or something. But how do you prove a gut feeling?

Making it all worse was that, way back when, someone on his mom's side of the family had slept with a White guy and George was born with green eyes. For other Cree kids at La Tuque Indian Residential School, who were made to study every day that White was much better than Cree, green eyes were a problem. They said he wasn't one of them, wasn't Cree at all, though he was starving and forcing down the regurgitated seaweed like everyone else.

Man, that really hurt.

Finally, after ten everlasting months, the blossoms unfurled, then June came around, and everyone went home. That year, over the winter, the road North had been finished, so George and his Indian Residential School colleagues were going to be bussed home. The counsellors woke them at 6:00 AM that day for an early breakfast. In the dining room sat a whole box of oranges for the ride. George grabbed one and put it in his pocket.

The bus left La Tuque at 7:00 AM, drove up Highway 155 to Lac Ste. Jean, and stopped in Roberval at another School for lunch. Everyone got a sandwich (egg or ham) and an apple, went to the bathroom, and then piled back into the bus that headed north on Highway 167.

It was a long trip, and the roads all gravel. The bus couldn't go too quickly and it didn't have the world's best suspension. Just to pass the time, everyone would go to the left side of the bus. And then to the right side. George sat at the back looking out the window and watching the road wend away from him. Finally, at five or six o'clock in the evening, the bus pulled into Perch River, the end of road. By then, everybody's everything ached.

George's parents were waiting for him at Perch River. His mom pulled him right off the bus step and into the longest squishiest hug of his life. Off to the side, George saw his dad smiling widely, so happy to see him but also eyeing him keenly: George was taller – and quite a bit lighter – than when he'd left.

No one said anything about it. At home, his mom just started feeding him.

"Eat this," she'd say, and shove bannock under his nose.

Or "Eat this," and it would be sliced grilled moose or barbecued beaver. With enough of her cooking, George looked once more like a boy his age was supposed to look.

George eyed his parents as keenly as they eyed him. They had changed. They looked weathered. Older than when he'd left. His mom seemed different – it was hard to put a finger on it – but he had changed, so why shouldn't she?

After supper one night, George and his dad sat out on a log watching the sun go down.

George Shecapio

"You know, George," his dad said. "Right after you left for School, your mom got sick. She was sick all winter long."

He picked up a twig and peeled off the bark.

A half minute later, he continued. "I've never seen a sickness like that before. It took everything out of her. Everything. She couldn't think clearly. She couldn't make the easiest decisions. She couldn't speak normally. Her words were so slow. And she needed so much sleep that she couldn't do her work. I did it. Turns out I can cook a fine goose. Right up until the snow started to melt and she knew you were coming home, she was sick. Never seen anything like that before."

Many years later, George did some research and realized she had slumped into a deep depression. While he was in School having the Cree squeezed out of him, his mom was really suffering too. It got better by the third or fourth year, when they knew George was looking after himself, but she suffered every year he was in School.

At the beginning of George's last School year, the teachers said that something called Expo 67 was coming to Montréal to celebrate the 100th birthday of Canada, and that the kids with the highest marks that year could go there in May. A trip to Montréal sounded like fun. George studied hard and got the highest marks – he still has the report card if you want to see it – and he was one of five or six kids chosen to go to Expo.

What an extraordinary trip that turned out to be! Over a hundred countries had exhibits. You could walk through and see how people in those countries dressed, you could taste what they ate, you could hear their music and watch their dances, you could see paintings and sculptures and photos from all around the world! There were so many places and people and foods that George had never heard of. And other pavilions held exhibits about space, about history, about how things used to look in Canada, about computers and other new inventions that were part of the future. It was really something.

At home the next month, around the fire, George told his parents all about it. They listened and laughed along with him, delighted at his delight.

When he was finished, his dad looked at him and said,

"Wow George. That Expo sure sounds wonderful. But – whose 100th birthday? We've been here eight or nine thousand years. At least."

George had nothing to say.

And that was George's last year. Even with the richness of Expo and the wonderful taste of baked beans and the sheer pleasure of studying, some of the things that happened there – well, they just crossed a line. George decided he'd had enough of La Tuque Indian Residential School. He would go on the land instead and study the ways of his people. The other kids said that his parents would be punished. They probably were but they never said anything about it to him. As long as he was home, his mom never got sick.

Forty years later, George learned that his gut feeling had been right, that the plan all along for the Indian Residential Schools had been to wipe everything Cree right off the Canadian map, starting with the kids. The words they used after the fact were *assimilation* and *genocide*, which really meant the same thing. It explained quite a few things about the School and how the teachers went about things. When he heard the news, he wanted to strangle the Deputy Superintendent of Indian Affairs, Mr. Duncan Campbell Scott, who had made Indian Residential School attendance mandatory, except that he had died before George was born. Instead, George and half of Eeyou Istchee, with all due respect, expelled a quiet sigh of relief when they heard of the death of the man who took them, the Abitibi Indian Agent who had stolen the identities of so many kids that the world was better off without him.

George Shecapio

George still shudders to think that that Indian Agent, who enjoyed his job too much, lifted him into the plane. Actually touched him.

The ice crystals in the air sparkled in the waning sunlight. forty-five degrees below zero. George sucked in a lungful, such a beautiful day, and bent to unhitching the sled and refueling the snowmobile. He and his dad were on the way back from a hunting trip. They had harvested a moose. His dad was planning to camp overnight on this side of the lake, but George, now forty-seven years old, wanted to get home for his granddaughter's birthday party.

His dad looked out across the lake, studying the horizon.

"Don't go, George," he said. "Bad weather's moving in."

"I'll be okay, Dad," he said.

For extra safety, George strapped some snowshoes to the back of his snowmobile, and took his chisel, hatchet, and safety pack. He put his cell phone in a pocket next to his body where it would stay warm. And set out across the frozen lake. The sky was going orange.

Well, wouldn't you know, his dad was right.

Just as the sun dipped below the horizon and the temperature began falling for the night, George's snowmobile got well and truly stuck in a puddle of the slush that forms on frozen lakes when water from underneath manages to work its way to the surface.

He dismounted and looked down at the snowmobile track and runners. They were freezing into place and more slush was working its way into the track crevices. No way George was going to be able to get the machine out that night. And he didn't have the energy to walk all the way home.

When surprises came up out on the land, his dad had taught, you had to keep your wits about you, no matter what. You had to use what you had, not panic about what you didn't have, then decide what to do and follow through.

So George looked around.

The temperature was below minus fifty by then and the wind was having a party. The ice sloshed this way and that, and water below pushed up through cracks and turned the ice surface to slush.

He couldn't walk around to keep warm, then, or his boots would soak through. Wet feet meant death. Building a fire wasn't really the best idea either – it would melt the ice, and besides he didn't have any wood to burn. He'd better not sleep because then his body temperature would drop. Also death. He had snowshoes and they'd be handy in the morning when he could see where he was going but they weren't much good at night.

What he had for the night was his jacket and the head on his shoulders. It was a good jacket and so far he didn't have any complaints about the head.

No matter how he looked at it, it was gonna be a long cold night on the frozen lake.

George left the machine where it was and snowshoed towards an island he knew was there. It was all white and he couldn't see a thing, but he walked so that the wind was always at his back. After a while, he reached the island.

He poked around there in the dark and soon found a small cave with some trees nearby. Using the hatchet, he chopped down some of the trees and lined the floor with branches. He fashioned more branches into a bit of a door at the entrance to ward off the winds. He decided not to build a fire because chopping that much wood would make him sweaty. And sweat at these temperatures, also death.

That night, he felt the temperature try to break a record or two, and the howling of the wind put wolfsong to shame. But he wasn't cold himself. His shelter was out of the wind altogether and his feet, separated from the extreme cold of the earth, were comfortable. He sat in the cave and enjoyed the night. His pocket had some snacks in it so he ate those.

George Shecapio

It was important to stay awake and think on good things, keep his wits. He thought about Expo 67 and how interesting it would be to see the Serengeti. And Siberia. There were Indigenous people in those places too who knew a thing or two about extreme weather. Wouldn't it be something to have some conversations with them?

Soon he began to think that maybe his cave needed a bit of ambience. And wasn't that a switch there on the rockface? He reached over and flicked it on. Yellow lights came up slowly, warming the place even more. And then five young women sauntered out of the back of the cave, laughing and laughing. Tracy, Monica, Jessica, Mary, and Triffona. Each was more beautiful than the last.

George settled right in, savoured the attention, and together they talked and laughed and stayed awake, stayed warm, stayed alert.

When the sun came up and daylight was brighter than the cave, the women faded away. It was still blizzarding outside but George could see enough. He strapped on his snowshoes again and headed out for a nearby camp where he knew he could get cell reception.

When he got there, people were already there. George walked to the tip of the camp, where he knew there was a signal, and he made some calls.

By the time George got home, his wife was at work. He called her to let her know he was home. Then he found a plate with leftover birthday cake. He ate it, ran a bath, and took a good nap.

He had survived a minus fifty night out in a storm without a fire. Had even enjoyed it. That was really something.

George was lucky. Some of his colleagues who spent many more years in La Tuque Indian Residential School had so many extreme experiences that their schooling has gone to waste. Even now, they have to spend their days either escaping bad memories that keep chasing them or recovering from trauma. George got out early; he could focus on being productive. He married young, at nineteen years of age, and he and his wife together raised seven boys. Everybody's healthy, life is good. He did return to school eventually, as an adult, to study management stuff. When he remembers things from those few years at La Tuque Indian Residential School that he'd rather not remember, he heads out on the land or talks through it with his wife or other supportive friends. His kids know about Residential School, and all the details that aren't in this story. They know how lucky they are to attend school in their home town where no one wants to rub the Cree out of them.

When George was interviewed by the Crown and Indian Affairs Representative for the Indian Residential School Settlement, they asked if he wanted a priest or minister present as he spoke. He realized then that, even though they were trying to address the Residential School wrongs, they really didn't understand what had happened.

No, he said politely, he certainly didn't need any more of that.

George is a baked-bean connoisseur. He researched many recipes, trying them out, adding a little of this and a little of that, until all the ingredients were in perfect proportions. Everybody loves his beans. His kids, his siblings, his neighbours. As long as five women aren't coming out of the back of the house to join the party, his wife loves them too. And when he serves them, he makes sure the portions are generous. Everyone can have seconds.

Plenty of food, plenty of life, plenty of love to go around.

George Shecapio

Stories Heard Along the Way:
Fire and Crossfire

A Catholic priest was stationed in Eastmain, but Eastmain locals never attended Catholic services. To entice them, the priest began screening black and white movies with stars like Randolph Scott and John Wayne. The locals enjoyed the films but still didn't attend services. After a few decades, the Catholic Church gave up. The priest, who had been working on a Cree dictionary, was transferred to Québec City, and his Eastmain home became a shelter for workers building the airstrip. Once the airstrip was finished, the building was left empty, ramshackle, and dangerous. One day in the '80s, the priest from the next community, Waskaganish, drove in to Eastmain, set fire to the building, and drove back to Waskaganish.

A Residential School screened a Formula Western film for the students, complete with cowboys and "Indians." One boy watched with interest, and, following the method of the Hollywood "Indians," fashioned a bow and arrow out of branches and feathers he found around the School. Soon after, he saw a farmer on a wagon, behind some horses. He drew an arrow on his bow and let fly. The arrow sank into the thigh of the farmer. And the young Cree boy was expelled.

Bows and arrows were used for hunting game as late as the 1960s. The best arrow shaft was made of birch because it's straight and light and sturdy. Any feather would do at the tail as long as it was strong and straight. The bow was usually made from tough, springy tamarack.

They work at the cork with the dinner knife until it's out and pass the bottle between them.

Artist: Jared Linton

mary shecapio-Blacksmith

Mary Shecapio-Blacksmith

MARY'S HUSBAND was not doing well. He had to be med-evacked south to Montréal, the doctor said, and she should go along. Mary went home and packed their bags, and, a few hours later, she pushed his wheelchair across the tarmac to the airplane. The nurse helped them get settled and the plane took off.

And then somebody started screaming.

High, loud, shrill. It sounded like they were being tortured.

Mary looked around the plane. Everyone looked fine. Except that they were staring at her.

Why were they staring at her?

"Mary, relax," her husband – who she was supposed to be taking care of – said. He was patting her hand like she was a little kid. "You're okay! Just relax!"

The lady who was in charge of safety came over. "Madame, Madame, you're perfectly safe," she said. "Just relax."

And that's when Mary realized that *she* was the one screaming.

Five years old all over again.

1960. Mary is living in the bush with her mother and father and brother. She is just five but already understands and loves the rhythm and seasons of life on the land.

One day her parents take her to the dock. Lots of other families are already there.

Her dad picks her up. He looks sad. Mary wraps herself around him because she knows he likes that. Together they look at a grey metal boat. It's a strange boat – it has arms and a roof but there's no place for oars or paddles. It just sits on the water and it's bigger than a house.

A strange man comes up and grabs her right out of her dad's arms!

"Baba!!" she cries and grips as tightly as she can.

But she's not nearly as strong as the strange man. Baba, crying as hard as Mary, reaches for her but he doesn't manage to get her back.

The stranger carries her away and throws her through an opening into the boat. Then he turns around. From inside, she watches him grab another kid who is screaming as hard as she can.

She looks around. Inside, it's a big grey room filling up with kids. Nothing to sit on but the cold floor. Nothing to play with or do. Somebody shoves in two metal round bathtubs (for vomit, she later realizes), and shuts the door. Now the room is black.

And then a loud buzzing drone, louder than anything she's ever heard. A sound like the world breaking up. The whole black room lurches and spasms and shakes. Somehow, without paddles, it's moving.

Mary, along with every kid squished in there, begins to scream.

After a while, the noise lessens, the door opens, and more kids are thrown in. A girl with hair sticking up all over the place sits down beside Mary. Then the door is shut, the room becomes dark, and the noise and lurching begin again. Mary is flung against the girl with the hair, and they scream together.

When the boat stops and the door opens again and everyone is pulled out, Mary is someplace else altogether. There are a few adults with white skin (white!) and a whole lot of Cree kids.

Mary Shecapio-Blacksmith

"Welcome to Moose Factory," the adults say.

That night for supper, she gets a glass of water and one small potato with a thin circle of baloney. The next time she will have enough to eat will be in ten months, when she visits her parents.

It will be much longer until she learns that the big grey boat was an airplane and that she actually *flew*.

A couple of days later, Mary is with a new friend when a guy in a black nightgown (*priest*, she later learns) comes and says to her friend, "Would you like to clean my office?"

Cleaning an office sounds very grown-up. Of course, Mary's friend goes.

A while later, she comes out of the office. She can hardly walk and she's crying harder than Mary has ever seen anyone cry.

"What happened?" Mary asks in Cree. She has to be careful – the guy in the nightgown will hit her if he hears her speak Cree.

Her friend just shakes her head and cries.

Wow, thinks Mary. *What was that?*

A few days later that same priest calls Mary into his office.

"Sit on the couch," he says. She doesn't speak much English yet, but he points and she understands.

Then – he pulls up his robe and shows her his private parts. Mary is revolted and turns away, her eyes wet, but then he shoves his long thing into her mouth. Right to the back of her throat.

She can't breathe. She has to breathe –

She bites down. Hard.

And breathes.

Instantly he's angry and throws her against the wall, then pushes her onto the couch. He reaches down, pushes her skirt up –

Her body splits apart like a wishbone. More pain than the world can hold.

Mary faints.

She comes to. A cloth has been placed on her face and she pulls it off. The priest is standing now, smoothing out his night-gown, looking pleased.

"You may go," he says to her, and points to the door.

The instant she moves, the pain twists her body again. She almost passes out.

She can't really walk, but needs to get away. Leaning on walls and furniture, she hobbles to the washroom. Bathtubs of blood running down her legs.

A senior girl is there and she has a thick white pad that says Kotex. *Hey that looks like it's for catching blood,* Mary thinks. *Maybe everybody gets one.*

"I don't have one of those," she says in Cree.

The big girl looks at her strangely and laughs.

Mary goes into a toilet stall and sits for a long time, bleeding into the toilet. Eventually it slows down. She cleans up as best she can.

She has never been so filthy. Shame, a totally invisible filth that she has never experienced before, fills up the new emptiness inside.

She can't go home to the beautiful land for ten months yet.

Later, when she tells this story to the Indian Residential Schools Settlement people, she could use one of those metal bath-tubs because she vomits several times.

There. Now, you've heard the second-hardest part of this story.

The priest in the black nightgown tries again. A few weeks later, everyone gathers for a wiener roast. Mary and her friends are sent into the bush to get some long thin branches for roasting. He is there and he spots Mary.

He leers at her, then follows her into the woods.

Mary Shecapio-Blacksmith

She is *so* scared. What if he does it again?

Just then somebody calls her, a lady's voice. "Mary! Mary?"

Mary sees her chance. She turns and runs towards the voice, past the priest, without any wood.

One way or another, Mary gets through the whole ten months and goes home.

The beautiful land. It will be a relief.

Until she gets there.

This is her family. She is safe. She can speak all the Cree she wants. She loves them, they love her –

But nobody knows how to *be*. Her brother, who was at the same School with her but they never saw each other, is a stranger. Baba, whom she clung to with all her fierce strength a lifetime ago, has become quiet and shy. Same with her mom. No hug or nothing. Invisible prison walls between all of them.

Mary doesn't even like being on the land anymore.

How can someone who doesn't like being on the land be Cree?

In the years after that, Mary is at a different School, in La Tuque.

It's still bad.

But, in her later years, this School gets one nice priest. His name is Father Bonnard.

He doesn't beat Mary. He doesn't twist her ears when she makes an English mistake. If she wets her bed, he doesn't rub her face in the pee. If she cries, he doesn't make her stand on her feet in one spot all through the long night. And he doesn't split her apart like a wishbone.

But another priest tries.

Mary is sitting at a table, away from other students, doing her homework. A priest in a long black nightgown comes up and pretends to help her.

What he really does is breathe in her ear and touch her arm and her shoulder and start working his way towards her breast.

What is it with White guys in black nightgowns who think her body belongs to them?

No way is this gonna happen again! She doesn't have room for any more shame.

Mary stands up quickly. Her chair falls back and pushes into him. She grabs her books and runs right past him.

"I'm gonna tell Father Bonnard!" she shouts.

"Mary!" he gasps, picking up the chair. "I'm sorry! Please come back. Finish your homework. Come back!"

But she is gone.

She feels better. Standing up for herself helps.

There is a chore that Mary likes to do. She likes to clean the chapel after a service. She likes the tidiness of it.

One day she and her two friends are cleaning the chapel. They put away hymnbooks and dust the pews and sweep the floor.

Eventually the priest leaves and they are alone. Now is their chance.

One girl stands guard upstairs and Mary and her friend sneak down into the communion wine cellar. She steals a bottle of wine and hides it in the folds of her skirt.

Back upstairs, they finish cleaning the chapel and leave, wine still tucked in her skirt.

There's a problem: the wine bottle has a cork. They have no corkscrew.

That night, after supper, one of the girls sneaks into the kitchen and grabs a dinner knife. It will have to do.

The next evening, they all go for a walk in the forest by the School campus and hide the bottle and the dinner knife in a patch of dense brush. They're careful. Anyone walking by will see nothing but brush.

Mary Shecapio-Blacksmith

The day after that, they return to the same place. They lean back against trees and get comfortable. Then they work at the cork with the dinner knife until it's out and pass the bottle between them. Every last drop.

Three girls, all way skinnier than they should be, a full bottle of wine. They get pretty tipsy.

It feels good to be tipsy. It's like forgetting.

1970. After nine years of Indian Residential School, first in Moose Factory and then in La Tuque, Mary dropped out of School.

She was so angry. The angriest person in the world that she knew was her.

But she had learned a few things. How to be punctual, for instance. She was always punctual.

She had learned that men were hideous. Men had penises. A man had hurt her so badly with his penis. There weren't words in any language to say just how hideous men were.

Her boyfriend happened to be man, and sometimes Mary just couldn't get past it.

She really liked him, he was such a good guy, but she couldn't tolerate proper sex. Every time they started fooling around, something went *hsssssss* in the back of her head and her heart began to race and then, there she was. Five years old all over again, a big man in a black nightgown on top of her.

Still, they muddled through and, when Mary was 16-and-a-half, they had their first baby, a girl. The most beautiful human being Mary had ever seen. Things were better for a while.

Eight months later, in a terrible accident, their beautiful daughter fell off a bed and died.

That day, Mary became the saddest person in the world that she knew. Sad and angry both.

She and her boyfriend mourned together, and got married the next year. She was already pregnant with twins.

Her husband sure was a good guy. Even though he was a man, even with all the *hsssssss*, Mary wasn't afraid of him at all.

He was afraid of her though. She beat him. She always felt bad about it later, but still she beat him. It got so that when he saw her getting a boil on about something, he quickly left the room.

Later he came back.

"Is it safe now?" he called. Sometimes he made a joke or two.

"Don't bug me," Mary warned. "I'm still mad."

"Okay," he said. "Call me when I'm safe."

And later they worked it out.

After the twins, both girls, they had another girl.

Mary loved being a mom. She loved the nursing and the cuddling and the playing and the feeding. Even the diaper changing. All of it. Those kids. They made her so happy that she got pregnant again.

This time it was a boy.

He had a penis.

Here comes the hardest part of this story:

Mary couldn't *stand* him.

He was still a baby who needed his mom, and he had asthma so he *really* needed her, but he was gonna grow into a man like the one who had hurt her terribly. *Hsssssss.*

She had to change his diaper and put his mouth to her breast. But she didn't want to touch him. Have anything at all to do with him. She didn't even want to be in the room with him. Five years old all over again.

So she pushed him away.

Mary Shecapio-Blacksmith

One day, when he was about six months old, the twins were at school and her other daughter was with a friend. Mary left him at home with a babysitter and went out to the bar. She needed to get away from him.

Tipsy is like forgetting. A few hours later she came home, completely smashed.

Her son was having an asthma attack. This little baby, he could hardly breathe.

Drunk as she was, she bundled him up as best she could, and called a cab to go to the hospital.

At the hospital, the doctors and nurses treated his asthma; he was gonna be okay. They also saw that Mary was nowhere near fit to be his mom.

They called a social worker who came to the hospital and took her son away from her. He stayed in a foster home until he was about three or four.

Honestly, it was a relief.

Even without her son at home, Mary was still the angriest person she knew. Filthy with shame.

Whenever she got scared, she just hit somebody. Once, in a bar, she worried that another woman might be flirting with her husband, so Mary beat the living bejeeses out of her.

"Honey, what's wrong?" her husband asked one day, after her ten-millionth meltdown. "Why are you always angry?"

He was sitting in the living room at the time, keeping a healthy distance. She was in the kitchen, pretending to cook but really just trying to calm down.

"You don't wanna know."

"I kinda do. Try me."

Mary sighed. She was so tired.

Tired of anger, tired of shame. Tired of the crazy hard work of secret-keeping.

"Okay," she said. "I'll tell you. When I'm done, do what you want. Hit me, leave me, rape me, whatever."

He was probably shocked when she said that but she didn't notice. Her heart was racing like it was trying to explode.

She collapsed into the living room cushy chair.

And she told him all about that day in the first week of the first year of her first School when a priest in a black nightgown split her body apart like a wishbone and filled up the gap with shame.

He listened carefully, kindness all over his face.

Then he got up and he squeezed into the cushy chair with her and he hugged her like crazy.

"I love you Mary," he said, "even more than I did yesterday."

Mary couldn't believe it. She'd thought for sure he was gonna holler for divorce or beat the crap out of her or *something*. And all he had to give her was love and hugging.

She started crying something awful. Shame leaking from her body, one tear at a time.

She cried for three days solid.

He sure was a good guy.

The days after that were filled with talking.

He had his own stories to tell – he had been at the La Tuque School for two years. He had seen some stuff too.

They had a couple more kids. A boy and a girl.

Even though her second son also happened to have a penis, Mary was okay. She loved him like crazy.

Mary went out and got herself some help.

She went through a Hoffman Process program.

She went through a Pic River anger management program.

Every time the counsellor came to her community, she went for a visit.

The counsellor said that walking for 27 minutes a day would do Mary good, so she did that. (Why 27 minutes, she never knew.)

Mary Shecapio-Blacksmith

The stress and starvation of School had led to some health problems and her doctor said that she was gonna lose her feet to diabetes if she didn't get it under control, so she and her husband switched to traditional food. Overnight, her blood sugar corrected. She thought the glucose meter was broken.

And, after a few years of healing, she had a long talk with her son, the one she hadn't been able to stand.

"I was a terrible mother to you. Because of my own pain, I rejected you. I'm so sorry," she said. "I am so sorry."

He forgave her.

A few years ago, Mary got her cheque from the Indian Residential Schools Settlement.

A whole lot of money. For what the priest had done.

Mary said nothing to her husband. She just put the cheque in her dresser. She didn't want to look at it.

Soon after, her brother got sick. In North Bay. She wanted to visit him.

"Are you coming along?" she asked her husband.

"I better not," he said. "We can't afford for both of us to fly and the truck won't make it that far."

"Let's just drive," Mary said. "We'll buy a new truck on the way."

Her husband laughed out loud. "Yeah. We can pay for it with spruce needles," he said.

"I'm serious," she said. "Trust me. And pack."

It was a rough drive. The old truck rattled and chugged and barely made it to the halfway point in Val D'Or.

"Just drive straight to the car lot," Mary said, "before it dies."

Her husband looked at her, kindness all over his face. "Honey, you are the best thing that ever happened to me," he said. "I love you no matter what. But – what have you *done*? Are the cops coming for us?"

Mary pulled the cheque from her purse and showed him.

"Standing up for myself at the Residential School Settlement thing helped. But I gotta get rid of this money," she said. "I really hate it."

He was happy to help her spend it. Such a good guy.

The best part of this story is now.

Mary has done so much healing. There's more to come, but she's not afraid of it anymore. She doesn't need to beat anyone nor push them away.

Her son, the one she rejected on the day of his birth, lives with her now. They look after one another. Her other kids and grand-kids visit all the time and her daughter, who loves to hunt, keeps the freezer full. She still visits the counsellor whenever he's in town.

A few years ago her wonderful husband passed away. She misses him so badly that her body hurts.

But life is pain. And also healing and forgiveness and love.

It sure would have been nice to have had the benefits of School without the rape. She wonders often about all the other little girls and boys whose bodies were split apart by priests. Have they coped? Have they managed to scratch back for themselves a little something Cree? Have they, like Mary, recovered enough to look forward to more days on this earth?

Much as she loves traditional food, she's still not a fan of life on the land; she'll probably never get that first love back.

Sometimes she hears people say, "Get over it already. Turn the page."

They weren't there, she realizes, they don't know better. And they don't know how much work she's done. Maybe they even think they're helping.

To them, she says, "Don't judge a book until you've read it. The whole thing."

Mary Shecapio-Blacksmith

Stories Heard Along the Way: Language

Many years ago, when colonizing missionaries first tried to translate the Bible into Cree, they ran into a problem: the Cree cover vast territories and have consequently developed many Cree languages and dialects. The missionaries chose to translate the Cree spoken in Manitoba, the geographical middle of the country, and hoped that the other Cree peoples would be able to figure it out. In Eeyou Istchee then, people will speak of Coastal Cree (Northern East Cree), Inland Cree (Southern East Cree), and Bible Cree (Plains Cree).

In one of the Schools, students were assigned to their dormitory beds according to the first letter of their names. Those with names at the beginning or end of the alphabet were closest to the doors and, since they were easily accessible, they were the ones most likely to be victims of nighttime sexual assault.

La Tuque Indian Residential School had one Cree supervisor and it was his duty to censor phone calls. Some students were able to speak on the phone to their parents, but he listened in on the calls to make sure that no one mentioned all the abuses that were happening.

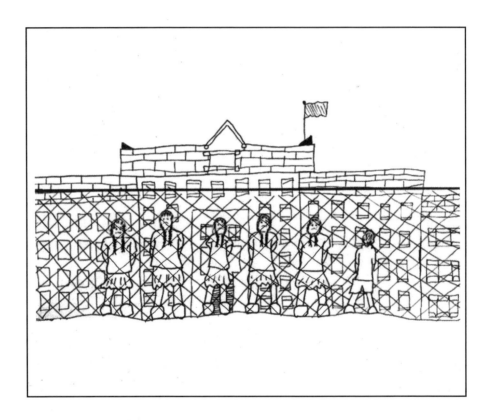

A few times a day, a line of girls in matching mud-brown tunics and bowl haircuts marched, single file, out of the dorm. And they never stepped out of line.

Artist: Tristan Shecapio-Blacksmith

Lloyd Cheechoo

Lloyd Cheechoo

BACK IN the fifties, before Lloyd was a little bit famous, he could've told you exactly what Cree was. *He* was Cree. He lived in the Cree town of Eastmain on the Cree territory of Eeyou Istchee in a Cree-style Eastmain house with his mom and his dad and his brothers and sister beside the great Eastmain River that emptied into James Bay. When his great-great-great-great-great grandfather had lived there, it had been called Stajun River but, other than the name, not much had changed. People spoke the Cree language and did Cree things. Their food came, as it had always come, from the saltwater bay, the freshwater river, and the vast land. Lloyd, who was four, watched his parents manage a boat in fast water, catch bass in the bay or sturgeon in the river, hunt geese or snare grouse or butcher caribou or smoke fish for winter stores. One day, he'd do all those things too. He wasn't scared of anything.

One summer evening, as the western sky over James Bay darkened to orange and then to grey, his dad laid a piece of green wood on the backyard fire to fend off mosquitoes and sat down on a log.

"Next week we're moving to Moose Factory Island," he announced. "All of us."

"Why?" Elmer asked. Elmer was Lloyd's older brother. He always asked why.

"When I was a kid, White people took me away and put me in Residential School. Now they want you and Lloyd. But there's a new rule. If we all move there, you can go to School in the day and sleep in your own beds at night."

He looked into the fire for a while. Then he spoke again.

"It's off-territory. We can't live off the land there. I'll find work. It'll be okay. Your grandparents live in Moose Factory." He flicked off a wood spark that had landed on his pants. "Yup, it'll be okay."

He didn't sound sure.

Lloyd looked over at his mom. She was chewing her cheek and her eyes were tight but when she saw Lloyd watching, she managed a smile.

The next week they left Eastmain, left the River and Eastern James Bay, left Eeyou Istchee altogether, and moved by plane to Moose Factory Island into another Cree-style house beside another great river. It was Lloyd's uncle's big house and it had plenty of room for everyone. Lloyd slept in his grandparents' bedroom. They were so happy to have him there. Even here, by this strange river, there was nothing to be afraid of.

In Moose Factory, Lloyd's dad looked for work. Cree people were supposed to get jobs like White people, the Government said, but businesses didn't always want to hire a Cree, especially one with Residential School education, so it took some time. Eventually he found work at the local Hudson Bay store, and he did what he had done in Eastmain. But they didn't pay him very well and he was a skilled carpenter. He kept looking until he found work that paid more – doing maintenance and carpentry at Bishop Horden Memorial Indian Residential School where he had once been a student.

Bishop Horden stood by the river, about a mile away from their house. Lloyd was still too little to go – his mom took him to

LLoYd Cheechoo

Kindergarten in Moose Factory Village – but Elmer and their dad went every day. Sometimes, between his chores, Lloyd walked out to the School. With the river behind him, Lloyd hooked his fingers through the wire fence and watched.

It looked like a jail compound. In Eastmain, the biggest building had been the Church. Here, two giant buildings stood side by side in an empty field, one about the size of sixteen Eastmain Churches smushed together and the other about the size of ten. The smaller one, Elmer said, held classrooms and the bigger one was a dorm. A high fence, as tall as three men and topped with barbed wire, started at the gate, circled all the way around the field, and met itself again at the gate.

A few times a day, a line of girls in matching mud-brown tunics and bowl haircuts or boys in matching mud-brown pants and buzz haircuts marched, single file, out of the dorm. Only girls, or only boys, never both. And they never stepped out of line. (How did that many kids never step out of line?) In magazines, Lloyd had seen pictures of convicts in prisons and prisoners in concentration camps. These kids looked like that. Even from fifty feet away, their eyes were hard. Like they *knew* something. Sometimes a whistle blew and then the kids broke formation and ran and kicked a ball around. It almost looked like fun – for a second Lloyd wanted to join – but then a kid would glance at him from across the field and, every time, Lloyd cowered. They might as well have been wolves.

Still. Even scared, Lloyd couldn't look away. If he hadn't had chores to do, he would've stood there, fingers hooked through the fence, and watched for hours.

Two years passed. His parents got their own house down the road and moved out. Lloyd stayed behind. His grandparents were aging and needed help. Lloyd lived with them, he chopped wood for the stove, he got coal for the lamps, he carried water from the town tap, and he ran to the store for groceries. It was important work for a kid and it was how Cree people had always looked after Elders. His grandparents, whose own kids had all been taken to Residential School, were so happy for a child to raise that whenever Lloyd came into the room their eyes sparkled like sun on snow. And, every day, he could walk three doors down the road and visit his parents.

Lloyd turned six. He could no longer watch the strange kids through the fence. It was his turn to go to Bishop Hordon School himself. Every weekday morning, a group of kids walked by their house and he and Elmer walked out to join them. They all walked to School together. In town, it was just a few kids, but more joined the further they walked. Some were tough, some were shy, some were Cree, some were White. And by the time they arrived at Bishop Hordon, they were a group of about fifty.

The walk was always the same. The closer they got to the School, the more tension Lloyd felt. And the instant his shoe hit the Schoolyard dirt, an invisible cold weight dropped on his shoulders like a burlap sack of wet sand. Sometimes he looked up to see where it came from. The autumn sun shone and the wind fluffed up his curls like nothing was wrong. There wasn't any sand on his shoulder. But the weight he felt was immense and took his breath away.

Inside it wasn't any better. The teacher was a tall White man with heavy glasses. He was stern and he spoke only English. He didn't shout at anyone. He also never smiled. Lloyd's grandparents always smiled. A clock hung on one classroom wall, a chalkboard on another, and in the middle were about twenty kids. Most of them said they were Cree. They looked Cree. But nobody spoke Cree. Nobody talked about Cree things. Nobody did Cree things. They just sat at their desks and did whatever the White teacher told them to do. How could *they* be Cree?

Lloyd could never figure out what was going on. Every day, all day, he was uneasy. He sat very still, watching everything carefully.

LLoYd Cheechoo

He was so busy trying not to be noticed that he couldn't think about learning. The invisible sand pressed down more than ever, and the clock surely moved slower than any clock had ever moved. It took five years for Lloyd to understand the language at all.

Starting in Grade Five, one afternoon a week, the boys went to Industrial Arts classes. In his regular classroom, Lloyd had struggled but *this* was worse. The teacher was a big man with a shiny bald head, bushy eyebrows behind thick glasses, a beard, and hairy hands. Every few hours, without warning, without reason, he hollered like crazy – and then beat on a Cree kid! He'd use his hairy hands or a yardstick or whatever he could reach. In an Industrial Arts classroom, there were quite a few things he could reach. It was so instant, so random, so out of control.

Sometimes Lloyd was the one getting hit. He'd be trying to do whatever he was supposed to do and *Whack!* a crack across the head. "You stupid donkey!!" the crazy teacher yelled. Or something like that. Lloyd couldn't always tell because his ears were ringing. In Industrial Arts, Lloyd never really did any work. He was too afraid to do anything but watch the crazy teacher and try to dodge the next crack.

Out on the Schoolyard, the kids divided into factions. The White kids – there weren't many – lived in town and slept in their own beds like Lloyd did. They were the elites. Everything in the classroom happened differently for them. They were fluent in English, so they were always far ahead. The teachers were kind to them, even in Industrial Arts. Those kids thought they were so important.

Then there were the Cree kids who lived in the dorm. They had strange scars and weird stories of kids being hurt or made to do awful things. Some of the stories were so extreme that Lloyd could never be sure they were true. Every one of those kids seemed off. Some of them, Lloyd figured, didn't want to be there. Even when he spoke nicely to them, they didn't answer. They didn't interact with anyone. Others seemed free, like they preferred to be in Bishop

Horden away from the land, like they were so much smarter, so much safer, and would never be afraid of anything. And some were terrified, always on edge, waiting for something to hurt them. Like even the grass might explode. The dorm kids were never allowed to speak Cree, and they learned English quite a bit faster than Lloyd did. After a couple of years, they couldn't understand Cree at all. So, how could *they* be Cree? And then there were the Day School kids, like Lloyd. Out on the Schoolyard, the factions really mattered.

One thing for sure: the best part of every day was running across that field away from School. He held his breath until he got through the gate just in case this time it was locked. A relief, every time. Then he ran home to his wonderful grandparents whose eyes sparkled like sun on snow and who fed him Cree food and spoke to him kindly in Cree. To where he slept in a safe and cozy bed and tried to play his cousin's guitar.

Not far from Bishop Hordon stood Tent City. Lloyd walked by it sometimes and peered in. It looked crowded and smoky from campfires. Nothing like his own home. Just strange enough for Lloyd to keep walking. Until one Saturday, when his School friend Reggie invited him to visit.

Reggie met him at the entrance by the last row of tents, and then led him through the rows and the deep muddy ruts between them. Everywhere, Cree people were doing ordinary things. Working with hides or cooking over open fires or chopping wood or cleaning fish or sealing wind out of their tents with sand.

Lloyd and Reggie played outside for a while, then went to Reggie's tent. His mom was making tea.

"Hello Lloyd," she said in English, "*Wachiya.* It's nice to meet you. Would you like some tea and bannock?" She looked Cree but she spoke English with some Cree words mixed in. Next tent over, private things were happening and Lloyd could hear everything.

LloYd CheechOO

Reggie and his mom, though, just spread jam on their bannock and pretended not to hear.

Lloyd and Reggie played quietly until the sky darkened to grey. Then Reggie walked Lloyd to the edge of Tent City and Lloyd headed for home.

He was a few steps down the road, not far at all, when a half-dressed man whose face had slid sideways charged out of the tents, right at Lloyd, hollering like crazy:

"ARNNGSSKKAAKKHH!"

What was he saying?? Lloyd had never even met this guy and he was so angry at him!

Lloyd turned and ran.

Later at his parents' house, after his heart had slowed a little and he could breathe normally again, Lloyd blurted everything out.

"Oh Lloyd, that man was just drunk and unhappy," his dad explained. "Our family lives in a house here because we have always been members of Moose Factory Cree Nation, even when we lived in Eastmain. But there aren't enough houses for all the Eeyou Istchee families who moved here to be able to keep their kids. They have to live in tents crowded together without real privacy. It's not easy. And that man probably went to Residential School himself and is trying to forget times when he was hurt. Drinking helps with forgetting. He'll sleep it off and his face will straighten out in the morning."

Lloyd thought about it as he practised guitar that night. Even unhappy, how could *that man* be Cree? If *he* was Cree, what was Lloyd?

Moose Factory sure was a rough town.

Years passed. Geese came and went. Lloyd learned to stay out of the way of drunk people. And of gangs and gang fights. And of other School factions and bullies. And of the teacher who hit kids. Of pretty much everyone but a few friends, his family, and his guitar. He got pretty good at guitar. What Lloyd didn't learn at all – way too scared – was math or English or any of the School stuff.

Later, when Lloyd was ten or eleven, Bishop Horden class-rooms closed, and all the students went to Moose Factory public school. There were no crazy teachers there, no invisible wet sand pressing down. Instead, there was a pinball team and a curling team and a hockey team and a soccer team.

Lloyd played soccer.

"Take off your shoes!" the coach yelled. "Kick that ball sky high!"

So Lloyd slipped off his shoes, ran the soccer pitch barefoot, and kicked the ball to the clouds. The coach had a point – it was exhilarating!

But even there, even where teachers were kind and fun, the instant Lloyd tried to concentrate on math or English, his heart raced and his breathing lurched and his skin turned white and pasty. He couldn't stop looking around the classroom for someone to hit him. He couldn't learn anything at all. Even though there was nothing to be afraid of anymore.

Eventually, Bishop Horden Hall closed down altogether. The dorm kids left for other schools. On Saturdays, Lloyd and his friends went out to Horden Hall and climbed the tall dikes that held ice back from the river. Up there, with the river at their backs, they sat and looked through the barbed wire fence at Bishop Horden Hall. The lights were off, the grounds quiet. It still looked scary, but lonely and abandoned too. He almost felt sorry for it. After a while, he jumped down, dusted off his pants, went home, and played his guitar.

Sometimes, on weekends, Lloyd went to the Moose Factory Movie House with his friends. There was one movie – *A Man Called Horse* – about a White guy out West who was taken in by a Nation and he had to do some painful ceremonies if he wanted to marry a girl. Lloyd couldn't stop thinking about it. About what it was like to be Indigenous out West. He sure would like to meet people

LloYd Cheechoo

from that Nation, see how they lived, maybe participate in their ceremonies. The James Bay Cree had ceremonies too, but they were different. Every day, for a long time, Lloyd thought about that movie.

For high school, Lloyd and Elmer were sent to North Bay. Some of the Bishop Hordon dorm kids were there too. They had been gone from their homes for years by then and had quite a bit to forget. Like the Tent City man, they found some relief in booze or drugs. As for Lloyd, it was his first time away from his grandparents. He longed for them so much that his stomach hurt. Everything was terrifying. Sometimes he almost envied the dorm kids, drunk as they were. They had been away from their families for so many years, scared for so long, that it all seemed normal to them.

Lloyd failed Grade Nine. And Ten. For Grade Eleven, Indian Affairs sent him to Timmons to take Grade Eleven while also catching up on Grades Nine and Ten. He passed Grades Nine and Ten but not Grade Eleven. Way too scared. Somewhere in there, he was flagged by the North Bay police. He didn't know why, but lots of Eeyou Istchee guys were being flagged. Was it just part of being Cree?

When Lloyd turned sixteen, he travelled alone to Sault Ste. Marie by bus to take Grade Eleven all over again.

His landlady met him at the bus terminal.

"I'm pleased to meet you Lloyd," she said. "Can you cook your own meals?"

"Yeah, sure," he said.

"That's good," she said, "Because I'm leaving tonight for a week. Going shopping in the US of A. Help yourself to anything you find in the pantry or freezer."

She showed Lloyd where the high school was, then she showed him where the pantry was, and then she drove off.

The house was stocked with foods he'd never heard of. *Pesto. Osso buco. Prosciutto. Saltimbocca. Gelato. Mortadella. Salami genovese. Pannetone.*

Lloyd tried everything. He went to school in the daytime. And came back at the end of each day and ate.

One night the phone rang and Lloyd answered it.

"What?? Who are you?" the guy on the other end said. "What have you done with the lady who lives there?"

"No no!" Lloyd stammered. "I didn't do anything! She's on a trip. She'll be back on Thursday."

"Did you murder her? I'm calling the cops."

"Look," Lloyd said. "I don't know why she didn't tell you. But I'm just – I'm a Native student. I'm boarding here this year. I go to the high school."

"Oh! You're her boarder! Well why didn't ya say so?" And he hung up.

Lloyd went back to eating.

It was a wondrous week. No scary people in that house at all. Just Lloyd and his guitar and a whole lot of food. At the end of the week, the lady's car pulled into the driveway again.

"Did you manage, Lloyd?"

"Yeah, I managed fine!" he said.

"Good. Do you think you could help me unload the car?"

"Sure!" he said, and went out to help.

They carried in suitcases and bags. When he thought the car was empty, she opened a secret compartment in the wheel well and pulled out boxes that had been stuffed in there. Then another compartment in the other wheel well. And a compartment in the back seat, where the stuffing was supposed to be. Another under the seat. And on it went. She had more hidey holes in that car than mouse nests in a woodpile. By the time they'd finally emptied it, Lloyd figured that she'd smuggled, across the US border, about as much stuff as a small truck could carry. Most of it was food.

Lloyd Cheechoo

Specialty things he'd never heard of. Salted meats, figs and lemons and olives and basil, bright green oils, ricotta, nuts, desserts, the works. Clothes and other things too, but mostly food.

"Every few months, me and my lady friends get hungry," she said. "Then we cross over and load up at the good markets. Now Lloyd. I'm gonna teach you to do real Italian cooking. Not that *spazzatura* people eat at 'Pizza House.'" She spat a little when she said "Pizza House." And then she cooked up a whirlwind.

Never before had Lloyd eaten gourmet food created by a trained Italian chef. Nothing had ever tasted as wonderful. Math and English didn't matter at all. Every day after that, Lloyd looked forward to dinner. He loved it when she cooked. She liked it when he played guitar.

"You're like Bob Dylan, but Cree," she said. Next to Lloyd's grandpa, Bob Dylan was his hero. It was the nicest thing she could have said.

At school Lloyd sometimes heard about the American Indian Movement (AIM) and National Indian Brotherhood. Vernon Bellecourt, Russel Means, Dennis Banks – those guys knew how to be Indian. They wore braids, looked the part, and talked about Native Pride. Long ago, they said, before colonization, the Nations knew one another, but now they were split apart, even though they had the same oppressors and similar obstacles. They reminded Native people about the other Nations around them. Now two women from different Nations could meet in a mall and recognize each other as Indigenous. Sometimes, the AIM leaders even got lumped in with Berkeley environmentalists or the Black Panthers. They were so confident in themselves that they didn't seem to mind.

Lloyd was so far away from home. So far from moose and bannock. So completely and unceasingly afraid. And with hair too curly to braid. Was he even Cree anymore?

Finally, after six years of high school across three cities, two credits away from finishing his diploma, nineteen-year-old Lloyd had had enough of fear. He packed his bags and went home to Moose Factory to live with his grandpa and grandma, and to work in construction with his dad. Sometimes, he missed gourmet food or city entertainment, but it was nice to be home where there was nothing to fear.

On weekends, he and Elmer and their friends performed at music festivals or fiddle dances or high school dances, doing back-ups and vocals for each other. Lloyd took up the drums then. If anyone around town needed a drummer, they called Lloyd.

"You wrote any songs?" one guy asked.

"Yeah, I got a song," Lloyd said. "It's called 'Winds of Change.' It's about change."

"Let's hear it."

Lloyd played it. The guy liked it. And recorded it. Just in case.

A couple of weeks later, the guy called him back.

"Hey Lloyd," he said. "We're making an album. We're putting your song on it. We're gonna back you up with a full band and produce it professionally, the works. Let's get a tribal drum in there. We're calling the album *Goose Wings: The Music of James Bay.* But it needs another song. Got any more?"

"I got one started. Maybe I could finish it."

"What's it called?"

"'James Bay.' It's about James Bay."

"Finish it now," the guy said. "I wanna hear it after lunch."

When the album came out in 1979, both songs were on it.

Lloyd and the other artists toured the album. Lloyd tried to dress the part. Sunglasses of course, because they made anyone look cool. He tried again to braid his hair but, with the curls, it just didn't work. So he wore a jean jacket or embroidered shirt and slung a leather thong with bone beads around the neck. Like Bob Dylan, but Cree.

Lloyd Cheechoo

Or, at least, Cree-looking. As much as he could manage with curls.

Thirty-three years passed. Lloyd's beloved grandparents passed away. He worked in construction, then moved into communications and started doing Cree radio shows. On weekends, he still played drums and guitar at dances or Churches or wherever he was needed. He got married and had kids. He went South and took the Hoffman Process program to take control of his panic and fear. And he sought out Elders and spiritual leaders to learn what he could about being a *real* James Bay Cree.

One day the phone rang. "Hey Lloyd," the voice said, "I'm doing a compilation of Native musicians. Sort of a limited Collector's Edition. Your two songs from that '79 album – they're just so authentically Cree. Would you let me include them?"

The album, *Native North America, Volume One,* came out in 2015 and included famous Native musicians. Willie Thrasher, Willie Dunn, Willy Mitchell, Morley Loon, and David Campbell. Some of the guys that Lloyd used to play festivals and dances with had songs on it too. It was like a reunion party on vinyl.

It took off. It was downloaded everywhere. Lloyd got media calls from CBC and New York. He and his friends, backing each other up once again, performed to massive crowds in Vancouver and Toronto. He wasn't afraid at all.

"Hey, can you wear a leather vest with strips?" somebody asked Lloyd.

"Naahhh," he said. "That's for politicians. I'm just Cree. I'm gonna wear jeans. And a t-shirt. Maybe a denim jacket."

The Guardian UK and *Der Spiegel* wrote about the album. It was nominated for a Grammy – against Bob Dylan. Dylan won.

And The Barenaked Ladies, who had heard Lloyd play, called and asked if they could perform his song live in concert. He hadn't even dared to dream something like that and the dream came true anyways.

These days, Lloyd lives in Mistissini. He works with Cree radio. He's still playing guitar and writing songs. And he's raising his grandson while his daughter goes to university. Sometimes he can feel his eyes sparkle when he looks at the boy. The house is full of love. He hasn't been afraid in years.

"I don't get it Grandpa," his grandson said to him. "You're a real star. The Barenaked Ladies and everything! But all you do is watch TV and talk on the radio."

If you ask Lloyd now what a real Cree is, he'll tell you what an Elder told him:

"What matters is the everyday. You honour people, you spend time in nature, you respect the people and the land, and you share. You look after one another. These things are what it means to be Cree."

Lloyd Cheechoo

Stories Heard Along the Way: Dam(n)

When ninety per cent of the Eastmain River flow was diverted to build a dam, the river itself turned brackish as the saltwater of the bay pushed upriver. For years, the people of the community collected rainwater or gathered water from rock caps on islands in the bay – and didn't always bring enough for the dogs. The Eastmain dogs, who were not yet able to canoe out to the islands, suffered. Now that Eastmain has fresh water, some people set water pots out in their yards for dogs to help themselves. The dogs are still working on their canoeing skills.

Ever since Hydro-Québec began building a dam on Cree territory without Cree permission, they haven't had the best reputation in Eeyou Istchee. Years of power outages in Oujé-Bougoumou, dating all the way back to the '90s, haven't helped the problem. In the fall of 2018, looking to improve their relations with the James Bay Cree, Hydro-Québec sponsored a show of Tomson Highway's Cree opera *Chaakapash* in Oujé-Bougoumou. At great cost, the entire Montréal Symphony Orchestra went North, along with the set and everything needed to mount a world-class opera in a small community. Ironically, just as the show was about to begin, the power went out. The musicians used flashlights to see their scores.

"Are you the water taxi?" Marni said. "Can you take me to Mistissini?"

Artist: Jared Linton

marni macbeane

Marni Macbeane*

ON MARNI'S eighteenth birthday, which was in January, the principal called her into his office.

"Your education stops today," he said. He raised his palms to say stop.

You say that, Marni thought, *as if it ever started.*

She had been at Indian Residential Schools for over ten years now, three different ones, but she still couldn't speak English very well or do more than basic math. What they had made her spend time on instead – well. She didn't want to talk about it.

"You can't go home yet, of course," the principal continued. "Tomorrow, you start working here, downstairs in the laundry. Unless – I was wondering – would you like to go to Montréal? I have friends who are looking for a nanny."

"Will my parents know where I am?" Marni asked.

"No," he said. "We can't reach them until June when they meet you at the boat."

It was risky. The principal could not be trusted. Neither could his friends. Cree kids had a way of disappearing when White folks were involved. Montréal was so far south.

But she would be away from School. Nothing could be worse than School.

And there was a chance, the skinniest chance, that from Montréal she could figure a way home.

"Okay," she said. "I'll go."

It was better than she had expected. In Montréal, Marni had her own bedroom. The kids she looked after thought she was the best thing ever. They woke her every morning and kept her busy all day and fell asleep in her arms. Her lady boss was kind and grateful for the help. She paid Marni a real wage and helped her to open a bank account. She taught her more English, a little French, and a little math. For the first time since leaving her mother's cooking fires, Marni even got enough to eat. And eating enough meant that, at eighteen years of age, she finally started her monthly periods.

Oh there was the usual trouble. She had been there a few weeks when the man boss came into her bedroom in the night. He pulled back the covers and tugged at her pajamas and demanded that Marni do for him what she had had to do for so many different people in School.

Ah. So *that* was why the principal had wanted to send her to his friend.

But this was not School. Marni was not helpless. She sat up in bed and pointed to the door.

"Get out," she said to him, in her best English. "Or I tell your wife."

His face shrivelled a little. He scampered away like a mouse.

She got up and locked the door behind him. The usual trouble was to be expected when White folks were involved.

The pussy willows were beginning to make Montréal smell like spring when Marni decided it was time. She and the lady boss were cleaning the kitchen together one day. Marni was washing the refrigerator racks in the sink.

"Ice is breaking up at home," she said. "My parents will be in Mistissini. I want to visit them. Just for a week."

The lady boss, who was on her knees scrubbing the oven, pulled her head out and turned to look at Marni.

"How are you gonna get all the way to Mistissini?"

"By train. I saved money. I'll come back," she said.

"Okay," the lady boss said, getting to her feet. "I'll help you find the right train."

A few days later, on a cloudy afternoon, Marni took a small bag and went with the lady boss and kids to the Montréal train station. It was the biggest building Marni had ever seen, made entirely of concrete, and churning with people. If Marni had been alone, she would have been too scared to step inside. But the lady boss walked right through the crowd, like she knew what she was doing, to a row of wickets. Marni followed with the kids.

"The Abitibi," she said, "To Senneterre. One ticket please," and the man in the booth gave her a ticket.

They made their way then to the row of trains – Marni counted seven of them – and the lady boss helped her find the right one. Marni stepped up, walked down the narrow train hallway, and found a window seat. As the train pulled out of the station, she waved through the window to the lady boss and her kids. They waved back.

"See you soon!" they called.

"See you soon!" she said. The first good White people she had ever met. She almost felt bad about lying to them.

Marni leaned back in the seat. The lady boss had packed her some sandwiches, and the scenery outside got better the farther they went. She would have liked to relax, enjoy the clacking and lurching of her first train ride, watch the countryside, maybe even chat with another passenger. But people were stepping on and off at each train stop. Any one of them could hurt her. She had to be alert.

The night went on and on. It felt like a week. She stayed awake for every single minute.

Early the next morning, about sixty train stops and twelve hours after she had waved to the boss family, the train whistled and clacked to a stop in Senneterre. Marni picked up her bag and stepped down onto the platform.

The Senneterre station was smaller than the one in Montréal. Two train tracks ran by the back of it, and windows and a plywood canopy wrapped all the way around. Marni wanted to look like she knew what she was doing so she walked right into the station and sat on a bench near the front.

The floor was pink and the walls were covered with pretty yellow tiles. There were a couple of washrooms, a wicket for buying tickets, and a restaurant. The smell of eggs frying wafted through the air. A dozen people with suitcases at their feet waited on benches. A bored White boy kicked at a bench leg. Out the front window the road stretched forward and beyond, into the open Québec countryside.

She was barely halfway home – the road was where she needed to be.

Marni ate one of her lady boss's sandwiches for breakfast, then went into the ladies' room where she washed her face, then walked out front to the road.

Right away, a taxi drove up. *"Où allez-vous?"* the driver asked.

"À Mistissini," she answered.

"I can take you 350 kilometres, as far as Chibougamau," he said, "but my wife wants to come along."

"Okay," Marni agreed. Safer with another woman in the car.

They agreed on a price, and off the taxi went, carrying Marni farther and farther north.

It was a dusty four-hour drive. She was more tired than she had ever been before, but these were strangers. They could try anything. She had to stay awake.

Finally, they pulled into a gas station just outside of Chibougamau.

ᒪᕐᓂ ᒪᒃᐯᑎ

She needed to use the washroom. The driver was filling the tank, his wife sleeping against the window.

Marni went inside and found the ladies' room. When she came out, she saw, through the glass in the gas station door, the driver out front, sitting in the car and waiting for her.

Marni didn't go out front. Quietly, trying not to be noticed, she snuck through the station diner out the other door, then ran across a field and a parking lot to a motel – she had always been good at running.

Another taxi sat there. The driver was smoking a cigarette and listening to the radio, waiting for a fare.

"Take me to Perch River," she said, getting into the car. "Right to the end of the road! And go now!"

"Okay, girl!" the second driver laughed. He didn't ask what the rush was.

Off they went, wheeling down skinny dirt roads, leaving the first taxi driver and his wife behind in the plentiful dust. Unpaid, still waiting for Marni to come out of the gas station.

In the car, Marni ate the last lady boss sandwich. She was so tired. But the trees outside looked like home. She couldn't have slept if she'd tried.

Nearly two hours later, at Perch River, the taxi driver rolled down his window and poked out his head.

All around was wilderness. Buzzing insects, hardworking squirrels, miles of black spruce. A couple of tents were pitched at the riverside, and a single curl of smoke rose from the grey left-overs of a campfire.

"Girl, you sure you wanna be here?" he asked. "Seems kinda *remote.*"

"I'm sure," she said, and paid him. "I'll be fine. Thank you for the ride."

Marni stepped out and the car pulled away.

She filled her lungs with spruce air and smiled. Here, at Perch River, everyone was Cree. She didn't have to be afraid anymore.

Someone was there, behind the first tent. He was cleaning a couple of fish.

"Are you the water taxi?" she said in Cree. "Can you take me to Mistissini?"

"Sure," he said, "but I was just about to cook this. Wouldn't you like to join me for roasted whitefish first?"

"I'd rather go right away," she said.

"Okay," he said. He left the fish with someone else and together they got into his boat and set out for Mistissini. Marni couldn't stop smiling.

Early that evening, just after frogs had begun to sing, she pulled the leather strap on the door of her own cabin and walked in.

Her mother was washing something. She turned when she heard the door.

"*Wh– What* are *you* doing here!?" she said. She was so surprised she had to sit down. "You're not supposed to come until June!!"

Marni gave her the short version.

Her mom hugged her about fifteen times, wet hands and all.

"Go get your dad," she said then. "And don't unpack. They're gonna come for you. We gotta get into the bush right away. And Marni," she said, hugging her again, "this is the best thing that's happened in a long time."

That night, Marni had the best sleep she'd had in years. Maybe in her life.

Early the next morning, they packed the big canoe and paddled north into the bush. In the boat, Marni told her parents all about living in Montréal and how she had escaped.

She didn't tell them about the usual trouble. There was no point. And besides Indian Residential School was done. She could forget about it and move on.

She had escaped.

Marni Macbeane

At last, Marni was learning something useful. Cree words melted on her tongue like bear fat. Knives and bush tools toughened her hands. Her nights belonged to her. Parts of her spirit that she had thought lost began to unfurl inside her like wildflowers. Good things were in her life again.

Still.

Once, her father returned to camp from the trapline with a beaver slung over his shoulder. He handed it to Marni, smile so wide, like he had been waiting half a lifetime to do exactly that. She took it from him but – what was she supposed to do with a dead beaver? From across the camp, her mom saw her confusion. She came over, took the beaver from Marni's hands, and prepared it in front of her, starting with the removal of the musk gland. She showed her every step along the way.

Her parents loved her so much. They were overjoyed to have her there. They never said a word about how strange it was to teach a child's duties to a grown woman. How any ten-year-old raised on the land knew more than Marni.

Sometimes, when she was alone, Marni got so mad that she shook. After everything she had gone through, for so many years, at least she should have gotten an education. A White education, a Cree education, she should have learned something. In all directions she had been cheated. Even with all the love around her now, her mind slid, like a goose landing on water, into the bad days.

To the boat ferrying kids from where the plane landed in Moosonee to the Moose Factory School. No one had told Cree parents that there would be a long boat ride so the kids weren't properly dressed and there were no blankets. They got so cold that their hearts raced, they got dizzy, they shook and vomited. Sometimes the next person's vomit fell on Marni.

Or to being too scared to speak in class. She missed a lot of class because of the usual trouble. But if she was in class and gave a wrong answer, the teacher hit her hands with a steel ruler and they swelled up like balloons. To this day her hands are scarred from that ruler. In class, she was terrified. Her insides quivered and her muscles didn't work. She couldn't even grip a pencil properly.

Or to nights in the dorms when kids cried into their pillows. The teachers or supervisors sometimes heard them anyways. Then they walked up to the kid's bed, yanked back the blanket, and shouted, "Shut up!!" If the kid couldn't stop, they beat her. Marni got used to lying awake at night, trying not to feel. If she didn't feel, maybe she wouldn't cry.

Or to a quiet conversation with a friend on the Schoolyard. A teacher overheard a Cree word, stomped over, and grabbed her friend's hair. "What're you saying about me?" she hissed. Then she dragged Marni's friend across the Schoolyard to the principal's office by her hair, her dragging feet carving little furrows in the dirt.

Or to walking naked, in front of all the girls, to the shower room and showering in public. They saw every inch of her. They saw her washing her private parts, they saw every teenage change in her body, they saw where she had been hurt by the usual trouble. It was humiliating. The only place in the whole School anyone had privacy was the toilet.

Or to being always unbearably cold. The blankets at her first two Schools were thin, grey sheets, the same in both Schools though the Brantford sheets had a narrow red stripe running close to the edge. Marni thought they had probably been worn thin in the war before being sent to the School. At least, at her third School in La Tuque, the blankets were actually blankets.

Or to getting mumps, then chicken pox, then measles, all in one year. She hardly went to class that year. She slept up in the infirmary. There were no nurses. Nobody looked after her. But sometimes a counsellor came and, with a strange expression, grabbed a handful of Marni's skin around the red blisters and twisted and pinched until the blisters broke and a small bruise formed.

Marni Macbeane

Eventually Marni recognized the strange expression: it was satis-faction. The counsellor liked hurting Cree kids.

Or to the usual trouble. It had started the first week of the first year of the first School, when she was still a very little girl. That time it was a priest and it hurt more than anything had ever hurt before. It kept on happening through three Schools right to the end. Men and women, nuns and priests, supervisors and teachers. She lost track of how many times, how many people. She never said anything about it. She didn't want anyone to know.

The bad days were every minute of every day at Indian Residential School. From stepping on to the August plane to step-ping off the June plane in Mistissini, Marni was afraid. It didn't mat-ter which School, they were all the same, nothing was good. Even her summers were poisoned. Sure, she came home for a couple of months, but everything was awkward. How did someone *be* a daughter? How did someone *be* not afraid?

Once she tried to tell her mother.

"Mom it's awful there. They do bad things to my private parts."

"Oh no, Marni," her mother said. "They're Government people. They can't do *that*."

But later, when her mom saw Marni flinch, she asked, "Why are you so scared? You know I won't hurt you."

Marni stayed quiet. Why bother? Even if her mom did believe her, what could she possibly do about it?

Her mom looked at her then, thoughtfully.

But now Indian Residential School was done.

She had escaped.

She was in the bush with people who loved her. She could forget about it and move on.

And yet – she couldn't stop thinking about Indian Residential School.

Here's the thing about the usual trouble. Even though it had been forced on her when she was very young, even though a five-year-old girl could never have defended herself against such giant men, Marni still felt like it was her fault. Shame crusted on her like swamp mud. If she showered for a hundred years, she still couldn't wash off the filth.

She tried to move on, she did, but no matter what, the instant she was in a room alone, it was always right there. In her head. Demanding to be remembered.

She just wanted it to go away.

One day, Marni's father said something strange. Every time Marni had left for School, he said, her mom got sick. She fainted, then her body seized and jerked around like a fish on a dock, foam bubbled from her mouth, and her heartbeat and her breathing were all over the place. He had never seen anything like it. Whenever it happened, he worried she might die.

What on earth.

In School, Marni fainted all the time. In class, in chapel, in the shower, wherever. Her eyes rolled back, her knees buckled, and the next thing she knew somebody was waking her up on the floor and she had some fresh bruises. But she fainted from hunger. Or fear. Lots of kids did. Fainting was part of the Indian Residential School experience.

Her mom was safe in the bush. She had plenty to eat. Nobody had threatened her or forced the usual trouble on her. Why had she been fainting and seizing and frothing at the mouth when Marni had been the one living in terror?

Right around Marni's twentieth birthday, a couple of years after her escape from Montréal, she was picking Labrador tea leaves with her mom.

"Marni, I have to ask you something."

"Okay," Marni said.

"Somebody wants to marry you. Do you want to marr—?"

"No."

Marni didn't mean to interrupt. It was disrespectful. But she couldn't bear to be away from her parents. She was still learning bush skills. And she wasn't nearly ready for anyone else's bed yet.

Her mom looked at her hard and long. And then looked away.

"Okay," she said.

Five years passed before her mom mentioned it again. This time, they were grinding dead wood into powder.

"Marni, somebody wants to marry you. Are you ready, do you think?"

Marni stopped grinding for a minute and thought.

"Maybe," she said. "Did he go to Residential School?"

"No," her mom said. "His parents hid him in the bush."

"I'll meet him," she said. "We'll see."

Her mom arranged for them to meet at the winter campsite. He was tall and gentle, funny and polite. He spoke Cree and English and French. He would teach her the White languages, he said, what she should have learned in School.

She liked him. Quite a lot.

They got married and lived out in the bush.

For a few years, they didn't have kids – Marni couldn't help but push him away. She couldn't bear to be touched.

"It's not you," she explained when he asked. "Bad things happened in School."

"Oh," he said. "I'm so sorry." He never pressed her after that and she didn't say anything more.

Eventually, it was okay. They had a couple kids. And then a couple more and then a couple more until there were five boys and three girls.

Those kids. Marni loved those kids to pieces and they loved her back, all eight of them. She made sure they learned all the bush skills and Cree and English and French, and that they never went to Indian Residential School. And she watched them carefully. Nobody better hurt them the way she was hurt.

As far as she knew, nobody did. They never knew what it felt like to be constantly scared of giant men and the usual trouble. She sure wasn't gonna tell them.

Just for fun, every year, in the Native sports tournaments that happened across the North, she joined in. Even if she was pregnant and her belly way out front. Her favourite sport was canoe racing, and she won in her division every year that she competed. She had ribbons and trophies and her kids thought she was famous.

With her kids and her husband and her canoe races, Marni could be a little bit happy. Not as happy as before she was taken to School, but a little happy is better than none.

One day, she was doing the washing, thinking – as she always did when she was alone – about Indian Residential School, when it struck her. No matter how tired and frustrated she got, no matter how many awful and unfair things had happened to her as a child, no matter what usual trouble her body had had to recover from, she had never even *wanted* to hurt a kid. All those priests and nuns and teachers and counsellors who had come up with a hundred and six ways to hurt Cree kids – they were rotten inside. Something was really wrong with them.

And then, just like that, Marni *knew* why her mother had been sick all those years ago: she had known about the abuse, about the usual trouble. Marni would sense if her own kids were being abused, she thought, and it would make her sick. Her mom hadn't wanted to believe it, but inside she knew it was true. And she had been terribly angry and sick with worry about what those rotted people were doing to her daughter.

That's the way love works.

M aɾhi M aℂbeàhe

Sometimes, over tea in the evening, as the fire worked through its last coals, Marni's husband asked her about Indian Residential School.

She told him stories then. Not about the bad days – and all the days were bad days – but sometimes she told him of fighting back.

Of Monday's fresh porridge reheated every day through the week. By Saturday, it had curdled and fuzzy mould spots floated on top and hunger was all she could think about. Then she sometimes stole apples from the trees that grew alongside the Schoolyard and hid them in the folds of her skirt. Or she snuck down to the kitchen at night to scrounge whatever she could find and run with it back to the dorm. Other girls were caught, but Marni could really run. She was never caught.

Of being strapped for something, who knows what, but just before the strap landed, Marni yanked her hand away and the full force of the strap, with all the tiny little ridges, struck the teacher's leg and tore through the cloth to the flesh below. The teacher cried out in pain. And Marni ran.

Of not being able to stand by when the supervisor attacked a smaller Cree girl. "You're so mean," Marni said, "to have to do that to a little kid." And she ran.

Of getting in trouble with a friend and being taken together to be strapped. The supervisor called in a second supervisor to help out. One of them held her friend's arm in place, tender wrist skin up, so that the other could use both hands to strike. Marni's friend faced them, raised her chin, and said, "Do what you wanna do." The supervisor's face turned bright red and she raised the strap – and Marni's friend pushed at the supervisor holding her arm. Just then, Marni opened the door and the pushed supervisor fell through the open door. The girls ran. They were punished of course, she was always punished, but fighting back was worth it. To know that they could do *something*. Even today Marni is friends with that girl.

Her husband laughed quietly then to hear her, and hugged her close to him. She could feel how very proud he was of her. To be a kid and so scared and so hungry and still look after herself and still stand up for smaller kids.

What she never told her wonderful husband about, all those years that they were together, was the usual trouble.

"Like this," Marni says in Cree, deftly slicing out the musk gland. She's teaching her granddaughter how to clean a beaver. Her kids and grandkids all know how to live on the land year 'round, and they all speak Cree. In Mistissini, it's easy to see whose parents or grandparents went to Indian Residential School because they are the ones who speak Cree the most fluently.

Later, back in the cabin, the girl wears Marni's old canoe racing medals, all of them at once, and prances around the room, her arms full of trophies and plaques.

"Thank you very much," the girl says, and bows to an imaginary crowd.

Talk of "reconciliation" is on the news every day now. Some of Marni's children probably wonder about her youth, the days before she was the canoe-racing champion.

She never tells. Maybe they think she didn't go to Indian Residential School at all, or, if she did, that it wasn't so very bad. She's not sure what they think. But she is sure that they don't know about what really happened to her, about all the usual trouble, because she has never told anyone.

And they don't know that the moment they leave the room, as soon as she is in a room alone, Marni's mind is back there, in those days, remembering. Reliving. In the most vivid detail.

She never forgets. Not for a day. Not for a minute.

Marni Macbedne

Stories Heard Along the Way: Reconciliation?

During the Independent Assessment Process (IAP) to address extreme abuses endured at Indian Residential Schools, a bishop from a School attended by Cree students was named in over 400 reports of sexual abuse. Another priest at the same School was named 300 times. The men had sometimes used holy water – a Catholic symbol of purification – as a sexual lubricant. The victims, however, never actually felt purified.

Some storytellers who participated in the IAP were cheated by their lawyers. Some lawyers who had already been paid took tens of thousands more from payments meant for survivors. Others didn't want to do the work involved in proving major abuses and tricked storytellers, who struggle daily with School-related scars and damage, into signing statements that only minor abuses happened.

Some Residential School students fought back when staff assaulted them and, tough from bush life, were able to overpower them or run away. The students who had managed to prevent further abuse were informed in the IAP that they could not be compensated. In some cases, the officials balled up the papers on which they were writing and tossed them into the trash, right in front of the storytellers.

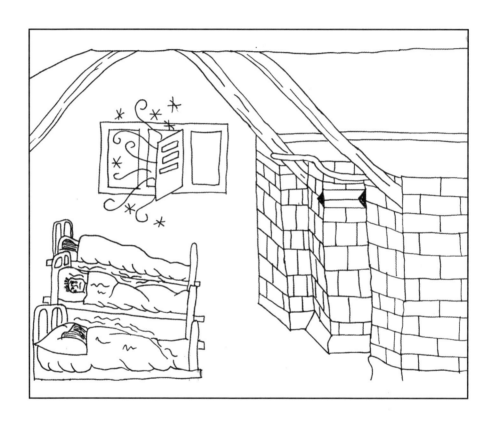

It's the dead of night and the room is freezing.

Artist: Tristan Shecapio-Blacksmith

Juliette Rabbitskin

Juliette Rabbitskin

As remembered by Emily Rabbitskin, Caroline Shecapio, and Kathleen Rabbitskin

THAT AFTERNOON it was hot inside the tent. The sun beat down on the canvas, and the women had a fire going inside to rend the fat off a moose. They threw open the canvas flap and let the fresh spring air in.

A bird flew into the tent. It was about the size and shape of a dove, but completely white. It landed on the bench right beside Juliette's mom and stayed.

"Look how white that bird is," Juliette's aunt said. "Even the bill is white. Even the feet."

"Never seen a bird like that before," Juliette's mom said.

The bird sat there comfortably for a while as they worked, like it was family.

Then, gracefully, like it wasn't any effort at all, it flew once around the tent, then dipped its wing and ducked out of the door and was gone.

"There she goes," said Juliette's aunt.

"Something's wrong," said Juliette's mom.

Of all the people in the world, Emily was the person closest to Juliette. They were cousins but were closer than sisters. They were always together.

"We have to be together," Emily explained when they arrived at La Tuque Indian Residential School for the first time. "I speak for her. She signs to me and I tell you what she says, that's how it works. Otherwise she doesn't talk. Her nickname is Juwah."

"Okay," the School people said, and gave them the same dorm room along with Caroline, Emily's older sister.

"Your bed is there," Emily told Juliette, "and mine is here and Caroline's is there. We will be here for a while and then we go back home to the Mistissini bush."

Juliette nodded, yes.

The School people tried a few times to separate them. It never worked. No matter where they put Emily, Juliette always found her. Even if Emily went to the toilet and locked the door, Juliette stayed just outside, knocking on the door. Eventually, the School people gave up and Juliette just went wherever Emily went. To class, to the gym, to bed. If, for some reason, Juliette wasn't with Emily, then she was with Caroline. Caroline also knew how to sign with her.

The only time Juliette wasn't with Emily or Caroline was when they were getting into trouble. Like when they stole cookies or apples or bread and jam. Anything the kitchen cupboards held that might quell the aching hunger keeping kids awake at night. Once Emily smuggled a huge spoonful of sweetened cocoa powder in her hand back to the dorm and shared it with Juliette. They transferred it from her hand into a bathroom cup and swished it around with a bit of water so it was thick and used their fingers to suck it back. Some powder had fallen on Emily's skirt and they dusted it off as best they could. Another time, Caroline snuck back with her hands all full of peanut butter. She tried to lick it off her hands to hide the sticky mess before she was caught, but it was hopelessly smeary. The sharp-eyed counsellor saw, and, after they had all laughed at the peanut butter everywhere, let her have it. Somehow, Juliette always knew when they would get into trouble, and that's when she stayed away.

Juliette Rabbitskin

It took about two weeks for Juliette to become everybody's favourite person at La Tuque. She was always doing kindnesses. Like helping someone make their bed. Or do their chores. Or get between them and the bullies. And she was always busy. If she saw someone doing something, she sat down beside and wanted to do it too. Every person at La Tuque wanted to be her friend. The scariest teachers, the cooks and janitors and counsellors, the bullies, the underdogs, everybody.

The things she made. They were so beautiful. She worked the brightest colours into the most unusual designs. Her stitching was perfectly spaced – it was like looking at the handiwork of a grandmother who had been sewing all her life. Juliette got all the sewing badges of the La Tuque Girl Guides program. She sewed them on a sash and hung the sash over the end of her bed.

The first half of April in 1966, Emily and Juliette's third year, was a cold one. The snow had not yet begun to melt and everyone longed for spring. And then, someone in the dorm got pneumonia.

Here's the thing about La Tuque Indian Residential School. It was crowded. Kids everywhere you looked. In about two days nearly everyone was wheezing and hacking and fevered and shaking. The Infirmary had maybe five beds, not nearly enough, and besides the germs had already spread, so kids stayed in their own beds. The few healthy kids carried food trays for the others until they got sick too. The dorms stank of sick people.

The Health Department quarantined the whole School. But they didn't send extra nurses to help out.

On the third or fourth evening of the outbreak, a Saturday, the evening nurse walked through the dorms, room to room, and opened all the windows and doors.

"We need fresh air in here," she said to everyone. "I want every window open. If you close them before I say so, the strap gets a workout. And don't you dare get out of bed."

And then, her shift finished, she went back to her own room and closed the door.

Click.

The cold night wind, still two months away from summer, blew freely through the dorm and whistled in the hallways.

Juliette and Emily and Caroline were sick. Their room, with a big open window, felt like a refrigerator. Their fevered breath puffed out in little clouds. They huddled under the blankets and shivered and waited for morning.

Eventually, they fell asleep.

Someone shakes Caroline awake. She opens her eyes. Her throat is parched from the cold dry air. It's the dead of night and the room is freezing.

Juliette is standing by her bed.

She seems desperate. Her breathing is weird. Fast and shallow and gaspy, like wind in trees. Her whole body is working so hard that her shoulders curl forward and back with each breath.

A drink of water? she signs to Caroline.

"Okay," Caroline answers.

They're not supposed to get out of bed – the nurse, the strap – but Caroline gets up anyways and takes Juliette by the hand – her hand is so hot! – to the dorm monitor, a girl named Mary who is two years older.

"She's asking for water," Caroline translates.

Mary sees right away that Juliette is really sick.

"The nurse still isn't back," she says. "Take her to the bathroom for a drink."

Juliette can't walk very quickly because she's working so hard to breathe, but together they make their way through the dorm to the bathroom. There's a big circular fountain where the girls wash their hands. Caroline steps on the fountain footbar and water falls in a curved row of thin round streams. Juliette bends over to catch a few streams in her mouth. She drinks and drinks.

Juliette Rabbitskin

When finally she has had enough, Caroline takes her by the hot hand back to bed and tucks her in.

She looks then at the open window – it's so cold she wants her parka – and almost closes it.

She doesn't want to be strapped.

Juliette curls up like a baby, shivering under her blanket. Her breathing doesn't sound like wind anymore. It sounds more like a train.

Caroline can't do anything else. She climbs back under her own covers and listens to the train-breath rumbling the bed beside.

Finally, after a night that lasts a lifetime, the dark sky pales and the air blowing through the open window warms slightly.

Adults burst into their room and touch their foreheads. Caroline is better, Emily is still feverish – and Juliette sounds like a train. She can't properly waken.

Caroline tells the adults about the terrible cold in the night, the trip to Mary and the bathroom for water. The adults pick up Juliette, now limp, and carry her out to drive her to the hospital.

Of all the kids, only Mary is allowed to go along, they say.

Mary is kind and Juliette likes her. But she is not family.

A few hours later, out in the bush, a rare white bird visits Juliette's mother and aunt.

That afternoon, the intercom crackled. Emily and Caroline were summoned from their sickbeds to the principal's office. On the way there, Caroline had a bad feeling, like something was wrong. Emily was still too feverish to think about anything except bed.

When they got there, their boy cousins and brothers were there too. They never saw the boys at La Tuque. Now, even Emily knew – this couldn't be good.

The principal who was also a priest closed the door, then turned and spoke softly. His face was red and streaked from crying.

"I'm so sorry to inform you," he said, "that our Juwah died in the hospital today. Just after 2:00 PM. The cause of death is pneumonia."

"No she didn't," Emily said. She set her jaw like a brick. "She's coming back and then we're going home to the Mistissini bush. You wait and see."

But Caroline didn't say anything. She believed him. Once before, at another Indian Residential School in Brantford, she saw the dead body of her good friend Sally. Floating face down in the pool, drowned. *An accident,* the adults lied, *because she couldn't swim very well,* though everyone knew she could swim better than anybody.

But this time was different. Caroline saw Juliette in the night, felt her burning hand, saw how hard she had to work for breath, how very sick she was. How everything was much more serious than a twelve-year-old dorm monitor could manage. She knew that, this time, the Indian Residential School adults were telling the truth.

The next day, the nurse who left a School full of sick kids alone changed the sheets in the girls' room.

"I wanted to close the window," Caroline said to her. "You weren't there and it was so cold. We were sick and shivering."

The nurse huffed. A little smile pushed up the edges of her mouth.

"You really shouldn't have given her water, Caroline" she said. "You weren't supposed to. If you hadn't given her water, she wouldn't have died."

For many years, so many years, Caroline believed her.

The next Tuesday, the day of the funeral, was a beautiful, warm, bright day. Finally the snow was beginning to melt. Caroline and Emily, still under quarantine, couldn't attend. The other people who went said the service, led by the principal-priest, lasted all of five sunny minutes.

Juliette Rabbitskin

The Shawinigan newspaper printed a short article. It said nothing about a pneumonia outbreak so bad the School was quarantined, nor about a dorm of sick kids abandoned, no adult looking after them. Instead, it said "Little Miss Juliette Rabbitskin," an "Indian child," had been "a victim of flu," and extended "deepest sympathy" to the family.

Later, when they had recovered, Caroline and Emily went to the La Tuque town cemetery to visit Juliette's grave.

At first, they couldn't find it. They walked the rows of graves and read all the markers but none were for Juliette Rabbitskin. In fact, none of the markers at all were for people with Cree names. They were about to give up when Emily noticed some fresh dirt way back in the corner. They walked over. There, out near the scrub, away from all other graves, as if the cemetery custodians had wanted to quarantine her all over again, was a grave with a wooden marker for Juliette Rabbitskin.

Juliette was such a social person. She would have hated where she ended up.

Out in the bush, Juliette's parents still didn't know.

Smalley Petawabano was the Chief of Mistissini then, when it was still called Mistassini Post. He said he couldn't think of many things more horrible than someone paddling in from the bush straight to the beach to pick up their daughter for summer, watching kids step down from the bus one by one, and finding out, when the bus was empty, that she was dead.

He asked around to find out when Juliette's parents were planning to return from the bush and which route they would take. That day he took his motorboat out early in the day and puttered up the lake to meet them on their way in.

When Juliette's mom saw his boat, still way off in the distance, her heart slowed right down.

"He's got bad news," she said.

And then she remembered the white bird.

A few years later, it came time for Juliette's younger sister, Kathleen, to attend La Tuque Indian Residential School. The next time her parents saw the Indian Agent, they approached him.

"Please," they begged. "Our Juliette died there. Please let us keep Kathleen safe at home. So we can have one. Please."

"Sure," the Indian Agent said. "No problem at all. She can stay. Of course, you won't be able to buy your trapping rations or your groceries. Nor ammunition for hunting nor any kind of blankets or winter supplies. And you can't see a doctor if anyone gets sick. But sure, if you can do without those little things, your daughter can stay home."

Then he laughed at them, openly.

Kathleen was too young to remember Juliette. She didn't even know Juliette had existed. But when her parents dropped Kathleen off or picked her up from the Indian Residential School bus, they hugged her and turned away and were terribly sad. More than the other parents. It was like they thought the world was ending. She couldn't understand it.

Later, when she was older, just about to have her own baby, she noticed that there was another little girl in the community that her parents were always watching and cuddling.

"That girl is so much like Juliette," Emily explained. "They can't help but be drawn to her."

"Who's Juliette?" Kathleen asked.

And then she heard for the first time about her sister who had never spoken but whom everyone adored, and that she had died at La Tuque Indian Residential School. And that at the moment of her death, out in the bush, a white bird had visited her mom.

When Kathleen's daughter was born, she named her Juliette.

For dozens of years, every spring, a lady named Louise who lived nearby visited the La Tuque town cemetery. She walked all

Juliette Rabbitskin

the way to the far back corner, among the bushes and away from the other graves, and she left big bright flowers on the single lonely grave there. Louise had once been a student at La Tuque Indian Residential School when Juliette Rabbitskin died. When everybody was reminded again that an Indian Residential School was a deadly place for Cree kids.

Louise was kind. Juliette liked her. But she was not family.

For years it bugged Emily.

She had promised Juliette that they would all go home. Emily had gone home long ago, Caroline was home, Kathleen was home. They had careers and families who loved them. La Tuque Indian Residential School had been razed to the ground long ago. Mistassini Post had become Mistissini, a busy town with paved roads and a big school and clinic and radio stations and stores and everything. But Juliette was still stuck there, in the cold La Tuque ground, out near the bushes, away from all the people. Alone.

Not long ago, Emily and Caroline and Kathleen sat down with a stack of forms and, with the Mistissini band office and the town of La Tuque, applied to have Juliette's coffin exhumed, hoisted onto a truck, and transported up to Mistissini. They re-buried her in a crowded part of the main cemetery on Sam Awashish Road, surrounded by people she knew and loved, and placed a stone there: "Let the little children come unto me," it says.

She is home.

If you go to the cemetery to visit Juliette's grave, take your time. Inhale the spruce air and get comfortable. Linger. If you're really lucky, a white bird – even the beak and feet are white – might visit the grave with you, stay for a while, dip her wing, then fly away.

Records: The Usual Trouble

May 1893. One girl "had her clothes taken up and [was] whipped in that state... [Her father] would not take her back [to School] as she was almost a woman and that was disgraceful." *Deputy Superintendent General H. Reed*

June 1896. The "moral aspect of affairs [in the Schools] is deplorable." *Agent D.L. Clink*

February 1905. Deputy Superintendent General F. Pedley calls attention to "questions of immorality" at a School.

October 1912. The sexual "pollution" of two young girls at [a School] has been "kept from the public... I trust, in the interest of the Department's educational system, that it will remain so." *Inspector W. Ditchburn*

July 1914. Principal McWhinney does nothing when a teacher has "sexual intercourse with [two girls]." *Agent Blewett*

February 1915. A letter to Deputy Superintendent General D.C. Scott raises concerns about "the breaking of the Seventh Commandment" (forbiding extramarital sexual activity).

July 1924. A Christian Brother undressed a boy, "whipping him naked until he became unconscious." *A letter to D.C. Scott*

October 1924. "We had one of the boys run away two weeks ago, and … found out that the bigger boys were using him to commit sodomy … I suspected this for sometime, but myself and the supervisors had not been able to check up on it." *Principal Lett*

April 1953. DIA advises "teachers to abstain from physical contacts with pupils either in anger or affection."

November 1953. A principal beats two boys, leaving "marks all over the boys [sic] bodies, back, front genitals etcetera." A doctor confirms the injuries. *Superintendent R.F. Davey*

May 1965. "[The principal] told me to kneel and then he pulled my skirt up and then pulled my pants down. He put my head between his legs and he started to give me the strap." *Student Letter to Indian Affairs*

1990-92. "It is important that [Indian Affairs] be seen as responding in a way that liability is not admitted, but that it is recognizing the sequelae of these events." *Indian Affairs Official*

June 1990. "The sad thing is that we did not know [sexual abuse in Residential Schools] was occurring." *Official J. Tupper*

July 2022. Priests with troubled histories with children were being frequently relocated, often ending up at Residential Schools. *Archivist R. Frogner, examining Oblate files*

The noisiest place in the world, that was the bush. Wind in black spruce, crashing rapids, scolding birds and squirrels – always things were moving, talking to each other, getting things done.

Artist: Tristan Shecapio-Blacksmith

Shiikun

Shiikun*

*Names and details have been changed to protect identities.

ON A SNOWY day in the late sixties, in one of the first log houses in Mistissini, the time came for a Cree woman to give birth. Four times she had done this already and didn't need much help, but someone called the Cree midwife and the French nurse anyway. And a good thing too, because, when the baby finally slid out into this world, she wasn't breathing at all.

Before anyone else in the room even realized what was happening, the midwife grabbed the biggest bowl in the house, ran out and scooped up snow, then to the big drum of cooking water, then back to the newborn. She wrapped her hand carefully under the baby's head and lowered the limp body into the ice water. A few seconds later, the newborn filled her tiny lungs with air and began to holler. Everyone in the room laughed. The midwife dried her off, wrapped her in a blanket, and passed her to her mom.

The French nurse filled out the birth certificate and assigned the girl the French name Mirabel. But it wasn't her real name and, after that French nurse, no one ever used it. Her real name was Shiikun.

The next week, Shiikun's parents and grandparents took her out on the land and that's where she grew up.

Each year, with the seasons, the family rotated through several camps spread across Eeyou Istchee, following game and fish

135

and living a traditional Cree life. The noisiest place in the world, that was the bush. Wind in black spruce, crashing rapids, scolding birds and squirrels – always things were moving, talking to each other, getting things done. Sometimes, as Shiikun went about her chores, she heard, through the clamour, her ancestors talking. They had been there since the time of the glaciers, they knew she belonged to them, and they were looking out for her.

For a few weeks every summer, two other kids came to their camp. They were Shiikun's older brother and sister, and most of the time they were away at a White place called Residential School. They hated it, but if they didn't go, her mom said, the family couldn't buy flour nor canned goods nor ammunition nor winter supplies.

Her mom never complained. But her back sometimes curved and Shiikun knew she was worried or sad. She was careful not to ask about it. If her mom wanted her to know, she would tell her.

When Shiikun was seven, her family moved to Mistissini into the log house where she had been born because she was supposed to attend school. The White people's rules were changing. They wanted the Cree to settle. Shiikun could go to a community school instead of Residential School, but the whole family had to move with her to that community.

Shiikun liked school. She didn't like the community. In the community, adults were strange. Their shoulders slumped. They walked funny. Their words were nonsense. They smelled sour and sick. Sometimes her own parents – who were perfectly normal in the bush – turned strange for days and then disappeared. Shiikun came home from school to an empty, silent house. All alone in a community of adults who smelled sick and couldn't be trusted.

On those days, she left her house and walked around Mistissini looking for the other children who had also been left alone. She could always find a few, hiding quietly somewhere. They scraped together whatever food they could find and one of them cooked it up. Those

Shiikun

nights, on the floor of someone's house, usually Shiikun's, the abandoned kids slept together looking after one another as best they could. After a few days, their parents came shuffling home with glassy eyes and nauseous faces and wrinkles full of shame.

It didn't take long for Shiikun to figure out that what made them strange was Homebrew. They cooked and drank it in Mistissini because there wasn't much to do and they had so much to be sad about. In the bush they didn't drink it, even when they were sad, because bush life was too busy. There wasn't time for Homebrew.

Shiikun lived for the bush. And a good thing too, because every year, when December came, her family moved back on the land. Shiikun's Grade Two report card said this: "Shiikun is a pleasant student to have. She is sometimes disruptive to other students and talks too much, but is doing very well overall. We don't know what happened to her after Christmas. She never came back to school and her parents didn't come by and report. We heard she flew off in a bush plane with her family but were unable to confirm."

Two years passed. Out on the trapline, it had been raining off and on all day and now the sun was shining. The squirrels had begun again their chitter, the air smelled of wet spruce, and everything was still a little muddy. Shiikun's mom had just cleaned two rabbits and set them to boil on the cooking fire inside the tee-pee. The skins draped over a branch outside, drying. Later, they'd be stretched for mitten liners. Shiikun, now nine years old, was washing the knives and butcher tools outside, taking her time and splashing in the warm water. She was thinking as she worked and what she was thinking about was all the new people in camp.

There were her older brother and sister, home for a few weeks of summer, like usual. There was also a man. She'd never met him before. Her mom, who smiled all the time now, said he was Shiikun's oldest brother. He'd been away at Residential School for fifteen years without a break.

What Shiikun couldn't figure out about any of these new people was why they were all so sad. They had been separated in the Schools, hadn't seen one another at all, but they all looked the same. Like old Mistissini adults on Homebrew. And another thing: in camp, they walked around, touching trees and tools and tents as if grateful to touch them again, but they were awkward. Simple camp duties that Shiikun had mastered years ago, they fumbled and looked embarrassed. Why couldn't they look after themselves in the bush?

Suddenly, before she knew why, Shiikun stiffened. Something was wrong.

Someone wants to hurt me, she thought.

She looked around. The strange man, her oldest brother, leaned against a tree and leered at her under half-open eyelids. Shiikun shifted the wash bowl to finish the chore facing him and tried to ignore the ice in her spine. A corner of his mouth turned up and he walked off into the trees.

That evening, everyone gathered in one of the cabins, a candle burned, and her grandmother was just beginning to tell a story. It was Shiikun's favourite time of day and she snuggled under her blanket against the tent wall.

Suddenly, she stiffened. Again. In the dark, something was crawling up up up her leg. Her same brother, sitting much too close to her, was touching her!

She pinched the back of his hand as hard as she could and he pulled it away. She heard a low snicker.

The first chance she had, Shiikun told her mom what was happening.

"Oh, just don't say anything. He's coming from that White School and doesn't know our ways," her mom said. "He's not used to this." She waved her hand to show that *this* meant life on the land. She smiled tolerantly – but her face drooped.

Shiikun

The season changed and the family moved back to Mistissini for Shiikun's school. Soon as they could, her parents fixed a vat of Homebrew and disappeared. The first afternoon, Shiikun was alone in the quiet house, and her oldest brother came in.

"Can you fix me something to eat, Shiikun?" he said politely. "I'm hungry."

She did as he asked. Then, in an instant, everything changed.

In a voice she had never heard before, he said, "Okay Shiikun. When I'm finished eating, you and I are gonna go into that room" – he pointed with his spoon – "and things are gonna happen. And you will never, as long as you live, tell anyone about them."

Something cold and heavy had gathered behind his eyebrows. *If I don't obey him*, she thought, *he'll kill me.*

Together they went into the room and the door closed.
Click.

He shoved Shiikun onto the bed and covered her face with a pillow – and then he attacked every part of her body but her face. He punched and pinched and slapped her, he grabbed handfuls of skin and corkscrewed with all of his adult strength, he twisted her arm almost out of the socket – and then he pushed up her skirt and began to do very strange things to her private parts.

At first, she couldn't move. She could hardly breathe.

And then, twisting her head under the pillow, she filled her lungs with air, and began to holler. She kicked wildly, with all her strength, and pushed him and the pillow away. When he bounced back, she squeezed her muscled legs together and protected her private parts as best she could. But she was nine years old and he was an adult. Things happened.

After that, whenever she heard him, Shiikun tried to hide, but the attacks kept coming. In the bedroom, in a crawlspace, in a corner, against a wall – the things he wanted to do to her! Any room he entered became a place of terror. Always he covered her face first – to this day, she cannot tolerate cloth touching her face – always he demanded her silence, always she fought back with everything she had and screamed until her throat was raw.

People in nearby houses could hear her, she knew, but no one ever came to help.

"Mom, he's really hurting me," she said, after her parents were back. She lifted her shirt to show the welts.

"Oh Shiikun," her mom said. "Those are schoolyard bruises. Don't say things like that. Your brother is new here." Again, though, her face drooped.

She knows I'm telling the truth, Shiikun thought. *But I'm not the one she'll protect.*

Briefly, she thought of telling a teacher. But the shame – she didn't even finish the thought.

Maybe her sister could help.

Then she saw her sister and oldest brother snowshoe out together into the bush. A few hours later they came back. His face was rigid and hers was empty. They didn't say what had happened but something plainly had and her sister couldn't help her after all.

Shiikun was alone. *This is my life now,* she thought. *Never again will there be a good thing about it.*

One day, when Shiikun was eleven, her oldest brother took a trip to Ottawa. He went to a house party, got into a drunken fight, and was knocked out. On his way to the ground, his head bashed a countertop. Someone drove him to a hospital, where a doctor telephoned Mistissini. In those days, all of Mistissini had one telephone, in the priest's house. A priest whose English was poor. He took the message and walked to Shiikun's house.

"So sorry, so sorry," he said to her parents. "Hospital of Ottawa telephoning to say your son has accidented. He has accidented his head. In three days he die."

The grammar was wrong but the message was clear. Shiikun's parents were distraught. Their beloved son, gone all

Shiik un

those years, had barely come home. Word spread through the community and people began dropping by the house to comfort Shiikun's parents.

But Shiikun couldn't stop laughing. *The nightmare is over!* she thought. *All the days, the summer and winter days, that will be my own!* Over the next week, she hid from visitors so they couldn't see her glee. And between guests, she walked through the bedroom, in the crawlspace, all the places around the house where she had been assaulted. *I'm safe here now,* she whispered and touched the doorjamb or the bedcover.

On the fourth day, a taxicab pulled into the yard. With his head wrapped in bandages and a corner of his mouth curling up, her brother stepped out.

The world stopped.

The priest, with his poor English, had misunderstood. That first day, with the midwife and icewater, if only she had not been revived.

Once again, horror. Always, Shiikun hollered for help and fought back with everything she had. No one ever came. Most nights she had to bandage something. A few times, she woke in the morning with severe head pain and no memory of what had happened. It was all the same. She was alone.

Sometimes, she acted out at her mom.

"Shiikun," her mom asked one day, as they worked together. They were making *boudin* and were mixing the blueberries into the cake dough. "Why are you angry at me?"

"Because someone is hurting me," Shiikun answered. "You know about it, but you protect only him and drink Homebrew. You're my mom and you won't even *listen* to me."

Her mom said nothing and turned back to the dough.

The story Shiikun never heard, not until she was a mother herself, went like this. Her mother's father was an excellent hunter and provider. Even in the hardest winters, his family wanted for nothing. He was funny and gentle and kind and teasing. Around him, the air was calm. He had just one rule: emotions – joy or rage or sadness – must be felt but never expressed. "Be quiet," he'd say, especially to the women. "Don't talk about that."

It might have been a good rule for life on the land but it was a terrible rule for life in the Residential School years.

By the time Shiikun was thirteen, she was a tough bush girl. She had thick ropey arms and powerful calloused hands. The family returned to Mistissini, as they always did in June, and her parents disappeared with Homebrew shortly after.

Again, her brother came into her room, weight gathering behind his eyebrows, as it always did before an attack. This time Shiikun planted her feet on the ground and faced him.

"You have to stop," she said. "I'm big now and I'm strong. If you try it, I will really hurt you. And I *will* tell someone. Our parents don't care, but maybe the police or a social worker."

He listened, curled up his mouth, then turned and walked out.

It was finished.

High school was in Val-d'Or, 500 kilometres from Mistissini. Shiikun stayed in a large boarding home with other Cree students.

A few weeks into term, on a cold and windy Friday afternoon, Shiikun and two Mistissini friends took their bags to the Val-d'Or bus station and boarded a silver bus to Chibougamau. A Cree School Board van would be waiting for them, the school counsellor had said, to drive them the last ninety kilometres home. The Cree School Board was new, gradually taking over from the Residential School system, and they wanted the youth to spend time with their families.

Late at night, after six hours of winding along narrow highways, the bus pulled into Chibougamau and the girls stepped down into the empty parking lot.

Shiikun

The completely empty parking lot. Van nowhere to be seen. The Val-d'Or Cree School Board had done their part and bought the bus tickets. But the Mistissini Cree School Board had messed up.

Theirs had been the last bus of the day and the station master was locking up the bus station for night. The girls were on their own in Chibougamau, over an hour from home, outside, in the cold October night. Under the street lamp, flecks of snow drew horizontal lines in the air. The wind smelled of winter.

Shiikun and her friends looked at each other, not really surprised. Without saying much, they grabbed their bags, walked to the road, and stuck out their thumbs.

It was risky. Late-night drivers, coming from Chibougamau bars, were too drunk to drive safely, and Cree girls disappeared along Northern highways all the time. But what choice did they have? By the time someone dropped them off at the Mistissini entrance, it was 3:00 AM and well below zero. But for the wind and barking dogs, the community was silent.

The girls' Mistissini homes were boarded up for winter, their families out on the land. They walked to Shiikun's house, wedged their fingers behind the plywood covering the door, and loosened it enough to wiggle inside. Shiikun tracked her hand over cold walls until, over by the closet, she found the electrical panel. She flipped a switch and turned on the stove but not the lights – she didn't want anyone to know they were there. In the dark, they lugged mattresses from the bedrooms to the kitchen and closed the door. By the time they fell asleep, still in their coats, the kitchen was warm.

The next day, they woke hungry. One at a time, they squeezed out the door and went to find someone who would share food. Shiikun found a cousin who was happy to give her a hot meal and a packed bag, and to hear about Val-d'Or. Afterwards, Shiikun wandered around Mistissini, community of bent shoulders and abandoned kids. It had never really felt like home. Eventually, she wiggled back into her dark house where the other girls were waiting and where they could all look after one another.

On Sunday morning, Shiikun turned the oven off, flipped back the electrical switches, and re-fastened the plywood over the door. They picked up their bags and stood at the roadside to hitch-hike back to Chibougamau and catch the bus to Val-d'Or.

Two weeks later, they did it all again. And every second weekend for the next two years. Never once was the van there to meet them. Sometimes, they missed the Sunday bus back to Val-d'Or. On those nights, they walked over to the Friendship Centre and spent the night downstairs, curled up around their bags on the Friendship Centre floor.

That left the other weekends in Val-d'Or. Sometimes Shiikun could go on the land with friends who had traplines nearby. On the land, she was safe and happy and knew what to do. But there were still weekends, one or two a month, when she was stuck in town. Unsafe. Bewildered. Lost. What was she supposed to *do* in Val-d'Or? Who was she even?

To stay off the streets in the evenings, Shiikun and her friends began to meet in bars. They were underage, but the bars never checked ID. Usually a few Cree politicians or consultants were there for meetings, and they took the girls out for a nice restaurant supper and then to the bars. They paid for everything. Important Cree men, decision makers, respected across Eeyou Istchee. Shiikun and her friends thought they were safe with them.

Sometimes one of the men would give Shiikun money. "Go buy yourself a necklace or a bracelet," he'd say, "and wear it tomorrow night. We'll go out for supper. You can be my date."

The next day would be filled with shopping and dressing up, and the evening with supper and then the bar or a house party – and the man's hotel room.

Where the door closed. And sex things happened.

Shiikun always hated it. But what choice did she have, he had bought her supper and a necklace.

Shiikun

Later, in bed in her dorm room, she reasoned it out. The men were feeding her. They were not ignoring her. They were not beating her. They didn't cover her face. By elimination, therefore, it must be that they – powerful Cree men – cared for her. She should enjoy it. She should be grateful.

Sometimes the girls tried to stick together, make a girls' night of it. When they managed it, no sex things happened. But more often, because of the drinking, or because Shiikun didn't understand city ways, or because she couldn't plant her feet and stand up to an important man who cared for her and had even bought her a necklace, the door closed and sex things happened. Far away from her oldest brother.

It was not finished after all.

Shiikun's back curved and she began to drink. All alone. No good thing ever again.

After high school, Shiikun moved to Toronto for university. She had her own little room, with a desk and a bright window with flowered curtains, a toilet, and a shower. Her family had been left behind.

One day, she saw a posting on a campus billboard:

Surviving Sexual Violence Symposium
Everyone Welcome
Room 632, Saturday 7:00 PM
Refreshments will be served

Shiikun stared at the posting for a few minutes. What exactly was it saying? Someone would talk about sexual violence? *In public??*

The following Saturday, Shiikun straddled a backwards wooden stacking chair in the corner of Room 632, sipped coffee from the styrofoam cup in her hand, and tried not to draw attention. At the front, a woman was telling a story so familiar Shiikun could have told parts of it herself.

A few weeks later there was another talk. A month after that, another. Each time Shiikun saw a posting, she attended. Each time, a different woman – or two or three or sometimes a man – told a story of pain and recovery. Sexual violence was everywhere. Shiikun wasn't alone. She had nothing to feel ashamed about.

Deep in her gut, something tight and hard and pinched loosened.

She made an appointment with a campus counsellor and, in a private room with one brick wall and a soft yellow light, she began to tell her own story.

It was *so hard.* With every word she spoke, she could hear her mother saying, gently, lovingly, *Oh Shiikun, don't talk about that.*

Maybe her grandfather had thought silence helped people recover from abuse. But for Shiikun, talking helped. Because she was finally talking, she was healing. She could feel it.

She didn't need to drink anymore.

She didn't need to believe the important Cree men had cared about her. They had attended Residential Schools, were themselves wounded, but they had hurt her terribly for their own pleasure.

If she could go back in time, she would give her younger self, whose choices were so few, a long comforting hug.

This part of the story is short, but don't be deceived. Working through so much shame, getting to where she could tell this story for you to read, was the hardest thing Shiikun ever did. That is really saying something.

Shiikun's oldest brother married, had kids, and found work. One day, while he was reading, the police showed up at his door with handcuffs. He had assaulted someone and she was pressing charges. He spent several years in prison.

One night, near the end of his sentence, from the prison telephone, he called Shiikun.

Shiikun

"I've been talking to a counsellor here," he said. His voice was tight and small. Shiikun heard people talking in the room behind him. "I want to apologize for what I did to you."

Now Shiikun was silent.

"Okay," she finally said, "but not on the phone. If you're gonna do this, it'll have to be in person."

"I'm out in two months," he said. "I'll call you then."

Two months later, she walked across Mistissini to his house. The instant she stepped in and the door closed behind her, her throat seized. She wanted desperately to leave. In that same instant, she saw her oldest brother had really changed. He had become quiet and self-reflective. Sober. The cold weight that had once gathered behind his eyebrows was gone. He was a frightened child in a man's body.

He brewed a pot of tea and carried three steaming cups into the living room. Sitting on a sofa, under a painting of a goose in flight, with his wife beside and Shiikun as far away from him as she could be, he listed the terrible things he had done to her. Most of them, he said, had first been done to him in Residential School, so he knew how badly he had hurt her. And then he apologized. She could see he meant every word.

Shiikun forgave him completely. Intellect, spirit, emotions, body...

The thing is – a body has its own memory. Her body can't forget. She has forgiven her brother but, whenever she is near him, her heart races, her throat constricts, her muscles clench, her ears ring, her spine is ice. Even if he's at the far end of a room, not looking at her, she feels it. Trauma, heaviest of glaciers, has carved a gorge in her too deep to be filled in a lifetime. Shiikun loves him, she's proud of how he has healed, how he has taken responsibility and cares for his family. But she can't be in a room with him and she can't allow her grandchildren to be near him.

They talk on the phone.

Not long ago, Shiikun's sister, who had once set off on snow-shoes with their brother, knocked on her door. Shiikun opened it. Her sister's right hand wrapped around an open bottle of gin. She smelled sour and sick. That was strange. She wasn't one to drink. They walked to the kitchen, but her sister didn't sit. She leaned heavily on the table.

"Shiikun," she said, through slurry lips, "Back then. I knew why you screamed. I heard you. I was afraid of him – of what he was doing to me – and I didn't protect you. I was older and it was my job. I'm so sorry."

Shiikun wrapped her arms around her beautiful sister in a long hug. "Tell me again," she said, "when you're sober. I'll accept your apology then. I really will." Her sister wiped her nose and stumbled out the door. Shiikun has heard nothing further.

Shiikun's mom never apologized for her neglect and dis-belief. She still won't talk about why she reached for Homebrew. Instead, she cooks and bakes for Shiikun and her family to show them her love. Shiikun visits her every day.

All of them, her beautiful wounded family. Their scars are as deep as her own. Glacial.

Shiikun works in the community. She has a loving family, a job vital to the Cree Nation, a safe house. She has broken the cycle of violence into which she was born.

On the land, her real home, she still hears the wind in the spruce, the crashing rapids, the scolding animals – and, under the clamour, her ancestors talking. They know all the stories that make up her own. They look out for her. Even with their terrible scars, her family will manage. Her grandchildren won't be silenced nor aban-doned. Good things, once again.

Shiik Un

Stories Heard Along the Way: Sight and Spirit

An old man with Sight had a vision that someone he knew was starving 500 kilometres away. He sent his son on foot with food to share. His son walked the whole way, found things exactly as his father had described, left the food with the hungry man, and then walked 500 kilometres back. The entire journey took about two weeks.

An aging Cree man, about 105 years old and still active on his trapline, had beautiful thick grey hair. One day, he called the local undertaker. "My time is near," he said, "and I'd like you to bury me in the traditional way. If you do that for me, I'll leave you my hair." Two weeks later, in the middle of January, the man died. The undertaker kept his promise and buried the Elder in the traditional Cree way. As tradition requires, he checked the gravesite first thing the next morning. There, in the fresh snow covering the grave, in a month when bears hibernate, was a single, clear bear paw print. A few days after that, a solid streak of grey hair suddenly appeared on the undertaker's head.

Traditional Cree shamans used a Shaking Tent practice in order to contact the spirit world. Once, a researcher from the South asked a shaman for permission to record the ceremony on an audio tape. "Not my decision," said the shaman. "It's up to the spirits." The shaman began the ceremony and the researcher recorded the whole thing. Later, when he played it back to listen once again to the voices of the spirits, he could hear his own voice, but the voices of the spirits and the voice of the shaman had not recorded at all. The spirits had not consented. The precious knowledge of the Shaking Tent ceremony is still kept within specific families in Eeyou Istchee.

There stood Matthew. Smiling, crying, a little bloody, dragging a fresh leg of caribou.

Artist: Jared Linton

Matthew Loon

THE YEAR after Matthew Loon was expelled from La Tuque Indian Residential School, there was hunger in the land. It was the late sixties, Matthew was about eleven or twelve, and he was spending winter in the bush with his father and grandfather. They had seen maybe one caribou that whole year. A few beaver swam under the ice, but they couldn't catch them. His grandfather set up a net for fish, but, after three days, the net was empty except for one fish. There weren't even any wolves.

It was hard.

Matthew's little brother sat down on the snow, piled it in heaps around him, and cried.

Their grandfather came over and sat down beside him. "Stop crying," he said gently.

"But my tummy hurts," his brother sobbed.

Matthew felt so helpless to see a little boy cry like that and to know there wasn't enough food in the camp to ease his pain.

That night, they all ate a few bites of bannock – that's all there was – and went to bed.

The next morning, Matthew's uncle called him over. "Let's go check our beaver traps," he said. "Maybe we'll find something."

The trip would take several days. They hitched the sled behind the snowmobile, loaded extra fuel cans, and left.

About four hours out, heading for the overnight camp, they were crossing a big lake when Matthew, taking his turn back on the sled, saw that the snow on the other side of the lake looked messy. Like it had been disturbed. His uncle hadn't noticed.

Matthew took off his mitt and threw it at his uncle, hitting him in the back of the head. His uncle stopped the snowmobile and turned around to look at Matthew.

"Look over there," Matthew said, and picked up his mitt.

He looked – and immediately cut the engine. They walked over.

The snow was disturbed by caribou tracks. Many tracks. Some going this way, some going that way. A big herd.

Matthew and his uncle hadn't eaten in many days. They were weak. They didn't have strength for a big game hunt and the sound of the snowmobile would scare the animals away.

His uncle returned to the snowmobile and sat down. Matthew silently followed, on foot, the few tracks going in the direction of their camp, ignoring the others, to scout the situation. Across the lake and through a narrow finger of woods and towards a bay and – there, on the bay ice, stood a single caribou. He looked a while longer, let his eyes adjust, and saw, further away, a small herd. Fifteen animals in all.

Matthew backtracked the way he had come and told his uncle.

Together they decided that Matthew would return to the bush with the gun, and take position at the narrow. Then his uncle would drive the snowmobile around and get on the other side of the caribou. They would be startled by the noise and want to pass through the narrow to get away. Even hungry and shaky and weak, Matthew might be able to fell an animal.

One animal would be wonderful.

Matthew ran back to the woods – he still doesn't know where the strength came from – and knelt in the snow, loaded and readied

matthew LOOn

his rifle, and signalled his uncle. His uncle started the engine and, as he came around the other side, the caribou began to run.

Bham! Matthew shot. The caribou's knees buckled and it fell.

He began to cry.

Bham! Bham! Bham! He could hardly see for the tears but he shot again and again. The next caribou fell and the next and the next. In about fifteen seconds, he shot fourteen animals. Every caribou but one.

Enough food to stop his brother's tears. Enough to feed the whole camp through the winter.

Matthew sat in the snow and wept.

His uncle approached on the snowmobile.

"Look at all the food! How'd you even *do* that? Hey – why're you crying?"

"I don't know!" Matthew sobbed. "I'm actually happy."

They made a small cooking fire and ate a few bites from the hind leg of the smallest animal. Then, with a little more energy than before, they opened the belly of each caribou so the carcasses could bleed out and freeze without going bad. Using all their strength, they cut up the smallest carcass and dragged it to the sled. Then they turned the snowmobile around and drove all the way back to the camp.

It was late at night when they arrived. The camp was dark. His uncle cut the engine and the night fell silent.

Matthew got off the sled and began to untie the carcass.

Inside the tent, something rustled.

"Light the candle! Something's wrong!" His grandfather's voice.

The tent flap opened. His grandfather peered out.

And there stood Matthew. Smiling, crying, a little bloody, dragging a fresh leg of caribou.

His grandfather's eyes opened wide – and then a grin the size of the tent stretched across his face.

"Honey!" he called to his wife. "Better start the fire!"

Together they lugged the caribou inside. Working by candle-light and the woodstove glow, Grandfather sliced off some pieces and handed them to his wife to cook right away. Then he continued to butcher.

Not too long after that, everyone in the camp was awake and eating.

The days of hunger were done. Young Matthew was not the only one crying.

Over the next couple of days, Matthew and his uncle made four trips back and forth to bring back all the caribou.

After that, whenever Matthew wished he could go back to School, he remembered that, if he hadn't been expelled, he wouldn't have ended the hunger in the land. Who knows how many would have starved?

One September morning, at La Tuque in the mid-'60s, when everyone was lining up for breakfast, Matthew's stomach was off. He kept running to the toilet and, every time he left it, he had to turn and run back. The last time, he didn't even have time to ask the counsellor for permission.

He stayed on the toilet for a while, just to make sure it was safe. And when finally his gut was really empty, Matthew washed his hands and came out of the bathroom.

There stood the counsellor. Red-faced, livid.

"I'm sick," Matthew tried to say, but the counsellor already had him by the throat. With one arm, he muscled Matthew up against the wall and held him there.

Everything went black.

Matthew woke in the Infirmary. His throat was badly dam-aged from the choking, they said, and he was going to a hospital for an operation to fix his esophagus.

He was gone for three months. The last thing the School people said was that he must never speak of this to anyone,

matthew Loon

especially not his parents. If he breathed a word of it, they said, bad things would happen.

By the time Matthew got back to School, the term was almost finished. He was behind in all of his classes. But he liked studying, so he crammed in as much as he could and passed his classes anyway.

Many years later, the Indian Residential Schools Settlement officials told him that he had been in hospital to have his tonsils removed. That he had imagined the whole thing and certainly they could not compensate for his imaginings.

His tonsils are still in his throat.

At La Tuque Indian Residential School, everybody was hungry. Some of the bigger kids were so hungry that, when the supervisors turned away, they took food from the little ones, just to fill their own bellies. Talking during meals was not allowed, so the little ones couldn't tell what was happening. And anyway they knew that, if they could just stay alive long enough, their turn to take food from someone else would come eventually. Matthew was little. He lost his food pretty often.

And Matthew was dark. Darker than anyone else there. Some kids beat him up over it every now and again. They had bruises of their own – maybe they just meant to share. Still, bruises hurt and Matthew wasn't especially fond of them.

One day, the students were lining up for something and a boy slugged him. Matthew spun around with his fist out. *Wham!* The other kid slumped to the ground, bleeding from the mouth. Even Matthew was surprised – he had never done anything like that before – and knew right away that this new hatred in his heart came from the principal's strap and the scars it had left across his back and his hands. The teachers came running, with their yardsticks that they swung like baseball bats, but that kid never bothered Matthew again.

And the sex stuff. The men who ran La Tuque Indian Residential School sure needed a lot of it. Pupils were supposed to provide this sex thing for one priest and that sex thing for another priest and another sex thing for the dorm supervisor and so on. Matthew wasn't especially fond of providing for men but some of the kids who were providing all the time thought it was normal. Some senior boys thought it so normal that they wanted to do sex stuff with Matthew. Matthew wasn't especially fond of that either.

In the dorm room was a closet. It had a bar on which to hang clothes and a small shelf above that. One night, after lights out, Matthew tiptoed to the closet, jumped high enough to grab the bar with both hands and hang there. Then he swung his legs back and muscled until he got his whole body up above the bar and on to the little shelf. If he'd been any bigger, he wouldn't have fit. He crawled back into the corner, deep into the closet, curled up, and fell asleep.

He woke to the sound of rustling. A senior boy wanted some sex stuff and was looking for a younger boy. But when the light from the door fell right on Matthew, back in the closet, he was dark enough that the boy couldn't see him.

After that, he climbed up into the closet and slept there nearly every night. Even with hunger, it was sometimes good to be little. Even with bruises, it was sometimes good to be dark.

One teacher at La Tuque Indian Residential School looked out for Matthew. She saw how he was being treated and she sometimes invited him to her home. On those days, they spent a few hours together just doing normal home things. Having tea. Making something in the kitchen. Reading books. Going for walks. On those days, Matthew had enough to eat and could take a break from School troubles for a few hours.

Outside the School was an enormous green field for playing soccer and field hockey and softball, and around the field ran a long running track. One beautiful fall evening, a counsellor gave

matthew LOOn

Matthew and another boy special permission to spend a half hour out on the track.

On their way back, another counsellor saw them and – without asking anything – took them by the collars straight to the principal's office.

They didn't struggle. They had permission to be outside. It would be all right.

When they got there, the principal was already sitting behind the desk in his big wooden chair. Matthew and the other boy sat and swung their legs from the two chairs opposite, while the counsellor leaned against the wall behind them. A tidy row of straps hung from evenly spaced hooks on the wall beside him.

"You're not allowed outside after supper," the principal said.

"Oh, we had permission from the dorm counsellor for exactly thirty minutes on the track," Matthew said. "You can ask him."

The two adults exchanged glances.

"The problem is," the principal said softly, "that we don't believe you."

He was already looking at the row of straps on the wall, choosing which one he would use. He pushed back his chair, walked around the desk, and reached up for a strap with little ridges on the contact side.

"Open your hands on the desk," he said.

First, he strapped the other boy while Matthew and the counsellor watched.

"Cry!" the principal ordered.

The boy cried and the strapping stopped.

Then he strapped Matthew's open hands. "Cry!" he ordered.

Matthew didn't cry. Why should he cry? He hadn't done anything wrong.

It was so confusing. Out on the land, his grandfather respected every person, every animal, and he expected the same of Matthew. When the Hudson Bay manager – who sometimes tried to cheat his grandfather – was coming to buy furs, his grandfather cleaned the place. "He's a person," his grandfather said to Matthew. "You have to respect him." What would his grandfather say about men like this who *wanted* children to cry?

"Cry!" the principal shouted. "Cry!!" And hit again and again.

The strap chewed up Matthew's hand and was soon coated in his blood.

Matthew didn't cry.

The two men bent him over the desk and raised his shirt. Then the bloody strap came down and grabbed some flesh from his back.

Still, he didn't cry.

Finally, the men got tired and the strapping stopped.

"Don't you dare tell anyone about this," the principal said.

Later, in the shower, the water coming off Matthew's body and pooling around his feet ran pink with blood.

The next day in class, Matthew couldn't hold a pencil. Mrs. Moccasin came over to see what the problem was and saw his hands, too swollen to bend and all scabbed. The strap marks were still sharp.

"Who did this to you?" she demanded.

"I'm not supposed to tell," Matthew said.

"Who did this to you?" She pressed again and again, until finally Matthew told her.

Her face got red and tight. "I'm going to talk to the principal," she said.

Then she gave the class an assignment to keep them busy and went over to the office, her skirt swishing behind.

That final swish of her skirt – it was the last Matthew or any student saw of her.

Even with all the troubles, Matthew liked School. He liked the classes, the studies, the books, the tests. He liked them so much that he wanted to go back and learn more.

Matthew Loon

But after Mrs. Moccasin was sent away, the principal said to Matthew, "I told you not to tell. We can't have this kind of trouble at La Tuque. You have to leave. You can't come back. When you're older and can't find work, you'll understand why you should have obeyed me."

Matthew moved out on the land with his father and grandfather to learn the traditional ways. And, as it turned out, to end hunger in the land.

He never told his parents or grandparents about what the priests and counsellors and other students had done to him. What would be the point?

Many years later, the Indian Residential Schools Settlement people flew him all the way to Calgary for a doctor there to look at the scars crisscrossing his back and write on a piece of paper that they existed.

By the time Matthew was thirteen years old, his family was out in the bush and he lived on his own in Mistissini, working as a dishwasher. He didn't mind the work and he made enough money that he never had to ask his family for help. He even had friends. Sometimes they sat around together and drank. Matthew didn't mind the way drinking could dull memories, but, after a year, it hadn't made anything in his life better. It seemed pointless, so he quit. Without the drinking, his friends disappeared. He didn't miss them.

He got married and had a family.

Around town, he saw people being badly treated. Women beaten, kids picked on, teenagers nobody understood. Matthew thought he might like a career in policework where he could do something about it. But policemen had high school diplomas.

He worked in construction, building houses for people moving out of tents and teepees into town, and liked it enough to get a diploma in carpentry. He got his driver's license, and that brought some work too. By then, wilderness tourism was taking off, and visitors were coming to Eeyou Istchee from Europe and USA. Matthew knew life on the land – his father and grandfather had made sure of it – and soon he was working as a wilderness guide.

The more time he spent on the land, the more he saw that every kind of life – plant, animal, the soil itself – was necessary. That all kinds of life were related, like siblings, and depended on one another. None could survive alone. He understood even more what his grandfather had meant by *respect* and why it was so important.

Sometimes Matthew's wilderness clients were kids or teen-agers having a hard time with the law. Their social workers warned Matthew that these were difficult kids and they would surely cause trouble for him. But Matthew knew about having a hard time with authorities. The kids that social workers found the most difficult were often the best company for Matthew and the most eager to learn what he could teach them. Sometimes, he'd hear later that his quiet conversations with kids out there, overlooking a river or a narrows, had changed their lives. In all his years of guiding, the kids never caused him any trouble at all.

One November, out on the land, Matthew was chopping wood and thinking about all kinds of things. He kept chopping and chopping until there were twelve full cords of wood. The pile was huge.

He laughed at himself. Why on earth had he chopped so much wood?

The next morning, he went hunting, and got three caribou.

The morning after that, he went out in the canoe, looking for beaver. Along the way, he broke up thin autumn ice with his paddle. His canoe had a comfortable seat that kept his backside away from the cold water. It also blocked his view of the canoe bottom. He couldn't see that a shard of ice had gashed the side of the canoe, and ice water was pouring in.

Matthew LOOn

Suddenly, his feet were wet and astonishingly cold. He looked down.

Two seconds later the whole canoe disappeared out from under him.

He was treading ice water.

The surface ice was too thin to carry his weight, and the canoe was gone. He had nothing to climb on to, no way to get out. Already his limbs were stiffening. The end of his life was minutes away.

In his belt, he had a folded pocket knife with a solid wooden handle. His hands could hardly move but he managed to open the knife and stab it into the ice.

He stayed in the water, gripping only the knife handle so that his hand didn't touch the ice, didn't freeze, and he held on.

In case someone was in earshot, he called out.

The morning sun glinted off the thin ice.

Underneath him, water. Dark as oil.

A steady wind from the west curved the trees on the shore-line and blew in a solid line of cloud.

It sure was a beautiful morning to die.

He couldn't feel his legs anymore. The sun disappeared.

He called out.

He couldn't feel his arms anymore.

His heart beat slower, his breathing got shallow. Nothing hurt. He felt warm.

Not so very long now.

He called out.

His wife. His kids. The people he would leave behind and who loved him. Tears slid down his face into the dark water below.

Such weakness. The wind so loud. He put his last strength, the little there was, into calling out once more.

And then he went down.

Somebody had him by the collar and tried to pull. The grunting sounded like his father-in-law.

"We're gonna tip!" a voice said. His mother-in-law. The pulling stopped.

A rope under his arms. He blacked out.

Matthew was in a tent, slowly warming under blankets. A fire burned nearby and people were talking. Someone asked him questions and poured something warm down his throat. He swallowed.

A bush radio crackled. "In the water for ninety minutes!" His father-in-law's voice. "We dragged him to shore and brought him to our camp."

Somebody was giving instructions. Matthew fell asleep.

The next morning, he felt a little warmer, but he couldn't stay conscious. Again and again, he passed out. There was another bush radio conversation.

"Not doing too good," his father-in-law said. "No, not fifteen! I said he was in the water for *ninety* minutes!"

"What?!" the radio voice said. "They told us fifteen! Hang on – we're sending a chopper. How is that guy even alive?"

Matthew lay in the Mistissini clinic.

The doctors were openly perplexed by him. How had he survived? Day by day, his organs slowly wakened and he felt a little better. His limbs wakened too and he learned again how to walk. Even his toes came around. He didn't lose any of them.

Meanwhile his family was out on the land without him. They used up every piece of the twelve cords of wood that he had cut.

For three years, he had to stay close to town for regular recovery therapies and checkups. In those years, he couldn't keep a job nor go out on the land to hunt for his family. They were very poor.

Eventually the doctors said he was okay. Right away, he went into the bush.

Matthew Loon

After three years away, the first kill he made to feed his family was a beaver. First shot and it dropped.

It felt good to be home.

Everything his dad and his grandfather had passed to him, Matthew passed on to his son. And, many years later, on a twenty-three-day winter walk with his daughter from Lake Albanel to Mistissini, he passed knowledge on to her too.

Not too long ago, Matthew got a letter from some medical researchers. They wanted to do research on his body and find out how he survived in ice water for so long. Matthew likes to help out, and is curious about it himself. But a doctor warned him that, if he signed the paper, they could do any experiments on him that they wanted and not worry about consequences. That sounded a little too much like Residential School, tonsils, and the Settlement process to him. He didn't sign.

His father-in-law sometimes tells the story of finding Matthew in the water that morning. It was the time of year when days first get to be really cold. He was outside, battening down the camp for the windy day. Clouds moved quickly across the face of the sun. Any time now, Matthew would paddle in with news of beaver.

For a few seconds, the wind let up. In the abrupt silence, he thought he heard something – something human – in the distance. He looked out, over the water – and before his eyes, a thin beam of yellow light poked out of the grey sky, cut smoothly through the day, and shone down on something far away.

He didn't question it. He called his wife and they ran to the motorboat and set out as quickly as they could. Their camp was on the shore of a sheltered cove, and they had to get out of the cove to reach the big lake, and then across the lake, and around a small peninsula. A couple of miles at least. Sometimes, he had to slow down and knock ice off the side of the boat, but the golden blade of light kept shining, showing him where to go.

He rounded a bend in the shore – and there, in the ice water, in the centre of the blade of light, was a person glowing white in the light like something from heaven.

He sped up. Just as the person went unconscious and slipped into the oily black water, he grabbed him by the collar.

Instantly the light went out.

From time to time, Matthew sees the La Tuque pupils who tried to give him bruises or do sex stuff with him. They want to be his friends now, to pretend it never happened. Matthew is cordial to them, respectful, and walks away.

Sometimes, his feet ache in the cold. Maybe that's the hypothermia, maybe it's just aging. He buys good boots.

The La Tuque principal made it hard for Matthew to find work. Even now, paying the bills is difficult. But out on the land, after he was expelled, he learned respect. And that, he tells his grandkids, is a much more important skill.

Matthew Loon

Stories Heard Along the Way: Dogs

A hunter with a dog team came upon a den of wolf cubs in the bush, parents nowhere to be seen. Thinking that the cubs would enjoy sled-pulling and that he could surely provide a better home than wolf parents could, he scooped them up, secured them gently on the sled, and turned the sled for home. There, he locked the wolf cubs up in his garage. Out in the bush, the wolf parents returned to their now-empty den. They put their noses to the ground and followed the scent all the way into town, right to the locked garage. Their paws were too big to pick the garage lock and rescue their cubs – so they jumped into the husky enclosure and killed every dog that had been forced to participate in cub-napping. Even wolves disapprove of Sixties Scoops.

Dogs have sharp memories, and they generalize. Eeyou Istchee dogs that have been hit by flying stones, or abused in some other way, have remembered – and later attacked other people who dressed or smelled like the person who hurt them.

Storytellers often identified strongly with dogs. Seeing a dog always tied up, always out in the cold, or without enough water or food, was intensely distressing because it reminded them of Residential School days when they were trapped, without enough warmth or food. At the same time, they said they were afraid people would laugh at them if they knew how great their agony was about dogs in distress. They felt pressured to "mind their own business," suffer silently, and not report abuse.

Albert and his father sorted through other people's leftovers to find Albert's summer toys. A three-wheeled truck. A broken-winged airplane. A one-armed toy soldier. They were perfect.

Artist: Riley Bosum

Albert Johnny

Albert Johnny*

*Names and details have been changed to protect identities.

IN 1963, before seven-year-old Albert left for La Tuque Indian Residential School, his father said to him, "Do as you're told. Respect the adults. Stay out of trouble. Remember that we love you."

Albert's older sisters had already taught him a few English phrases. *My name is Albert. I am from Mistissini. Can I use the bathroom please? Thank you.* And they had said he would be in one of the boys' wings: Lynx, Beaver, Raccoon, or Porcupine. (The girls' wings, in a different part of the School, were Marigold, Thistle, Daffodil, and Cosmos.) He thought he knew what to expect.

It was going to be fine.

The very first night there, just before bed, Albert put on his new pajama uniform. Then he folded his clothes and put them away on his shelf in the storage room where clean laundry was kept.

Suddenly, someone ran into the storage room and, in one movement, killed the lights and shut the door. Instant darkness.

Albert froze.

And then an enormous hand wrapped his neck and pushed him face-down on the floor. Hot breath shot into his ear. Then somehow Albert's new PJs weren't on his bottom anymore. And a great big man wedged himself into Albert's wee body. Right there on the storage room floor.

It hurt so badly that Albert stopped breathing.

When it was finished, the man ran from the laundry room. In the light of the hallway, Albert saw his face and he burned it into his brain.

He lay there on the cool floor, waiting for his organs to move back into place, learning again how to breathe.

It hurt just to move. After a while he pulled up his pants, got to his knees, then to his feet. He closed the door and found the light switch.

In summer, when he would be home again and his loving father would ask him how he had got into such terrible trouble, what could he possibly say?

Somehow – even today he doesn't know how – Albert got himself to the bathroom and into a toilet stall. He collapsed onto the toilet, trying to stay conscious. After a while, he lowered his pants and sat down again.

Blood everywhere. On Albert's underwear, on his PJs, on his feet, on the floor. Every drop had come from his own body and it was still leaking out.

Albert stayed on the toilet until the bleeding stopped. He wiped himself and cleaned up as best he could.

Then he flushed.

The toilet was still red, so he flushed again.

If he washed his bloody clothes in the sink, someone might see and he would get in trouble. He wasn't supposed to get in trouble. So he washed his bloody underwear in the toilet and flushed again.

Then he washed his bloody PJs in the toilet and flushed again.

Still it was red, so he flushed again.

He dressed in his wet clothes, walked gingerly to bed, shoved his head under the covers, and cried.

Before that day, life was good. After that day, it was not.

Albert Johnny

Albert told no one about what had happened but the word must have spread among the adults because his bed became a popular place. Nearly every night, as the evening train rolled by and rumbled the School walls, Albert had Visitors. Men helping themselves to his body, one wanting this, another wanting that, opening him up like a Christmas present. They must have worked out a schedule between them since there were so many men and they never overlapped.

Once, out on the Schoolyard, Albert heard his name over the intercom: a care package had arrived for him and he should go to the dorm to collect it. Other kids had got care packages from their parents – now it was his turn! He ran inside, met the supervisor, and followed him to his room.

No care package there.

The man just pushed Albert's face down on the bed, yanked down his pants, and did as he pleased. Then handed him a chocolate bar in payment.

Another time, Albert was sick and feverish. The supervisor looking after him said a warm bath would help. Together they walked to the shower room, ignoring the twenty shower heads on the wall, and went into the little private room at the front. It had a single clawfoot bathtub and a door that closed. Albert took off his clothes and waited, shivering, aching, while the supervisor drew a bath and carefully tested the water for the perfect temperature. When it was full, the supervisor gently helped him into the tub.

Instantly, Albert's chills eased and the aches in his bones began to soften. He closed his eyes for a minute.

When he opened them, the supervisor had undressed.

"Open your mouth," he said to Albert. Albert who was sick and trapped in the tub.

And the man did as he pleased right there in his fevered, gagging mouth. The lollipop he gave Albert after didn't cut the taste at all.

One Visitor taught Albert to masturbate. "Now let me do you a favour," he said, before they began. "It's only fair," and handed him a package of licorice twists.

Another Visitor was a Cree man who had once been a student and who now worked at the School as a supervisor. "I know your mother, I know your sisters," he said to Albert. "They asked me to take care of you. That's what I'm doing here. When I touch you like this, that's me looking after you." He usually left a pack of bubblegum.

Always they behaved as if it were a proper transaction, as if the candy were fair payment. One appetite for another.

After a while, it seemed normal to Albert. Routine. Just everyday life at La Tuque Indian Residential School. His feelings sometimes got in the way – shame, dread, the deepest aching sad-ness – so Albert shut them down. He turned something off in his head and tried not to feel anything at all. And he did what the men asked because he didn't want to get into trouble.

Above all, stay out of trouble.

Night after night.

Year after year.

In June, Albert always went home. On the first morning, right after breakfast, Albert and his father and Uncle Willie piled into Uncle Willie's truck and drove the dusty dirt roads all the way to the Chibougamau dump. There, Albert and his father sorted through other people's leftovers to find Albert's summer toys. A three-wheeled truck. A broken-winged airplane. A one-armed toy soldier. They were broken, these treasures, just like Albert was. They were perfect.

Every time it was the best day of the year.

The men who visited Albert's bed talked to God quite a bit. God was there for everyone, they said, and he loved Albert. If Albert ever needed help, all he had to do was ask God for it.

Albert Johnny

Albert considered it. In the Bible, God razed entire cities with fire and brimstone. He stopped an army by moving a sea. He opened the earth and caused rebels to slide down its throat. He even stopped the sun from setting. For someone like that, ending night visits should be easy. It had been going on for years now – Albert was nine years old – it was high time somebody helped him.

So he prayed as the men had taught him to pray. He asked God to make it stop.

It didn't stop. It didn't even slow down. This was just another of their tricks. Bibles for land. Candy for sex. False comfort for prayer. An economy of deceit.

If it was going to stop, Albert was going to have to make it stop. By himself.

In Albert's dorm was a window from which he could see the gymnasium. Not far from that window, which was always closed, stood a ladder that went to the top of the School. One night, using all his strength, Albert managed to pry the window open, crawl out onto a ledge, then down to another ledge, and over to the ladder. He climbed it to the roof of the School. He walked along the roof all the way to the front entrance where there was a parking lot that led to the front door.

Albert stood at the edge of the roof. If he dove to the ground and landed headfirst on the concrete driveway, then the nightly Visitors would finally have to stop opening him up like a Christmas present because he would be dead.

He would dive. It was the only way out.

He stood there, preparing.

The train rolled by and rumbled the roof beneath his feet. In the setting sun, the iron of the track took on a rich deep red. Then, as the sky fell dark, the spruce needles began to shimmer in the silver moonlight. Such beauty, this world. Albert wiped his tears and moved to the edge and prepared to dive –

His father, his mother. Suddenly they were right there, in his mind.

They overflowed with love. Being near them made Albert calm, they didn't even have to say anything. They had been deeply wounded by the Schools taking child after child, and yet they warmed and lit up the world.

Albert did not want his beautiful parents to hurt more.

He turned around, climbed back down the ladder, snuck back along the overhang, back through the window, back into bed, where he fell asleep.

Until a nightly Visitor woke him up.

There's a story. One day, in the sandbox, Albert and his friends built a series of roads and highways and pushed their cars and trucks along them.

Albert had more cars in his closet.

"Wait here," he said. "I'm gonna get my cars from the closet." And he was off, running through the front entrance, up to the Lynx Wing, and right to his closet.

"Hey Albert!"

He turned around. On the floor, between the beds, sat one of his friends. In front of him on the floor was an open box. Bubblegum. Lollipops. Chocolate bars. Licorice twists.

"Do you want some?" the boy asked.

Albert was ten years old. What ten-year-old says no to candy?

He sat down beside his friend, they ate together, then he ran back outside with his toy cars.

After a while, the intercom system crackled. "Albert Johnny. Please come to the office."

Albert left his friends and ran inside. There was the principal, a few supervisors, the boy with the candy, and the boy's older brother.

Albert Johnny

The older brother looked at Albert. His face curled up. "Why'd you steal my candies?" he asked.

"I didn't," Albert said. "He gave them to me." And pointed at the other boy.

"No I didn't," the boy lied. "You took them."

Albert looked from one face to another. He already knew no one would believe him.

The principal looked at him and said, "Albert, you are in big trouble. You have committed one of the worst possible crimes you could do."

Albert was sent to his bed without supper.

Once, long ago, his father had punished him. Albert had slingshot a stone into the head of a bully. Slingshotting people was not allowed – but the precision of that shot had been immensely satisfying. That evening, his father came into the family tent, quietly took Albert's slingshot from the shelf, and tossed it into the woodstove fire. No shouting, no hitting, no scolding, no hunger, no shame. And Albert had actually done the thing he was punished for.

After the supper that Albert didn't have, a supervisor came to his bed. "Come with me," he said.

Albert got up and followed him through the dorm – the hallways were weirdly empty – and over to the gymnasium. And when the gymnasium door opened, Albert saw, standing in a tidy row against the walls, every single La Tuque student. Even the girls. He never saw the girls. La Tuque strictly kept boys and girls separate. To prevent inappropriate sexual behaviour.

At the front of the gym stood a chair for all to see. A canvas running shoe with a rubber bottom sat on it.

Albert wanted to take his place along the wall, but the supervisor kept him close by. He clapped his hands to get everyone's attention and the room hushed.

"In La Tuque Indian Residential School," he said, his voice booming around the gym, "there are certain things we don't allow.

We don't allow stealing. Taking what doesn't belong to you is one of the worst things you can possibly do. Now this is what happens to people at La Tuque Indian Residential School who steal."

He turned to Albert then. "Pull down your pants and your underwear. Then bend over the chair."

Of course Albert obeyed, and, in that instant, as he exposed to everyone in the School that private part of his body, his mind jumped to his first night. When his underwear was soaked in blood and a supervisor had helped himself to Albert's wee body as if it had belonged to him.

The supervisor picked up the shoe and, in front of everyone, beat Albert's naked bum.

Every person in the room was silent.

Albert pulled up his pants, walked out of the gym, straight to his bed, and covered himself with blankets. There, in what meagre privacy he could manage, as the train rolled by and rumbled the walls, he cried.

To fall asleep after his nightly Visitors, Albert often thought of his father's love. It made him feel better. This time, he fell asleep thinking of his father's axe. His shiny beautiful guns.

One Sunday, in the little room beside the chapel, Albert, about eleven years old, changed into his altar boy gown and waited for the supervisor who led the Sunday services. One of the other supervisors (who was a Captain in the Salvation Army) showed up instead. There had been a last-minute switch, he said. He quickly pulled on his gown and together he and Albert stepped out into the chapel. At the front of the chapel, Albert lit the candles and the Captain preached Jesus, saving grace, hell and all its brimstone, all the usuals.

So many times the Captain had helped himself to Albert's body. Had opened him up like a Christmas present.

But now Albert had in his hand a long, heavy, sturdy metal pole with a weighted hood on the end to snuff out candles. Now

Albert Johnny

Albert was no longer a wee boy. With some precision and a bit of force, he could sink that hood right into the Captain's head. How satisfying it would be to fell him like a tree in front of the whole congregation. To do this beautiful world that one great favour.

Albert took a deep breath and raised the pole –

Something stopped him. His father's face. Nick of time.

The Captain never knew how close he came.

In 1968, a new principal came to La Tuque all the way from Switzerland. His name was Father Bonnard. He brought big changes.

The first big change he made was to get rid of the strap. There would be no more lash scars. The second big change he made was to stop the haircuts. The boys' brush cuts and the girls' bowl cuts reminded him of people in Nazi concentration camps, he said, and he never wanted to see anything like that again. Their hair was allowed to grow. The third big change he made was to bring some genuine kindness and safety to La Tuque. No one could learn, he said, without kindness and safety. If Father Bonnard found out about all the nightly visits happening in Albert's bed and other beds around campus, Albert never knew, but finally the visits stopped.

For so long, whenever Albert was away from his parents, he had longed for them, for the great comfort of their hugs. But years of nightly Visitors had done something to Albert. Now a young man, he hated touch of any kind. In the summers at home, if his sisters rubbed up against him at the dinner table, he cringed. If his father or mother hugged him, he wanted to vomit. Even a handshake bothered him. He had shut off his emotions years ago. But emotions, like children with slingshots, are not always obedient, and when they flared Albert could hardly breathe for despair.

One night, in his last year at La Tuque, he returned to the window by the ladder, pried it open – it was easy now that he was big – and climbed out as he had so many years before. This time, he stepped down the ladder and walked to the railway tracks that ran by the School. He lay down on the tracks and rested his hands on the iron rails and waited for the nightly rumble. The rumble that had masked the screams of so many nightly visits, that had marked so many key moments in his life.

Soon the rails quivered under his fingertips, and then they shook his hands and arms, and then he could hear the train. It was almost there, his troubles almost done –

His mother, his father.

Even after all these years, though he couldn't bring himself to touch them, they were still so beautiful. He couldn't hurt them.

Albert sucked in a big breath and rolled off the track just as the train rumbled by. Nick of time.

He got up and walked back into the School. He changed into pajamas and went to bed.

Cree Elders will tell you that the land itself can heal you if you let it affect you. Not quickly, not like magic or a miracle, but slowly, steadily, it will find the wounds in your spirit and heal them.

After School, Albert moved onto the land with his parents. Over many years, he learned their traditional ways. There, a "nightly visit" meant nothing more than the hoot of an owl or the howl of a wolf. There, he had time to absorb the warmth and light of his parents. There, even the smallest leaf or the greyest day was beautiful. Every day brought many things to love. It changed things, and slowly the fear and betrayal inside of Albert began to dissolve.

It wasn't always enough. The nightly Visitors had scarred his life and now despair still sometimes clamped him right down. When it did, he thought back to the view from the top of the School building, or from a railway track – and then he supplemented the love from the land or his family with love from a bottle or a hash pipe or a sparkling white line of cocaine. No question, the supplements helped.

Albert Johnny

But they weren't always enough, either. For fifteen years, Albert saw a psychotherapist in Montréal. To her he spoke, in great detail, about nightly visits and railway tracks and diving from the School roof, all of it. Telling stories of pain to a White woman in a Montréal office was not exactly a traditional Cree way but, after he had told them, the memories hurt him less and he stood up straighter. She had moved to Montréal from England, and spoke with a British accent. The same ocean that dipped down into James Bay and fed his people had brought her to help him mend. Another beautiful thing in this world.

He began to write poetry then. Thousands of poems. And in his poems he talked about his beautiful parents, about broken toys, about surviving La Tuque, about the medicine of land, about meeting his wife at a juke box, about having a son, about whatever came to his mind. And with time and therapy and poetry and the land and his wonderful family, all of these things together, he needed the supplements less and less.

Until he didn't need them at all.

There's a story. Albert was a grown man with a son whom he had vowed to protect. When his son was a teenager, Albert finished up his schooling in Montréal while his son stayed with family in another community. They were good friends, Albert and his son, and talked often on the phone.

One evening, his son mentioned that a new White guy in the community had given him a ride home from School that day.

"Well that's neighbourly," Albert said. "What's his name?"

His son gave a name. "He used to be a supervisor at La Tuque," he said.

Albert froze. That supervisor had hurt so many kids. His son had been driving around the community with a child molester.

Albert stopped breathing. Time stood still. Helpless again.

"Dad?" his son asked.

Albert forced himself to inhale.

"Are you hurt? Did he do anything to you?"

"What? No! He just picked me up as I was walking on the side of the road and dropped me off at home."

"Son," he said, "I don't want to get into details, but I need you to remember his face. Burn it into your brain so you always recognize him. And never ever get into a vehicle with him again. It's a small town. When you see him, get as far away as you can. Promise me."

"Okay Dad, I promise," his son said.

Albert could tell from the tone of his voice that his son was probably rolling his eyes at the phone, at his weird old man. But that was okay. The nightly Visitors were still out there trying to find their ways into little Cree bodies – there would always be men like that – but his son was okay.

Albert's beautiful parents are gone now. He has instead two grandsons and one granddaughter whom he loves more than he thought a broken man could love. He would give his life to protect them.

Sometimes despair still clamps Albert down. To this day, whenever he's alone, he has a radio or something playing in the background. It lessens his fear of the night, the part of his brain that forces him to remember the faces of his nightly Visitors so that they never catch him off guard. There are still wounds.

But Albert knows now, with the deepest conviction, that he will come through the other side. It takes his breath away to think of all the love he has had in his life, all the wounds it has healed. He will keep on healing, he knows, until the day he draws his last breath on this beautiful earth.

On that day, as he slips into the next life, he will be entirely healed.

Albert Johnny

Stories Heard Along the Way: Skipping School

In the '60s, a hunter went into the bush north of Chisasibi. It was winter and a fresh coat of beautiful snow covered everything. By the lake, he saw a set of child's tracks and followed them to a campsite. Everything was still. The hunter called out. No response. The child's tracks went into the tent, so he poked his head inside. There lay an entire family, dead of starvation. The parents and older children were frozen solid, but the youngest child who had made the tracks still had some warmth under the armpits. Had the hunter come an hour earlier, he might have been able to save the child. In those days, there were multiple reports of entire families dying on the land because they had refused to send their children to Residential School. As punishment, the Indian Agent had forbidden all stores from selling them winter supplies or ammunition.

In the '50s and '60s, people in the South read about a famine in Northern Ontario and Québec. They attributed it to weather and to overtrapping in the North, even through beaver preserves had been set up two decades earlier. What they didn't know was that parents who refused to send their children back to Residential School were forbidden to buy groceries at any store – and so they trapped much more than usual in order to survive. In those years, neighbours also often shared of their own supplies and everyone went a little hungry.

Wally tied on his shoes, walked out the front door, put one foot in front of the other, and ran.

Artist: Tristan Shecapio-Blacksmith

Wally Rabbitskin

Wally Rabbitskin

WALLY woke up. It was still dark. He had been dreaming. His hands had been on the steering wheel of a big old car with leather seats and there was a stink in the air. The car wasn't going very quickly but his heart had pounded like mad. And then he was awake, drenched in sweat, heart still pounding. His wife lay fast asleep beside him, her chest gently lifting and falling with each breath. Wally looked at the ceiling for a minute, then at the moonbeam lighting up the 1992 *Cree Nation of Mistissini* calendar on the wall. His mouth tasted like metal.

He got out of bed and went to the bathroom. Under the bright light, he looked at his tongue in the mirror. Everything was normal. He shuffled back to bed. It had just been a strange dream.

The next morning, Wally and his wife packed the car, strapped their kids into their car seats, and drove south to Montréal. It was a beautiful fall day, the leaves just beginning to turn. They stopped in Roberval to gas up and grab coffee, then kept driving. Soon came La Tuque and the smell of the pulp mill. It was fine, it was fine, Wally didn't live there anymore –

And then it was not fine. His knuckles turned white from his grip on the steering wheel, his heart raced, and the taste of metal filled his mouth.

"You okay?" his wife asked. "You're all sweaty."

"I'm fine!" he shouted. "It's this stupid car in front of us!!" And then he rammed his palm into the horn, punched down the gas, and swerved around the car in front and the car in front of that, shouting at the drivers through the glass.

His wife grabbed the dash to keep from falling over.

She stared at him. "Wally!" she said, "they're just driving. What's wrong with you? In two seconds, you went from normal to a crazy person."

"I'm fine," he said. "Fine! They're stupid drivers!!"

"Why you always angry these days?" She asked. "What's up with you?"

Later, in their Montréal hotel room, calm once more, Wally turned to his wife.

"I'm sorry," he said. "I was angry. I *am* angry. Something happened to me in Residential School that I can't forget and – I don't wanna talk about it. I've been trying to make sense of it."

She put down the phone in her hand and looked at him.

"Oh," she said. "Something happened to me too. If you ever do wanna talk about it, I'm here."

She believed him, Wally could tell. Instantly, he felt better.

She turned back to her phone. "But Wally?"

"Yeah?"

"No matter how bad it is, you have to change your behaviour. You're a good dad and a good husband and you work hard and I love you but it's not safe to have kids around somebody who's always angry and it's not safe to have you driving like a maniac. You gotta do *something*."

"Okay," he said.

It was 1972, and ten-year-old Wally's first night in La Tuque Indian Residential School. He hadn't fallen asleep easily – everything was strange – and now someone was waking him too soon. He forced his eyes open. It was still dark out.

Wally Rabbitskin

"Wake up Wally," the night watchman was saying. "It's 5:30 AM. You're on toast duty."

Then he woke Wally's three roommates too.

Wally and the other three got dressed and followed the watchman out of their bedroom and past ten more down the stairs to the kitchen. There, on the counter, sat more bread than Wally had ever seen in his life and a giant toaster, already on and glowing red hot. It was a wide metal box with an open mouth at the front and a metal grill inside that slowly went 'round and 'round. One yawning boy stood at the mouth of the toaster and fed the bread slices, three wide, onto the grill. Like a giant tongue, it took up the bread and moved it slowly across the red elements and then dropped it, crisp and toasted, on the shelf underneath where a second boy picked it up. He handed it then to the other two boys who stood beside, each with a paintbrush and a bowl of melted butter, and painted the butter onto the bread and stacked it.

An hour later, a hundred other kids filed into the dining room to eat it. By then the toast was cold and a little bit soggy, but no one really minded. Just a few years ealier, La Tuque students were being starved and now they got enough to eat. A little sogginess was okay.

That whole first week, early morning toast-making was Wally's duty. On Friday, he walked to the director's office with a paper saying he had made toast all week, and he received $2.00. The next week, he had to do a different chore.

At first, School was overwhelming. So many rules and categories, everything was so regulated. At home he didn't even know who else was ten years old, and now he was supposed to do everything with (and only with) other boys who were ten years old. At home you never stood in line for anything, but at School you had to stand in line at least ten times a day. Wally had always made his bed at home – his mom liked things tidy – but at La Tuque his bed was tested every day to make sure it was so tight a dime could bounce on it, and not a single wrinkle. Even now, Wally makes a tight bed. It bugs him to see one unmade.

The best part of La Tuque Indian Residential School was the sports. Hockey or basketball or swimming, there was always something to do. In the basement of the School was a swimming pool, but to get there Wally had to walk through a dank and narrow passageway that smelled of mould. A creepy, scary dungeon. But he loved swimming so much that he held his breath and forced one foot in front of the other through the dungeon corridor until he came out into the bright swimming area. Eventually he got used to the dank passageway and after a few years he didn't even notice.

Wally was so good at sports that the physical education teacher encouraged him to go to the town nearby and try out for the local teams that had nothing to do with School. So he did. And the more sports he played, the better he felt. If he was running or swimming or skating and breathing hard, he could always forget about the bad things, at least for a while.

About the counsellor with an explosive temper, for instance. One Saturday, during free time, a bunch of kids were playing floor hockey. The counsellor wanted to join in, and that was okay, the more the merrier. But halfway through the game, he pushed a kid out of the way to try and score a goal. The kid, about eleven years old, played good defense and pushed back, blocking the counsellor from scoring.

Everything stopped.

The counsellor dropped his stick and shoved the kid to the floor. Then he reached down, grabbed a thick handful of the kid's hair, gripped it tightly, and dragged the kid – by only the hair – across the whole length of the floor to the stairs where he dropped his head to the floor. There, he screamed and screamed at the kid and finally sent him to his room.

So much for Saturday afternoon floor hockey.

That sort of thing happened once or twice a month. Just often enough for everyone to know that La Tuque – though it was better than it had been a few years before – was still a dangerous

Wally Rabbitskin

place. Everyone had some sort of scar. The worst was when a kid was taken away and later came back crying – but without visible bruises or welts or burns. Then you knew that whatever had happened was probably sexual, the kind of scar you couldn't see.

You were careful then not to ask. You didn't want to make it worse.

One of the counsellors was also the coach and he was always hanging around Wally and his friends. "Hey George," he'd say. "Do you wanna go into town for some fries?" Or "Wally, how'd you like to learn how to drive?" In this way, the boys were sometimes able to get outside the School, do something fun, and see the surrounding area.

Once, during a driving lesson, Wally and the coach had traded places so that Wally was in the driver's seat and the coach in the passenger seat. From where he sat, the green hood of the car looked even longer. Wally applied gas gently, and the car began to inch forward.

"Turn here," the coach said, after a while. "You should get some experience driving on gravel."

So Wally rotated the wheel to the right, and drove slowly down the middle of the road.

"It's harder to drive on gravel," the coach said, "but you still have to stay on your side of the road."

"Okay," Wally said, and moved the car over to the right half of the road, where it slanted towards the ditch, and kilometre after kilometre they drove.

Many kilometres down the road, in a remote wooded area where Wally was pretty sure no one ever went, the coach told Wally to pull over.

Wally slowed down, pulled over, put the car in neutral, and looked at the coach.

"Turn it off," he said.

Wally did.

"Ever think about girls, Wally?"

"Uuummm, ye–eah." Wally blushed and looked away. What did girls have to do with driving?

And then, with gruesome slowness, reaching from across the car, the coach slid his hand down the front of Wally's pants, rubbing his most private parts. His breathing went funny and his eyes half-closed.

The car was suddenly much too small.

He reached for Wally's hand then, and, in a weird strangled voice, said "Touch me too, Wally. Here, like this."

Wally managed to yank his hand away from the coach – but the coach was a strong man and Wally was a kid who couldn't do anything about the one giant hand still down his pants, nor about the other one with which the coach was now rubbing himself. There wasn't enough oxygen in the world.

And when it was done, they both got out of the car and traded places. The coach drove the car back to La Tuque Indian Residential School.

Wally was quiet.

"Oh come on now, Wally," the coach said. "How come you don't wanna say anything? You enjoyed it! It's normal!"

But Wally had *hated* what the coach had done. He felt hurt and angry and desperately confused. The one thing he could do in that moment was not talk, not pretend everything was okay, not give the coach what he wanted to justify his brutality, and so that's what Wally did. He said nothing and the drive back was silent.

That evening, thinking about what had happened and how repulsive it all was, a hot metal taste flooded Wally's mouth.

After that, Wally avoided the coach as much as he could. He approached Wally a few times with the how-about-a-driving-lesson expression. Wally saw him coming and moved away. But on

Wally Rabbitskin

Saturdays, when they all played basketball or hockey together, the coach joked with Wally's friends.

"Oh Wally's always mad," he would say. "Don't play with him, he's not a good friend."

Sometimes, Wally's friends listened to him. All Wally could do was promise himself that he would never be like the coach. No matter what, he would be better than that.

Many years later, when Wally thought back, he remembered how very often the hands of the counsellors lingered on a boy's skin or on his waist. How their arms draped around the boys in something more than camaraderie. How they wet their lips and got a look of euphoria on their faces just watching everyone play hockey. And how his friends did not know how to avoid the counsellors, and continued to go on trips with them and come back to the dorm, drawn, silent, flushed. And later still, many years after Residential School, how one of them would be a substance abuser and another would be accused of sexual assault, and Wally would know that – though no one spoke of it – his friends had been abused too. Driving lessons, fries, whatever. What choice did they really have?

His wife was right. All this had happened a lifetime ago – Wally had since finished a College certificate in Physical Education and a university degree in Social Work and he had a good job – but in some ways he was still a student in La Tuque Indian Residential School, living that driving lesson again and again. The coach's face kept dropping into Wally's dreams at night, or in front of his face in the day, always without warning. Each time it made him sweat right through all of his clothes, it brought a hot metal taste into his mouth, and it made him suddenly inexplicably enraged.

Wally didn't want his life controlled by a man long gone from it. He didn't want to be the kind of guy whose wife was scared of him. And he didn't want to die in a car accident. He really did have to do something.

Long ago, sports had cleared his mind. So he did the only thing he could think to do: he tied on his shoes, walked out the front door, put one foot in front of the other, and ran. During the whole run, he still thought about horrible things but afterwards he really did feel better, as if he had left some bad stuff behind. And even though his muscles burned – he was a bit out of shape – it had actually felt meditative. It helped.

After that, when Wally felt frustrated, or when the coach's face showed up, or when he wanted to clear his head, he ran. With each run, and then each year of running, he felt better still. So much better that Wally decided he would never talk about the coach and what happened during driving lessons. He would never give him any air time. Instead, he would talk about his athletic life now, and how fitness and exercise had helped him cope and change.

A couple of years later, Wally was walking into Adel's Restaurant in Mistissini. Coming out of the restaurant was a young Cree man whom Wally had seen around town. He always looked sad, desolate, utterly without hope. He was a bit unsteady on his feet. *Probably tipsy,* Wally thought. The man came right up to him.

"Hey man, I see you," he said to Wally. "I see you running around town all the time. I've spent my life in and out of foster homes, not good ones. I've been beaten, sexually abused, the whole gamut. Every time I see you running, I think *There's a guy who has no problems. He's never had any trauma, never seen any bad stuff, never had to work through anything. Nothing keeps that guy up at night.* That's what I think when I see you run."

And then the man was gone.

Wally stood in the parking lot open-mouthed. Then he went into Adel's.

That week, he told his wife about driving lessons with the coach.

She believed everything he said and told some stories of her own. That made him feel better still.

Wally Rabbitskin

Right around that time, the time he told his wife, Wally realized that he hadn't seen the coach's face or tasted hot metal for a long time.

And that he really wasn't angry anymore at all.

In 2013, the Indian Residential Schools Settlement officials came to town. They wanted to hear the stories of Residential School survivors, they said. They wanted to compensate, to reconcile.

Wally began to receive phone calls from the officials. Did he remember a boy named George? A boy named Fred? A boy named Matthew? Could he confirm that this boy had attended La Tuque in the years that he was there? And of course, he always could.

But there were problems with the process. For one thing, many Cree people were being told that they had attended Residential School for fewer years than they actually had. And when that happened, unless the Cree people could produce official documents for every single year, the Government would not pay them for the full time. They were saving themselves some money.

For another thing, how could a Truth and Reconciliation Commission, or an Independent Assessment Process, or a Common Experience Payment address the ways in which his life had been affected? The ways in which his puberty and dating years became agony any time he thought about a girl and suddenly that coach's face had slammed into his head? The ways his wife and kids had suffered in the years before Wally started running? How the stuff he couldn't talk about had for years been the main thing he had thought about? How La Tuque Indian Residential School had for years stolen even his sleep? How he still felt uncomfortable sitting beside a man, any man? How could any of that be compensated for?

Still, Wally got ready. He dug through his old boxes and he found old report cards, neatly filed away, dating all the way back to his first year there.

And then it was his turn.

On a cold November day, sleet plopping from the sky, Wally walked into the Assessment Process Room. Six or seven people sat at the front behind a long table, and Wally sat behind a little table facing them. A lawyer sat beside him.

"Mr. Rabbitskin, at what age did you begin attending La Tuque Indian Residential School?" the official, a man in a dark suit, asked.

"At age ten, sir."

"No, Mr. Rabbitskin," the man said, smiling and peering at him overtop his glasses, "I'm afraid that's not correct. You started at age twelve. The file says so."

Wally smiled politely and handed the official a brown envelope then. The official turned it over and all the old report cards tumbled out onto the desk. He thumbed through them.

His smile faded.

"Ahem, okay," he said, clearing his throat. "Perhaps umm a cleric at some point made a mistake. This panel will acknowledge that you began attending at age ten. Now, to your experiences."

And then, to these strangers, Wally told the details of some of the things he had seen, and some of the things that had happened to him, including driving lessons with the coach.

They listened quietly, respectfully, all the way through his story, taking notes all the while. He thought then that it would be okay.

He was wrong.

"I'm sorry, Mr. Rabbitskin, but your medical files show no permanent damage from this, uh, event in the car. Why should we believe it happened at all? Did anyone see the coach do these things to you?"

Wally knew they were trying to confirm the truth of his story, in the same way they had called him to ask if Matthew or Fred or George had attended La Tuque in the years Wally was there.

But the way they were asking, as if it were his responsibility to prove that his life happened, felt like they did not *want* to

Wally Rabbitskin

understand, they did not *want* to believe him, they did not *want* to reconcile, and, no matter what they said, they *did not want* to pay. Cheaper to treat him like a criminal.

Immediately, he wished he hadn't told them.

"Mr. Rabbitskin, how many times did this coach sexually assault you?" they continued. "Was he always alone? Did he ever penetrate you sexually? If so, with what and by how much? Did he coerce you to penetrate him? If so, with what and by how much? Were you ever hospitalized for injuries related to sexual assault?"

They were most humiliating questions. His experiences were being ranked. If he had been permanently disabled or physically scarred, like others he knew, if he had not avoided the coach in the years after the driving lesson, if the coach had had his way with Wally more often, if more counsellors had taken a liking to Wally, then he would receive more compensation. The memories that had swallowed so much of his life were now minimized and dismissed for not being worse. Like the boy who had played defense in the floor hockey game, he was being punished for looking after himself. The shame of the original driving lesson washed over him again. Thank goodness it had not been a public process.

He knew immediately that, even with the payment, if he had the chance to participate in any of the Indian Residential School Settlement processes again, he wouldn't.

And then he tied on his shoes and went out into the welcoming sleet for a long, long run.

Wally kept running. Each year, he wore out three or four pairs of running shoes. People in Mistissini got used to seeing him in his shoes and gear running out by the lagoon or on the long gravel path along the main road or just around Mistissini at nearly any time of the day or evening. Each run cleared his mind a little more and freed up mental space to think about other things.

He was thinking quite a bit about his brother.

Back when they were kids, they had often played hockey with their friends on the frozen lake. One day, the puck had slid out onto thin ice and Wally had skated out to get it. He stayed on stable ice and stretched and stretched his hockey stick but even so he couldn't quite reach the puck. He inched out a bit further then – and the ice collapsed. In Wally plunged. Freezing water up to his neck.

Their friends panicked and ran away, but Wally called to his brother. "Stay here! Help me out!"

Wally's brother called their friends back. Together the boys lay down on stable ice and held out their hockey sticks to Wally until he could grab one. Then together they got up, dug in their skates, and heaved back, pulling him until he flopped out onto solid ice.

Wally couldn't move easily anymore. He was too cold. So his brother, moving as quickly as he could, ripped off Wally's skates, pushed his feet into his boots, and helped him stand. Then he half-dragged soaked, frozen Wally – who could move less with each passing step – home. He left Wally there beside the stove that still had some glowing embers, and ran to Church to get their mom. By the time she arrived, Wally had managed to change into dry clothes. She built up the fire and fed him hot tea and broth and slowly warmed him up again.

Now his brother, who had once saved his life, was dying. Back in the '90s, diabetes had set in and now he was in renal failure, on dialysis, too sick to go into the bush. Wally couldn't stop thinking about him.

Late one night, after a long run, Wally turned to his wife.

"I'm healthy and fit," he said, "I want to donate a kidney to my brother. I think maybe this is supposed to happen. Maybe that's another reason I've been running all these years."

She was quiet for a while.

"Okay," she said, "but he has to take care of it."

The next day, Wally called the transplant clinic. They told him that his years of fitness made him a good candidate to donate

Wally Rabbitskin

a kidney and they ran tests to make sure Wally's kidney would be compatible with his brother's body.

When the tests came back, he telephoned his brother. "Remember when we were kids," Wally said, "and I broke through the ice out on the lake and you pulled me out?"

"You were a frozen mess," his brother said. "Your clothes and hair were all stiff by the time we got home and your face was covered in tiny icicles. I pretty much carried you the whole way."

They both laughed.

"Remember how great it felt to play hockey all the time? To be that fit?"

"Yeah," his brother said. "Or to go into the bush. I really miss that."

"Okay. Here's the deal. Our tissues match. I'll give you my kidney, but I want you to get that fit and healthy again. You have to exercise and eat properly and drink lots of water and no alcohol and take care of your family and make my kidney last until you're an old man. I can't donate twice."

His brother didn't say much, but Wally could hear his voice wobbling through the phone and knew he was tearing up. The relief came in quiet ripples through the phone.

A few weeks later, still a bit sore from major transplant surgery, Wally got a call.

"Hey Wally!!" His brother was laughing through the phone. "I'm on our trapline! Can't do too much just yet. But I'm here!"

Wally smiled. It felt good to hear it.

And then he tied on his shoes and went for a run.

Stories Heard Along the Way: Officials

A White game warden was behaving badly and causing trouble in a community, so the Chief ordered him to leave town. He didn't. The Chief kept hearing complaints and was finally fed up. One lunch-hour, he called a few friends. They went over to where the game warden sat in his truck. They all got on one side of the truck – and pushed it over into the snow with the warden still inside. Then they went back to work. After the warden righted his truck, he drove off and was never seen in the community again.

From time to time, the RCMP randomly entered Cree homes, pretended to search for something, made an enormous mess, and left. Sometimes they found packages of yeast used by fine bakers everywhere for doughnut- or bread-making. The officials fined the Cree homeowner for making moonshine and for owning a still even if there was no still there just because yeast is a moonshine ingredient. If the homeowner couldn't pay the hefty fine, she or he stayed in prison for a while.

From a circular sent to Indian Agents on December 15, 1921, by the Deputy Superintendent of Indian Affairs: "It is observed with alarm that the holding of dances by the Indians on their reserves is on the increase. ... I have, therefore to direct you to use your utmost endeavours to dissuade the Indians from excessive indulgence in the practice of dancing."

Back in the 1950s, Indian Agents built a registry of First Nations people of Canada. Often, members of the same family had their names recorded by different Indian Agents, each of whom spelled the names differently. Today, some common Cree surnames still have many different spellings. For instance, Chakapash, Chaakapesh, Tshakapesh, and Chakaapash are all variations of one surname. Other common Cree names, such as Iserhoff, didn't sound Cree enough to the Indian Agents, and those families had a difficult time being recognized as Indigenous by Government officials. Some weren't recognized until the 1980s.

On a number of occasions during the Independent Assessment Process of the Indian Residential Schools Settlement, officials telephoned the abusers who then confirmed, over speakerphone, that they had committed the crime. Despite the admission, the storytellers found it painful to hear the abuser's voice again. More difficult still was when the abuser wasn't charged: "Oh he's old and disabled and can't hurt anyone now," the officials said.

A boy with tuberculosis came home from Residential School for summer and died. The family buried him at the camp, but, since they were two weeks' travel away from an official, they did not register the death. In fall, they returned South to buy winter supplies. Because the boy's death hadn't been registered, the Indian Agent didn't believe he had died and the stores were forbidden to sell supplies to the family.

A plane landed on the lake. A man in a suit stepped out, pulled spectacles from his chest pocket, and set them on his nose.

Artist: Jared Linton

George Blacksmith

George Blacksmith

NINETEEN FIFTY-FOUR. A Cree trapper lay at the side of the Eastmain River, dying of tuberculosis. Loosely, he held the hand of his four-year-old son. They had been in the bush with their family and he had fallen sick, so they had packed up and started the two-week trip home. Overland on portages, his brother had carried the big canoe alone, and had then come back and carried him too. Now the trapper, too sick even to be carried, had been left by the river holding the hand of his son, while his brother went ahead to call an airplane.

Together, the trapper and his boy watched the pontoons of the Otter settle gently onto the river and taxi to shore. The door opened and his brother and the pilot stepped down. Efficiently and without fuss, they rolled the sick man onto a canvas stretcher and carried him onto the plane. The boy clambered up behind and took the trapper's hand again, his brother said goodbye, and the plane taxied up the river, lifting the trapper and his son into the air.

At Mistassini Post, it set down temporarily. The trapper was weak, his breaths laboured and slowing. It was difficult to speak.

He called for his sister Louisa and her husband Charlie. Someone went out to fetch them. They came quickly and boarded the plane.

In one hand, the trapper still held his son's hand and, in the other, he took his sister's. Then, with great force of will, he gathered into his weak lungs all the air he could manage.

"Louisa, Charlie," he said, "the next world is close. I hear my wife calling me from there."

He paused, still holding their hands, to fill his lungs again.

"Will you raise my son? Teach him life on the land? Love him as your own?"

"Of course," Louisa said.

"I'm honoured," Charlie said, wiping his eyes with a free hand.

The trapper took a few breaths.

"George," he whispered to his boy, placing his hand in Louisa's. "Now you have a new mom and dad. Respect them, listen to them. Love them."

The boy nodded, his eyes leaking saltwater all over the place.

The tension in the trapper's face eased visibly, as if a great urgency had passed.

Charlie reached down, lifted the boy, and held him close to his chest.

"George Blacksmith, we are a family now," he said into the boy's ear. "You and your Aunt Louisa and me. We belong to each other. I am so grateful."

For several minutes the air was still. And then they said their goodbyes to the trapper one last time, stepped down onto the earth, and waved the plane into the air.

Soon after, in a hospital far away, the trapper heard again the call of his wife. This time, he reached for her hand and let her pull him into the next world where his breaths came freely and his pain was gone.

"Here, George."

George's mother-aunt handed him a fish that she had just filleted on a tree stump. He took and laid it carefully over the smoking rack that straddled a low fire of green tamarack branches. They were at McLeod Point on Lake Mistassini. Cree cabins and teepees clustered around them. She passed him another filleted fish, and he draped it over the bar.

An airplane buzzed overhead and came in to land on the lake.

George's mother grew quiet. She wiped her hands on a cloth then passed it to George to do the same.

"Come," she said, and stepped into the teepee. Inside, she handed him new clothes she had laid out. He put them on and she ripped off a price tag still affixed to the collar of the red-checked shirt. Then she took his hand, and together they left the tent and smoking rack and walked to the water's edge. Other families were doing the same.

Out on the lake, a group of men, strange men carrying guns and heavy sticks, were stepping down from the plane into canoes that ferried them ashore. To George, the plane seemed huge. Big enough to hold inside of it the whole single-engine Otter that had taken his father. The canoes hit dirt and the men climbed over the gunwales onto land. The man at the front – "Indian Agent," his mom said – swaggered like he owned the world. He looked around, took a deep breath, and raised his arm.

"You! You! You! You!" he shouted, and with each word he pointed to a different child.

The other men lunged forward and – grabbed the children he had pointed to! These men were *taking children!*

George turned away and held onto his mom's leg with the ferocity of a five-year-old but it was no use. One of the men grabbed him from behind and carried him down to the water. He reached out towards her but there was nothing she could do. He saw then that the men, with their fists and their weapons, were bashing the mothers still clinging to their children, they were knocking over Elders, they were throwing young men down to the ground. They roughed up anyone who got in the way of the children they wanted. Everywhere people were hurt and bleeding.

"George!" His mother came to the water. The man with the gun permitted one last hug. She gathered him into her arms.

"This is for you," she whispered.

She gave him a shiny new quarter. He took it carefully and slid it deep into his pocket. That quarter, he knew, was all the money she had.

"Now go and stay safe. Be quiet and do what they say. We'll see each other again in summer."

Then George followed the other children into the big canoe that ferried them out to the plane. It took off, circled once over McLeod Point, and flew south.

George had lived with them for less than a year. Just like that, he was gone.

A person who carves a paddle knows that, in the early stages, when the wood is taking on the shape of a paddle, it's very rough. If you try to paddle with it, the shaft will push long splinters into your hand and it won't move much water. But take heart. As the carver keeps working, it gets better.

Nineteen fifty-five. It was the strangest day of George's life. First there were the rough shouting men. Then there was the cold airplane ride, sitting on the fuselage of a World War II amphibious water bomber that didn't have legs or pontoons but sat right on the water. Then the cold open-boat ride from airplane to shore. Then the cold ride on the back of an International stake truck from the shore to the School. He and the other children peered out between wooden slats to look at the passing landscape. When finally the truck rolled to a stop and the doors at the back of the box swung open, everyone was shaking with cold.

Following the others, George jumped to the ground, rubbing his arms to warm up – and stared at the biggest, squarest, oddest building he had ever seen. It wasn't made of logs or canvas but of

George Blacksmith

something white and completely flat that looked like stone. It was as tall as four Cree cabins and as long as ten. He wanted just to stand and stare at it, but someone was pushing at his back, urging him forward. George fell into line behind the other boys – the girls had a different line – and followed the feet in front of him into the building.

"There's Bishop Horden Hall," someone said. "Moose Factory's foulest place."

The floor inside was shiny and smooth, nothing like the springy pine bough floors of every home he'd ever had, and the ceiling was three times higher than the head of the tallest man he'd ever seen. George stood quietly in line, taking in the size of it.

A man in a green and white robe with a shiny thing in his hand walked up to the boy at the front of the line, put the shiny thing to his head, and made it buzz. Wherever the shiny thing touched, the boy's silky dark hair fell away. In hardly any time at all, the boy was completely horrifyingly bald, his eyes fixed longingly on his curls on the floor. Then the hair of the next boy in line submitted to the shiny thing, then the next, and then George's own head was buzzing as his hair fell and twined with the other boys' on the floor, a carpet of dark long moss.

It felt indecent, this naked scalp in a room full of people.

The line was moving again. He followed the boy in front of him into a room with a hole in the shiny floor.

"We have to take off our clothes now," the boy in front said.

"Why?" George whispered. "They're new!"

The boy just shrugged and began to undress. A few minutes later, George's clothes had been tossed in a pile along with everyone else's – he remembered to hold on to his quarter – and someone took the whole pile away. To be burned, probably, someone said. Then suddenly he was wet and the water raining down – rain! inside! – on his naked skin smelled like poison. DDT, he found out later. An insecticide.

Someone shoved a worn and greyed uniform at him. He dressed again and followed the others to line up against the wall.

Out of the side of his eyes, so as not to have to meet anyone's eyes in this disgrace, George glanced down the row.

Every boy there looked exactly the same. A row of little brown Indians. No one looking at him would know how much his mother loved him or that he already knew how to fillet and smoke a fish or that his first parents lived in the next world or that at home he had a golden lab called Nipiichon *(He-who-smokes-a-lot)*. Even canoe paddles had more distinctiveness.

A tall man in a long robe stood in front of them.

"THOU SHALT NOT SPEAK CREE," he shouted, but George and the other new kids had never heard English before and didn't understand.

A few days later, one of the boys said something in Cree to a friend, and the tall man overheard him. He clapped his hand on the boy's shoulders and turned him around. "Thou shalt not speak Cree," he reminded gently. Then, he pulled a pair of pliers from his belt, where they always hung on a comfortable hook. He worked his fingers into the boy's jaw, forcing open his mouth, and gripped his tongue firmly with the pliers. With his other hand, he fished a dirty needle out of a packet in his pocket, and slowly forced it through the boy's tongue. In the top, out the bottom, placidly ignoring the screams.

And so it began.

George and his friends were made to eat things that weren't food. They were given so little food that they went home lighter than when they'd arrived, though they were in their growing years. They were punished often without knowing why. Made to stand frozen like a rock for hours until they crumpled unconscious to the floor. Made to scrub filthy toilets using only their bare hands, or to spend days cleaning a large gymnasium floor with a toothbrush, knees and hands scraped and blistered and bleeding, and then use

George Blacksmith

the toothbrush on their teeth. Kids had their legs and arms broken by priests and teachers and counsellors. The wounded were sent to the hospital, sometimes for months, and everyone was told that the injury had been recorded as an accident. George saw a boy beaten until he slipped into the next world just to escape the blows; "Death by Accident," the records said.

Once, when a girl was shy about singing nursery rhymes, the music teacher came to her desk.

"Come, I'll teach you," he said gently. He took her five-year-old hand in his and led her to the front of the room.

Then he opened the desk drawer, pulled out his pliers, and wedged the point underneath her fingernail, got a firm grip – then ripped the whole fingernail out by the root.

She screamed and screamed.

"Oh-ho! You're hitting the high notes now!" he laughed. "You've really learned something!"

He moved on to the next finger. His forearms strained at the effort of tearing young tissue and the desk was covered in blood.

George was appalled. He got out of his desk and walked to the front of the room. The music teacher was concentrating on the fingernail and the screaming girl's eyes were rolling back. She was about to pass out.

George tapped him on the shoulder. He turned around to look.

"My name's George," he said. "One day I'll be big."

The teacher stared at him. Then he set down the pliers, straightened up – and punched George hard in the face. Knocked him right out. When George came to, an incident report was pinned to his shirt. "This unlucky accident happened when George was running indoors, in a classroom," the note said. "He fell and hit his face on the desk."

The worst minutes of Indian Residential School, though, the minutes that went on for years, had nothing to do with punishment or hunger. They were the minutes the counsellors spent doing things for their own entertainment or their own pleasure. Like hold George by the feet and dunk his head in a toilet bowl of feces and urine until he opened his mouth and swallowed a mouthful while they laughed and laughed. Like bring pubescent girls into the boys' dorm and strip them naked and force the boys to fondle their private parts, while the priests and teachers and counsellors stood and watched, breathing heavily and licking their own lips all the while. Like come into the dorms at night and slide into the boys' beds, spooning them from behind, and stick their rigid fingers – or whatever – into any part of the boys' bodies they wanted, right in full view of the other boys in the room. One of the night watchmen with a very big hat had a taste for George, used his little body for all kinds of things. And if George resisted, he would not be permitted to sleep. Or he would be carried out into another private room where the watch-man and sometimes other men did much worse.

For a while, the chapel, where everyone spent an hour each day, seemed the only safe place. But it didn't take long for George to realize that chapel times were just more abuse. More efforts to exterminate anything Cree, anything distinctive, anything real in him whatsoever. Spiritual, psychological, but abuse all the same.

On and on it went, much more than can be written here. For nine years in Moose Factory, and then for another six years in La Tuque. And in between the assaults, so many assaults, George learned to speak and read and write English.

More than anything, George wanted to DO something about it. Punch somebody. Dunk their heads in toilet bowls. But he didn't want to end up dead with another George-Had-an-Accident note pinned to his shirt.

He wasn't ready for the next world yet.

Nineteen sixty-three. A La Tuque teacher told George's class that an important Government man was coming to the School

George Blacksmith

to inaugurate a new building. This was an honour, he said, and everyone ought to be on their best behaviour. George didn't know what "inaugurate" meant, but this, he knew, was a chance. An opportunity.

There could be no point in saying anything about the physical and sexual abuse. The Government man was White and would surely not believe him. Nor was there a point in complaining that he could hardly speak Cree anymore – that was why Indian Residential School existed. But he could do something.

George asked a counsellor for advice on how to write a letter and he asked a teacher for a clean sheet of paper and an envelope and to borrow a good pen. Then he sat at a classroom desk and wrote, in his finest hand:

Dear Mr. Jean Chrétien,
We have heard you're an important man. We would like you to know that the food here at La Tuque Indian Residential School is really something terrible. Could you please do something about it?
Respectfully yours,
George Blacksmith, President, Student Council
La Tuque Indian Residential School.

When Mr. Chrétien arrived, George handed him the letter in the envelope. He half-expected to be punched in the face again, but Mr. Chrétien took the letter, shook his hand, and smiled.

"I'm pleased to meet you, George," he said. "I will read this letter later." And he slid it into his jacket pocket.

Whether Mr. Chrétien – who eventually became the Prime Minister of Canada – actually read the letter or not, or if it had anything to do with the changes that came, George never knew. But soon after, the food at La Tuque really did get better and the students finally had enough to eat.

One day, a woman visited the School. She was from Social Services, she said, and she went right up to George.

"So you're George Blacksmith," she said, stroking his head, cupping his chin in her hand, looking him up and down like she might buy him. "We have you marked, you know. You're one of ours."

George got away from her as quickly as he could. What was she *talking* about? He would never be hers.

The next summer out in the fishing camp, a few weeks after George got home from School, a plane landed on the lake. A man in a suit stepped out, pulled spectacles from his chest pocket, set them on his nose, and approached a woman there.

"I'm from Social Services, and I'm here to pick up a boy, about ten or eleven. His name is –" he checked a paper "– uh, George Blacksmith. He's an orphan. He belongs to us now. I have papers."

Other than the pilot who still sat in the plane, the man was alone. No RCMP team with guns and sticks.

"Hey Charlie!" the lady called to George's father-uncle. "This here fella wants to take George!"

George's father and another man, Smalley Petawabano, slowly turned, nodded to one another, and walked up to the man with glasses, getting very close, so that he stepped backwards. They were much taller than him.

"George isn't an 'orphan,'" his father said. "He's my son."

Whether the Social Services man understood his father's thickly accented English, George didn't know. They stepped forward again, and the Social Services man stepped backwards.

"B-b-b-but he's going to N-N-New York!" the Social Services man whined, pushing his spectacles up his nose. "To a m-much b-b-better home!"

They stepped forward again, he stepped back, and again, and again until he was on his plane. Without George.

George Blacksmith

"Get the hell out of here," Smalley said. "Don't ever come back."

Many years later, when Smalley Petawabano was the Chief, George learned about the Sixties Scoop, how Cree children were trafficked South into the homes of White people. How very close he came to losing altogether the wonderful family to which he belonged.

When you paddle through rapids or very rough water that wants to drown you within itself, you need a long paddle of a strong flexible wood like birch. A paddle like this is for pushing hard against the water. It doesn't break in the rapids, no matter how fast or twisty they are, nor from how many directions they come. And when surprise currents and whorls yank your canoe in unpredict-able ways, if you hold on to it tightly, this paddle will help you stay true and find your way.

Nineteen sixty-nine. "Brrrruuugghhh!!" George belched, then shifted so that the tree trunk he was leaning against didn't dig into his ribs. Early morning, sun coming up. Gonna be a nice summer day.

He lifted the lovely bottle to his lips again. Still empty.

Damn.

He was gonna have to head into town and find more hooch. But standing was a tall order at the moment. He was pretty sure he couldn't manage it and he didn't want people to see him when he was like this. Drinking was best done in the bush, alone. Just him and the lovely bottle and all that black spruce. The occasional raven or squirrel was okay too. Over the last seven summers of bushtime drinking, the ravens and squirrels had always been perfectly well behaved.

Still. He needed more. Without it, he'd start to remember and absolutely the most important thing in his life was not to remember. Especially not to remember a man in a big hat.

He waited a few minutes for the edge to wear off, dozed a bit, then he got to his feet and stumbled towards town.

Next thing, he was leaning against the doorjamb of a house. How had he gotten there? Last thing he remembered was the bush. Still, there he stood, empty bottle in hand.

Right. Hooch.

The door opened. He was at the house of Chief Isaac Shecapio.

Damn. No hooch then.

"George! I'm glad to see you! Come in."

Even drunk, you don't say no to the Chief. George stumbled in.

"Sit! I'll get you some food." He motioned to the kitchen table.

George collapsed into a chair. A couple of minutes later, a plate of barbecued moosemeat was before him. He picked up a chunk, sprinkled it with salt, and ate. With each bite, his mind cleared a little more – never a good thing because then some guy in a big hat was there, right there, doing things to his body, running everything in his brain.

"Uuh," George groaned.

"You're no different from anyone else here, George," the Chief said.

"Uuh – ?" George said.

"Almost everyone here has problems from Residential School. What happened there, and what happened here in silent communities without kids – it's too big for just about everyone. You're like a wounded bird right now. Hurt, confused, torn between two worlds. Lots of things you can't talk about, and maybe you'll never be able to. But your spirit is not yet broken – you came here. The time will come, soon I think, and you'll have to decide if you want to heal and where you want to belong. Only you can decide. Only you will know how to do it."

George Blacksmith

"Uuh," George groaned.

"It'll be okay, George," the Chief said, rubbing his back. "You'll know."

When George left a little later, the plate of moosemeat was empty. He felt better. He didn't really know what the Chief meant by knowing how to heal, but he definitely felt better.

A couple of months later, another beautiful morning, George sat outside the family tent with his parents. A pot of tea steamed over a campfire. Sunlight flashed off the lake surface where gulls were coming in to land. Soon, he would have to begin gathering his things. The bus would come one of these days to take him South, down the new road, for School. His mandatory elementary School was finished, but he had chosen to enrol and finish high school.

A raven landed by the tent and began pecking at the dirt.

George was thinking about something his father had said long ago. That each August, on the first nights after the kids were taken away, the community had been so silent that someone paddling by would think no community there at all. Adults said nothing, and kept their weeping to themselves. Birds didn't sing. Even the dogs were silent. No matter how bright the moon, they didn't bark at it.

The community was always so noisy. To imagine it silent seemed impossible.

"Mom," he said, "I don't wanna go to School this week. I wanna go into the bush with you and Dad. I want to know Cree ways. I wanna speak Cree again."

It was a surprise even to him. He hadn't really been thinking about it. It had just tumbled from his mouth. But instantly, he knew it was true and that this is what the Chief had been talking about.

His mom didn't answer. George looked over at his dad, who was also silent. Then he heard a caught breath.

They were both crying!!

Eventually, his dad spoke.

"Sixteen years," he said. "Sixteen years ago, your mother and I promised your first father that we would teach you the skills of the people. But then the Indian Agent came and took you before we could really start."

He got up and stirred the coals.

"That promise has been burning up my chest for sixteen years. I have never been this happy."

Winter was setting in, lake water thickening like chilling fat. George paddled back towards camp, a fresh beaver in the canoe. Last week it had been a moose.

His brain was tired. There was *so much* to learn. Hunting, foraging, trapping, snaring, fishing, carving, building. And geography. For years he had studied by reading and writing things down. Now he had to memorize a massive territory with over 5000 lakes – and be able to navigate it all from a canoe. Without a map! And then there was Cree history to learn (thousands of years of it), and food preservation practices, and land-based medicines, and wildlife management, and migration routes. And, and, and. It would never stop. At least the Cree language, which he had spoken fluently as a child, was coming back quickly.

George belonged in the bush. It was his home. His brain was tired but he had never felt this healthy and whole. The land took away from him even the faintest longing for drink or forgetting. It turned the lock on the man with the big hat and left him in the past. It returned to George the fullness of life.

And so began his reconciliation. To this day, for George, healing on the land and reconciliation mean the same thing.

In the fall, when temperatures drop and ice forms easily on the canoe, you have to be careful. The weight of ice can roll the canoe like a log and dump you in the ice water. Then you need a thick paddle made of a strong wood like spruce with a wide, slightly rounded blade and greater surface area near the bottom. Each stroke moves plenty of water. You can use this paddle to smash the ice off of the canoe and paddle your way home.

Nineteen seventy-five. George was in Mistissini for the summer gathering. Everyone was there. New babies to see, new stories to hear, new friends to make. But autumn was on the wind and George itched to pack up the tent and head home to the bush once more.

"Hey George!"

He looked up from the fish he was cleaning. It was the Chief.

"Good fishing today?"

"Yep," George said.

"Getting ready for the bush?"

"Yep. Can't wait, to tell you the truth."

"That's what I wanted to ask you about."

George stopped working. The Chief had something to say.

"Not too many folks here got as much White schooling as you did."

The Chief looked out over the water. He kicked at the stones on the beach.

"Thing is, George," the Chief continued, "White folks are here to stay. We run our own schools now but if we don't get more Cree teachers, they're gonna send up White teachers and then it's the same damned thing all over again."

"That's not good," George said, bending again to the task.

"Not good," the Chief repeated. He kicked more stones.

"So, uh, George, how d'ya feel about *not* going out on the land this time? About staying in town and teaching? Maybe we can bring our language into the classroom. If you need more schooling to make it happen, if you can stomach it, we'll support you."

George looked down. He didn't want to be disrespectful.

"But – the bush..." he said.

"It'll be there," the Chief said.

George had been on the land just five short years. It had nourished him, ended a lifetime of hungers. Leaving it so soon made him want to cry.

Thing is, you don't say no to the Chief.

George became a teacher, then the principal, and then he worked in Montréal for years – pushing, politicking, harassing, cajoling, doing whatever it took to bring Cree language education into Eeyou Istchee elementary schools. Along the way, he picked up a Bachelor's degree, then a Master's degree, and finally a Doctorate of Philosophy in Education. He learned to move nimbly between his own Cree world and the world of White Schools. Like a hunter using the lightest paddle of all – blade tapered at the end, thinner and narrower than the autumn paddle, made of a springy wood like tamarack – to come up swiftly and silently on water behind animals on land. An unexpected dexterity.

When George's son was born, George's uncle asked that the walking-out ceremony take place in the bush, on the trapline, and that the boy walk out with both George, his White-educated Cree father, and George's uncle, a renowned Cree hunter.

"If a child walks with two sets of knowledge," he said, "that child can become a great leader."

Twenty nineteen. George sits at his computer desk in Mistissini, writing. The snowplow lumbers by outside, piling road-side snow so high that George can't see the neighbouring house. It's been a snowy winter.

Sixty-five years have passed since the Indian Agent first ripped him from his mother's arms, fifty years since his father took him out on the land, taught him the old Cree ways, gave him back his words, and forty-four years since the Chief asked him to leave his home and the land so that future generations could speak Cree.

George Blacksmith

Younger George from the early 1950s would never have recognized this Mistissini. He would have thought it impossible. Thousands of people, paved roads, houses instead of teepees, a clinic and a bank and a recreation centre and stores and restaurants. And so much hockey. Younger George wouldn't even have recognized Older George, sitting at a desk, writing books of all things. In desperate need of the kind of healing that only the land brings, Younger George would never have believed that he would one day return for more White schooling, and that, in their own way, his degrees would bring healing too.

For someone who spent so much time in Indian Residential School, healing takes a long time and a lot of work. It's a bit like carving a paddle. At the beginning, it's rough. If you try to paddle with it, the shaft will push long splinters into your hand, and it won't move much water.

But take heart. Keep carving. It gets better.

On February 11, 2020, Dr. George Blacksmith passed into the next world.

Stories Heard Along the Way: The Hunt

Traditionally, an animal killed on the land was entirely used up. Even after the bones of a moose or caribou had been boiled for broth and there was no marrow left, the cook would take a joint bone with a circular divet in it, like a hip bone for instance, and tie it to another smaller straight bone – and that became a little game. You could hold the divet bone with one hand and toss up the other bone and try to catch it in the divet. In archaeological digs that prepared for dam-building, they found remnants of the game that were several thousand years old.

One beautiful sunny morning during Goose Break, a husband and wife straddled their snowmobile and headed out across a frozen lake to their goose camp. Suddenly, without warning, in a place the ice was usually thick and strong, the ice gave way and their snow-mobile dropped through into the water, taking them with it. They both struggled to climb out but the ice water was sapping their strength, the ice was slippery and smooth, and they couldn't pull themselves up onto it. The husband then got behind the wife and told her to set her feet against him and use him as a step while he tried to stay afloat treading water. She did and, with lots of effort from both of them, she eventually flopped out onto the ice. "Now go," he said. "Run to the shore there, follow it to that camp, and send someone back for me." She set out for shore. After a few steps, she glanced back – and he was already gone. He had used the last of his strength to help her out and to tell her where to find safety and warmth for herself. He was a seasoned hunter and surely knew he couldn't make it.

A long time ago, when people killed a caribou or moose, they boiled the bones a couple of times to get out all the marrow. Then they packed the dry empty bones into a pail made of birchbark and buried it by a common portage path. The next party dug up the bones that they knew would be there, crushed them, poured in some water, and added red-hot cooking rocks to bring it to a boil in the birchbark pot. It was a hearty, nutritious, tasty broth that gave energy and nutrients to the person who ate it.

A hunter gave a Cree woman fresh moose for her freezer, but she had spent her youth in Residential School and didn't know what to do next. She couldn't lift it onto her table, she didn't know how to cut it into smaller pieces, and there it was, bleeding all over her kitchen floor. She called her sister for help but couldn't speak for the tears.

"Why are you crying so hard?" her sister asked.

"Someone gave me a moose – I don't know how to butcher it!"

"Well stop crying!" her sister said. "You should be happy you have moose!" Then she got in the car, came over, and taught her what to do.

Two friends were out hunting. One saw a moose, shot it, and it fell. He dropped the gun and grabbed his knife and they both ran to field-dress the animal for transport. They knelt down beside the moose, and, just then, the moose sat up, looked at the two of them, and walked away, apparently unhurt. The two friends looked at one another and then back at the tail end of the moose.

"Shoot it again!" one friend said.

"I left the gun back there!"

They chased it on foot but the moose was already gone, deep in the bush, alive for another day.

Ally walked out to the woodpile, carried in as many pieces of firewood as she could, and dropped them by the stove.

Artist: Lexie Mîkun Saganash

Ally Lowell

Ally Lowell*

*Names and details have been changed to protect identities.

ALLY LOWELL did not go to Residential School. Her two sisters and three brothers did not go to Residential School. If her parents went to Residential School, they never talked about it.

Instead, Ally spent the first four years of her life in a tent in the bush. In the mornings, she woke to the smell of the fresh pine boughs that covered the tent floor, and to the sound of a snapping woodstove fire. Her mom was there, feeding wood into the fire, and her dad too, oiling his gun and preparing for the hunt. Ally pushed back her covers, slipped on her shoes, walked out to the woodpile, carried in as many pieces of firewood as she could hold, and dropped them by the stove. By then, the water was boiling and her mom was brewing hot Salada tea. Ally helped her serve it, first to the hunter and then to the others. Into her own tea, after everyone else had been served, she always scooped big spoonfuls of powdered sweetened milk from the rations her family received. She loved it there.

Ally sometimes wondered why her dad spoke perfect French when the rest of his family spoke Cree. And sometimes she wondered why people said her dad came from the South when she knew he was Cree and came from Eeyou Istchee. It was nice wondering about things. In her parents' tent, she always felt safe.

One morning, when Ally was four years old, her mom packed all of Ally's clothes along with those of her brothers and sisters into two big grey bags. Then the whole family went down to the lake – her dad carried the bags – where an airplane sat on pontoons. Her parents chatted a bit with the pilot, and then everyone climbed into the plane. Up they flew, above the trees and thousands of small lakes, for a long time. Ally could tell from the shadows that they were flying south. Finally they landed on a big lake and pulled up to a dock. They all climbed down from the plane and straight into a red truck. And, after a few minutes, they pulled up in front of a long white trailer house that Ally had never seen before.

It was a boarding house, her mom said, handing one of the grey bags to the lady who lived there. Ally was going to school. She was going to live in this boarding house with one of her sisters – their other brothers and sisters were going to a different house – and her parents were flying back out into the bush.

They were going home.

Without her.

In the bush, Ally's parents could collect income security. They didn't have to worry that Ally was suffering the horrible abuses of Indian Residential School because the Residential Schools were finally closed. Now, Cree School Board ran the schools. During school months, kids from the bush lived in a community with someone they knew. The lady was her mother's best friend and Ally would be safe and looked after in that house. She would sleep behind a little closet divider in the lady's bedroom, she would have enough food, she would have a warm place to stay, she would be with good people, and she would get a fine education. Her parents seemed to think it was a pretty good idea all around.

Ally thought it was a terrible idea.

She missed them badly. How could they have just left her there and flown away?!

She was so upset that she wet her pants the very first day.

Ally Lowell

She didn't eat for days.

She got sick. Very, very sick.

Ally's sister saw her getting sicker and shutting herself away from people.

One day, she came into Ally's little room behind the closet divider, sat on her bed, and held her hand.

"Ally," she said, "it's always gonna be like this now. Every fall, we go to school and our parents fly back to the bush without us. In spring, after school finishes, we'll go home again too. But it's gonna be like this for a long time now. It sucks. You gotta get used to it."

There was no point in fighting it. School was important. She didn't want her sister to worry. And some people would think Ally lucky to be there.

So she forced herself to eat again and tried to stop crying.

She even fooled the lady and her sister into thinking she was okay.

Ally was not okay.

The house was awful. Oh, it was clean and warm, and she liked learning things in school. But other kids in that house were used to living with people who had been badly hurt in Indian Residential School. The kids were unhappy. They would bug each other. Punch each other. Fight and shout and bully. They would do some of the same horrible things that had happened in Residential School. Without realizing it, they made the boarding house feel like a Residential School dorm even though it wasn't.

To try to feel safe, Ally hid under the blanket and covered herself with pillows. Or she sat perfectly still and pretended to disappear. Or, at night, she left the divider open so she could see the lady sleeping close by in her own bed. Nothing helped. In that house, she was always terrified.

The lady who lived there did everything a house parent was supposed to do. More, even. She wanted Ally to be happy. But she couldn't send the other kids away for Ally to feel safe. And Ally couldn't stop wondering – was the lady doing this because she loved all the kids? Or was she in it for the money?

In June, after ten months of eternities, Ally's dad drove up in the red truck once more. She ran out the door and he scooped her up and laughed and laughed and said she was so big now and hugged her closely for the longest time. The next day Ally was back out in the bush, far away from the long white trailer house, snuggled around a fire with a cup of milky tea in her hand. Then, finally, she felt safe again.

Until September, when it started all over.

One summer, when Ally's family was visiting Mistissini for a few weeks, her parents took her to a Church camp meeting. In the space between the Anglican and Pentecostal Church buildings, the Church people had set up an enormous white tent, the kind you might see at a circus. It had a square canvas roof with a point in the middle, and it was held up at each corner and along the sides by long metal poles. It was so big that almost everyone in the community could fit under it. Inside were folding chairs set in straight rows.

Ally sat on a chair in the middle, under the peak, safe between her mom and dad, and looked around. Other kids were playing between the rows and out on the grass, and she wanted to run and play with them, but her mom was stern.

"Pay attention, Ally! Sit right against me here," she said.

The evening began with music. A lady sang and then a man and then a group of people with a banjo. They sounded pretty good. Ally's dad gave her a quarter and sent her to the front to drop it into the offering plate. By then it was raining outside. The drops thwacked the canvas and a cool breeze kept the mosquitoes away and freshened the air. Altogether, it was strange but kind of nice.

Then, a tall White guy in a suit and tie stepped to the podium. He took a deep breath, looked right at Ally – and started shouting.

Ally Lowell

"The end of the world is at hand!" he yelled. "The Lord is coming, like a thief in the night. He will take his followers to heaven and the rest of you will be left behind, alone and abandoned!"

The speakers crackled in her ears and rumbled through her bones louder than thunder. He punched the podium. She felt the force of his anger like a wind on her face.

"Repent!" he shouted. "Repent and follow him! Or spend eternity in the great lake of fire! You will burn and burn and never die! You will be in torment! You will be in agony!"

He was furious. His face was so red! He didn't stop shouting for a long time.

Ally was terrified. What was *repent*? Why was that lake on fire? Had someone poured gasoline on it? What happened to the fish? She had watched a movie about people burning alive in their cabins – it was the worst torture she could imagine. And now the world was going to end. Nothing she could do about it. She was going to burn. Her parents would not be there. She would be left behind to suffer terrible things *again.* Why did everything have to be so scary? Whatever happened to feeling safe?

When all was said and done, the world didn't end after all. But that knot of cold terror in Ally's gut did not unfurl. Septembers were the worst, when her parents left her at the lady's place for school again and again and again. But really, the fear was there all the time now.

Every single day.

For years and years and years.

Until high school finally finished.

The year after high school, when Ally was nineteen years old, she lived in Nemaska, down the road from her parents. She could see them any time she wanted. Sometimes she dropped by twice a day for no reason other than to hug them. She was so relieved she wouldn't have to leave them in fall that she walked around half the time with a silly smile on her face. September had nothing to dread.

But when it came around, that cold, sick fear was there all the same. As if her body were bracing for abandonment and neglect.

Ally pushed the bad feelings out of her mind. What did she have to complain about? She had been lucky for her schooling and now it was done. She could get on with her life.

One morning, she woke up with stiff, swollen knees. It felt like someone had buried hot needles in them.

A week after that, it was her elbows.

And, a few weeks later, her knuckles and neck and toes.

Sometimes she felt as if she were eighty years old.

"Inflammation," the doctor said. "Your immune system seems to be attacking your joints. Hmm. Could be diabetes, or lupus, maybe a sclerosis, or ... something. Let's run some tests. For now, take cortisone pills to ease the swelling. And we'll give you another medication that will support the cartilage in your joints. Together, they should keep the pain in check so that you can function."

Ally hated the medications – they made her feel *off* – but they did help. And if she wanted to walk, she had to have them. So she took the pills and got on with her life.

After a few years, the medications no longer dulled the pain. The doctor gave her oxycodone.

Then, when that didn't work anymore, morphine.

Ally didn't really want to think about how powerful the prescriptions were. She didn't like to think about what was happening to her body. She took the medications and got on with her life.

She went to college. She got into a serious relationship and gave birth to a little boy. She found good work in a Government office. She spent time with her parents. All was well.

From time to time, her mind flitted back to boarding house days or to the lake of fire. When that happened, she willed herself

Ally Lowell

to think about something else. Every September, when that cold terror knotted her gut again, she pushed it from her mind and spent time with her parents up the road. Or her son. Or her wonderful partner. And every few months, when the inflammation got so bad she couldn't walk or sleep for the pain, she went to the clinic for more medication.

After a few years, the oxycodone and morphine weren't touching the pain.

Ally turned then to cocaine and heroin and other street drugs. They helped. They even cleared some of her bad memories away. She was grateful for the drugs and got on with her life.

As best she could.

One day, when Ally was in her early thirties, she came home from work and began cooking supper. Her boyfriend had had a bad day. He wanted to buy drugs to feel better – but the only money Ally had was their rent money. They started to argue, it escalated quickly, and, for the first time ever, he beat the living crap out of her.

Next morning, she stood in front of her mirror. It had been cracked in the fight but she could still see that her left eye looked like one of her son's shiny rubber balls.

Well.

She had heard about abusive men. They didn't stop. And she knew how women in her community dealt with it. They stayed with the man, they kept the family together, no matter how bad it got. This was part of her life now. Nothing she could do about it.

She drove all the way down to Montréal, bought some turtle-necks, scarves, and expensive makeup, covered up the bruises, and got on with her life. She didn't want her son to see her being beaten or taking street drugs, so she was always careful to close the door if she thought either of those was going to happen.

And she was right. After that first beating, it happened pretty regularly. She still loved him. And she loved doing drugs with him. But there were regular arguments and she always had a few bruises to cover. Just another thing to look after.

Four years passed.

One day, her boyfriend, in one of his moods again, picked Ally up like a bean bag and threw her against the wall. She crumpled to the floor, turning instinctively to dodge the next blow – and froze.

Their son was standing there, watching it all, gripping his favourite teddy bear tightly to his chest. His face was white and rigid and he was utterly silent.

Ally's boyfriend whirled around to see what she was staring at.

And – in an instant – he grabbed their son over his huge shoulder and ran out the door.

The teddy bear dropped to the floor.

For about twenty seconds, Ally did nothing.

Then she picked up the phone and called the police.

The cop who showed up at the door was one of her friends. She let him in and watched him look around her house. He saw the mark where minutes earlier she had slid down the wall. He saw a fist-shaped dent in the wall from a previous conversation. He saw the teddy bear on the floor. He saw Ally's face, beginning again to swell.

And then, with all the gentleness in the world, he said, "How long're you gonna take this, Ally? Your scarves and makeup don't hide anything. Everyone knows. We wanna help but you're the only one who can do anything about it. What're you gonna do about it?"

Ally couldn't meet his eyes and stared out the window instead.

Her phone rang.

It was another friend. Ally's boyfriend had gone to her house with their son. Her friend could see he was high and had taken the little boy away from him.

Ally passed the news to the policeman.

Ally Lowell

"I'll go get him," he said. "Think about what I said." He picked up the teddy bear and took it along.

As soon as he was out the door, Ally began to cry. Hard. She had no excuses now. This was the day she had to do something about it.

The next week, she left her son with her parents and checked into a traditional First Nations lodge on managing anger, recovering from addiction, and healing from abuse. It didn't use Cree traditions, but the traditions it used were close enough.

And when the lodge was finished, Ally came back to Nemaska.

The first thing she did was find a different house and move into it. She didn't want to think about all the things that had happened in the old house.

The second thing she did, after she had settled into the new house – she kicked her asshole boyfriend right out of her life.

Many years passed.

Ally was in her late thirties and had built a good life. She had a house in Nemaska, a job she liked, a kid she loved, and she saw her parents nearly every day. She had been sober for years and worked now with a naturopath to accept and learn about her inflammation and to exercise and change her diet so that she didn't need painkillers. Her next goal was to get off the medication altogether.

Septembers still made her sick. She talked herself through the dread. And she learned to accept the contradiction that, yes, her parents loved her, and, at the same time, they had left her behind every single year. By choice.

From time to time, she went back to the traditional lodge for more healing.

In town, the Indian Residential School Settlement process was underway. One day, at the grocery store, she felt someone touch her arm. It was a friend of her father's.

"Did your dad apply for Residential School compensation?" he asked her.

"No," Ally said. "He never went to Residential School."

The old man looked away, as if deciding something.

Then he took a breath and met her eyes again.

"Ally," he said, "I think you should know. Your father nearly died in Residential School. The very first week. A really big priest picked him up like a bean bag and threw him down the stairs. One of the scariest things I've ever seen. He spent five years in a hospital in the South with a crushed esophagus. His neck and throat were so mucked up he couldn't eat. All those years, they fed him through a tube."

Ally tried not to show her surprise.

"Oh! I didn't know that," she said. "Thank you for telling me!"

She paid for her groceries and left.

In the grocery store parking lot, she sat in her car.

A crushed esophagus? *Five years* in a hospital?

Her dad's sister lived in Nemaska too. She would know more. Ally put the car in gear, drove right over to her aunt's house, and asked her about it.

"Oh yeah," her aunt said, "I thought you knew."

In her kitchen, she opened a drawer and pulled out an old photo. It showed her as a little girl visiting a small boy in the hospital. The girl sat on the chair and the boy sat on the bed. They both looked right at the camera.

"He was the favourite with the nurses, you know. They thought he was lovely. They taught him French and English and math and religion and everything. They read him stories and bought him birthday presents. They thought he was special. They loved him."

She ran her finger over the boy in the photo. She obviously envied him.

"An injury like that – one single injury – to get him out of School right away. In those days, back in the '40s and '50s, we were being killed in there all the time."

Ally Lowell

She put the photo away again.

"That's why he *could* love you, you know. Because someone had loved him. The way you and your dad would hug, like nothing else mattered. The rest of us tried but really we were flapping around gasping, like fish on a dock. Didn't know the first thing about love."

Ally thanked her aunt and went out to her car. She sat quietly behind the wheel. It was shocking.

And yet, it wasn't.

Her dad was never one to talk about bad things at all, especially if they were in the past. He just kind of kept quiet and got on with his life.

The lady's boarding house.

The ease with which her parents left her there, as if abandoning your kid every fall were normal.

Her dad's perfect French. His perfect English.

His White religion.

That stupid lake of fire.

It all fell into place.

After a while she started the car and drove home and hugged her son for the longest time.

Records: Failure

June 1858. The *Head Commission Report* concludes "with great reluctance [that] this benevolent experiment [of Indian Residential Schools] has been to a great extent a failure."

April 1891. Despite the high cost of the Schools, Indian Affairs has not seen "that any commensurate results are being obtained." *Indian Commissioner E. Dewdney*

November 1902. That "our schools have failed in their object is generally admitted." *Indian Affairs Official M. Benson*

June 1903. "Any lad who has never left the reserve, is at the age of 18, far better off than a lad who has been in school for years, and what is more is very much more self-reliant and able to make his living as easy again as any of these school lads." *Blood Reserve Agent's Report*

1913. "Fifty per cent of the children who passed through these schoos did not live to benefit from the education which they had received therein." *Deputy Superintendent General D.C. Scott*

October 1922. "These Indian schools are the biggest farce to be called schools I have ever seen. They appear to be all pretty much the same... I have seen some very crude teaching but I think I can safely say that I have never before seen in the finished product anything put forward as teaching that touched quite a low level as that which is to be seen in these Indian schools." *L. Hutchinson, School Inspection Report*

October 1923. "The ex-pupils of our Indian schools have such faulty education that very few of them are capable of interpreting Cree into English, or vice versa. A story is told of a clergyman who attempted to preach to an Indian congregation through an interpreter, from the text (Math. 14-27): 'It is I be not afraid.' When this came to the ears of the congregation in their own language, it was: 'Hit him in the eyes, don't be afraid.'" *Principal R.B. Heron*

July 1930. It is "discouraging … to go back year after year and find no improvement [in the Schools], although suggestions have been made to the Department." *Official W.M. Graham*

November 1957. "I would sooner have a child of mine in a reform school than in this dreadful institution." *J. Parker, Northwest Territories Council*

1960-1961. "The paradox, over-simply stated, is that we are educating Indian youth for uneducation." Even after spending millions, "the lot of the … Indians has not improved during the past twenty years: it has worsened." *Report to Indian Affairs Education Division*

January 1968. "[T]he fact remains that we are not meeting requirements as we should nor have we provided the facilities which are required for the appropriate functioning of a Residential school system." *R.F. Davey, Superintendent of Education, Indian Affairs*

1997. The last federally funded Residential School closes.

Such a treasure, this photo. Harriet would like to give everyone in her family a copy, wouldn't that be a nice gift.

Harriet Snowe

Harriet Showe*

*Names and details have been changed to protect identities.

HARRIET swirls her coffee around in the cup, savouring the morning sunshine a moment longer, then turns from the window and picks up again the photo in the pink frame.

In the photo, six-year-old Harriet, wearing smart new pink pants and a crisp white top with matching scarf tied under her chin, holds up a small burlap bag of oranges. On one side, her older brother stands tall in his new pants and dark green coat, smiling stiffly, his fist also curled around the handle of a bag. On the other side, her older sister smooths down her new flower-print skirt and smiles at someone outside the frame. Behind them, not in the picture, floats the huge grey airplane that will fly them away. Harriet is leaving for her first airplane ride and her first day at La Tuque Indian Residential School.

Standing behind them is their mother, trying to smile. A few minutes after this photo was taken, Harriet recalls, she cried bitterly. Every time Harriet left, her mother squeezed her tightly to her chest and wept, like she wanted never to let go. Residential School was hard for mothers.

If only there were a way to make copies. Such a treasure, this photo. Harriet would like to give everyone in her family a copy, wouldn't that be a nice gift, but for the tape. Years ago, when her dad made the wooden frame and painted it pink, he coated the whole thing, photo and all, with clear protective tape. Now the tape has yellowed and bonded to the photo, and she can't peel it off without ruining what's beneath. And it's better to have the photo with its shiny brittle veneer tinting the scene than to lose it altogether.

That grey plane had no seats. They all crammed in and sat on the bare cold fuselage. Harriet doesn't remember taking off or flying, but she remembers transferring to a bus, and stepping off at La Tuque Indian Residential School. A few years later, once the gravel road was built, they went by yellow school bus from Perch River all the way south.

Just look at the three of them in their brand new clothes. What did their parents sacrifice to pay for those beautiful clothes? Of course, the moment the kids arrived at La Tuque, all their belongings were taken away. Even the socks, even the underwear. Harriet was given a dark tunic and ugly white underwear, like every other girl there, to wear every single day. Except Saturdays, when she could wear something else, something second-hand, not her own. Still, she had worn those beautiful new clothes for a day. One whole day to look like Harriet and not just another little brown girl. They took her precious oranges too. So costly up North. Harriet never told her mother that she didn't get to eat a single one.

She smiles about it now – the funny things we remember – and takes an orange from the fridge for her lunch bag before reaching for her coat.

Isn't it just the loveliest winter morning. Several feet of snow have already fallen. Harriet works at Meechum but this morning the postmaster called her with a cold. She went by his house, picked up the keys and a list of what to do and where things are, and she's helping out. On her way to the post office, she pauses to look at the lake. The December sun, barely able to push itself off the horizon, glints off the last ripples. Soon even those will be frozen.

Harriet Snowe

Once inside, she stands in the door of the back room. What a heap of boxes! You can sure tell it's Christmas. Every one of these boxes probably holds a present for someone. Harriet steps gingerly around them. She moves a parcel off of the desk chair and sits down to register them and print labels.

Back in Residential School, her brother always went home for the holidays – one of his aunts picked him up for a few days – but Harriet had to stay. She really cried when he left and she couldn't, but he always brought her something nicely wrapped. And, after she carefully peeled back the clear tape to save the pretty paper, the gift would be in a brown box just like these. One year it was a book of animal stories. She can still picture the cover.

Harriet smiles softly. At Christmastime, she always thinks about La Tuque.

Ding! Oh that's the bell on the counter. Look, it's already past noon. Harriet steps into the front room.

A young girl, about six, missing her front teeth, stands at the counter holding her mother's embroidered coinpurse and an envelope she has addressed herself. It must be school lunch break.

"You're the Meetthum lady," the girl says.

"Yes I am," Harriet smiles, "but the postmaster is sick today and I'm helping out."

"Oh. I hope he'th okay. Can I buy a thtamp pleathe?" Her missing teeth have given her a lisp.

Harriet finds the right drawer and pulls out the stamp folder. The girl chooses one with a caribou. A reindeer, the Santa stories say, but, really, a caribou. One at a time, she counts out nickels and dimes, and pastes the stamp on the envelope.

"I made thith card for my Gookum," she says. "She livethe in Chithathibi."

"You know," says Harriet, "I think she'll really like it. I like homemade cards best of all. I bet she'll show all her friends."

The girl smiles widely, then waves goodbye with her finger-tips. Harriet drops the card in with outgoing mail and returns to the computer work.

What a nice girl that was. When Harriet was a child, she would have liked her for a friend. The first day she arrived at La Tuque, she had no friends. Right after her belongings were taken, and her older brother and sister sent away to their dorms, a tall lady told the youngest girls to pair off and check each other's hair for lice. Harriet had no friend to be her partner.

"Oh, please let *me* be your partner," someone said. She was a senior girl, almost grown-up, and from Mistissini.

"Okay," Harriet said softly. Together they sat on a bench.

All around, girls were squirming and complaining about pulled hair. Harriet undid her braids and braced for pain. But the girl took the comb and, with a gentle touch, a few hairs at a time, she meticulously searched Harriet's hair. When she found a live bug, she combed it out onto a piece of paper and squished it, all without hurting Harriet even a little. Then the girl rubbed a solution into her scalp to kill the nits. It found every mosquito bite or scrape on Harriet's scalp and really burned. Harriet's eyes quietly filled with tears.

"At my sister's School," one of the girls said, "they cut their hair right off."

Well, Harriet thought then, *it burns, but it's better to have hair.* And, a minute later, it was all done.

Harriet turned then to clean the girl's hair, but she didn't need it. And in the end, of all the girls, Harriet had the cleanest hair. That day she was lucky not to have friends yet.

A few years later, though. Harriet's mom sent along waffle cookies – each cookie was filled with the most delicious strawberry or chocolate or vanilla filling and, because Harriet was an Intermediate, they weren't taken away. Instead, they were set on her shelf in the storage room and on Saturday nights, after her shower, she could go into the storage room and ask the counsellor for one of her waffle

Harriet Snowe

cookies. Harriet could bring one friend and her friend got one of Harriet's cookies too. The two girls took their cookies to the bedroom and ate them in tiny bites to make them last. Then everyone wanted to be Harriet's friend. And if she didn't pick this girl or that girl to be her 'friend,' she really paid for it on the playground.

Funny the things you remember.

Years later, when Harriet looked after children herself, she saw them making the same deals. It's the way of children. Well, maybe the bullies wouldn't have been so intent on her cookies if La Tuque food had been better – Harriet would sometimes scoop spinach slop up in her hand, drop it into her pocket, and run to the washroom and flush it away – but even well-fed kids will barter for more sweets. She saw it with her own eyes.

Now when Harriet craves waffle cookies, she buys them at Meechum. Last week they had some in special Christmas packaging.

Really, Harriet got a good education at La Tuque. Oh, it was strict – there were so many rules. And they were so *different* from Cree rules that they could be hard to follow. Cree rules were about respecting people, or staying safe on the land in the hardest of times. La Tuque rules were about control. About when you were allowed to sleep or talk or use the toilet, or in which fifteen minutes you could eat. About who you could see (never your brother). And about what you were allowed to say (nothing in Cree, ever).

But in the classroom, Harriet's teachers wanted her to learn and they helped her to do it. Sometimes now she meets people who, for all the years they spent in Residential School, struggle to read or to do math. Their teachers failed them. But Harriet's teachers really taught.

Well, they were a little rough sometimes. Maybe that wasn't necessary. When Harriet looked after children herself, she spoke softly to the misbehaving ones, and gave them choices. It always worked. Roughness teaches roughness, nothing more.

It was easier for Harriet than for some of the other students because of her father. He had rules of his own. Anything he set his mind to doing, he did well – trapping, hunting, fishing, carpentry – and he expected the same from his kids.

"Education is what White people have," he would say. "It's a real tool and it's how they are taking what belongs to us. You go to School, you study hard, you learn all you can. And then you come back. You help strengthen the Nation. You don't stay in that world, you don't lose your Cree language, you don't assimilate. You can't be two things, White and Cree," he said. Boy, he would really lecture sometimes.

And he meant it. In the two months that Harriet could be home with her parents, they taught Cree ways on the land. She had more to learn in those two months than in all the ten months of School.

Her father's rules were not like other Cree rules. Not many Cree kids had curfews, but Harriet did. Once when she disobeyed, her father even spanked her. It was more humiliating than painful – the shame of it really bugged Harriet sometimes – but spanking wasn't something that happened in Eeyou Istchee. And the way he went on about pregnancy. "You better not get pregnant! Not while you're young. You can have babies after graduation. And marriage." Harriet's friends had boyfriends and children while they were still teenagers, but Harriet studied. Sometimes that bugged her too. Now she knows that her father's rules weren't about him or what he wanted: he made rules so that her time in the White School would be easier. That some of their strange ways would already be famil- iar and she could focus on studies.

How did he know that? He didn't go to Residential School himself, and people didn't really talk about what happened in the Schools. How did he know to prepare her so well?

Years later, when Harriet looked after kids, she had some rules too. Not nearly as many as La Tuque had, but enough to make the work a little bit easier.

Harriet Showe

There was one especially wonderful afternoon. One of Harriet's teachers was so pretty. She had white hair that she arranged in waves around her face with blue sparkly combs on either side and then pulled back into a tidy bun. She invited Harriet to her place for supper on a Sunday evening. She came to the School to pick Harriet up, and she and Harriet walked to her home together.

Harriet had never before been in someone's apartment like that. From the outside, the square cement building looked cold and rigid, so different from her own cozy homes and camps across Eeyou Istchee, but the inside was comfortable. There was a bright kitchen, with a small table and chairs, a living room with a plush rust-coloured sofa and wooden coffee table, and an inviting bedroom that they looked into from the doorway. Someone had spread a handstitched quilt across the bed. Even the bathroom was pretty: on the back of the toilet sat a glass dish filled with colourful bath beads that looked like candy.

Harriet and the teacher sat side by side on the sofa. On the coffee table, the teacher had set a plate of ginger cookies. Into a blue-flowered china teapot, she poured boiling water over tea leaves. Harriet drank the tea from a matching china cup. She had never held anything so thin and fragile as that cup, but, in a place so comfortable, Harriet wasn't nervous about it at all. Together they paged through a photo album of pictures from when the teacher was young. She had lived in places Harriet had never heard of and she had done things that Harriet had never done. She shared with Harriet where she had come from, showing her the world outside Eeyou Istchee and La Tuque. It was so interesting. They ate supper at the kitchen table, and then walked together back to the Residential School up the road.

Late that night in bed, Harriet thought about her wonderful afternoon. Maybe one day she would live in an apartment like that.

And then she remembered. *You come back to help our Nation. You don't stay in their world, you don't lose your language, and you don't assimilate.*

Still, she thought, that teacher was very kind. She took care of Harriet.

Funny the things we remember.

Ding! Ding! Ding!

Harriet steps out from the back room. The front office is suddenly full of people, all on their mid-afternoon break from work. For the next thirty minutes, Harriet runs back and forth from the front room to the back, giving people their parcels, one at a time, and printing out labels and stamps. She's much slower than the postmaster, but people are patient and she gets it done.

Near the end of the line stands a mom, holding her son's hand. When Harriet hands her a parcel, a small knowing smile bends her mouth.

"What's in the box, Mom?" the boy says.

"You'll see."

"Can I see now?" He tugs at her sleeve.

"You have to wait. Until Christmas morning."

"Can I at least see where it's from?"

"Yes! On Christmas morning."

"Moooo-oooom..."

And they're gone. The room is empty again. Nothing but the slow tick of the clock on the wall.

Such a lovely thing for a child to be home at Christmas. There was one year Harriet stayed home in fall and attended the day school in her community. Now, why was that allowed? She can't really remember, but it was so lovely to wake up each morning in her own bed, eat breakfast with her own parents, wear her own clothes, and go to school like a regular child. Now

Harriet Snowe

each Eeyou Istchee community has a school, but in those days they turned the community hall into a class room with tables and chairs as desks.

That year, home for Christmas with her family, Harriet got a backpack from her dad and it was *red.* Shiny, delicious, candy-apple red. It was *beautiful.* And it was *hers.*

Harriet's whole world took on a candy-apple glow.

Of course, as soon as she stepped back into La Tuque, they took it away and she never saw it again, but, for a few days, Harriet was a Cree girl with a red backpack. Now, whenever she's in the South, she looks for that backpack. Or something like it. Once, in Kingston, she found the shape of it in a backpack store but in green. It has to be *red.* She's still looking.

Christmas at La Tuque could be fun too. Really, it could. Of course, Harriet would rather have been at home, but the teachers and counsellors did their best to make it nice for the few kids left behind. On Christmas day, after morning Church, they all played some games. And in the evenings they were allowed to stay up later.

Some of the School bullies couldn't go home either. That wasn't great. Harriet would have enjoyed a break from them. They were different, though, without their friends. Less mean. Almost sad.

One Christmas, when she was about eleven, the counsellors said there would be a movie on Saturday night!

The thrill of it! Kids who went home to their families didn't get a movie. Maybe it would be a Disney film – Harriet had heard Disney films were nice. She counted down the days until Saturday, and on Saturday she counted down the hours.

At seven o'clock, right after supper, all the kids who were left behind gathered in the gym and sat cross-legged on the hard floor, boys on one side and girls on the other. A counsellor walked up and down the wide space between. Boys and girls were not even supposed to wave at each other. And then the lights went down.

It *was* a Disney movie. Harriet doesn't remember which one, but she remembers that pacing counsellor making sure she didn't even wave.

A few years later, they showed another movie. Again, Harriet looked forward to it all day, hoping it would be Disney. This time, it was girls only and the new house master set up a portable movie screen downstairs where there were some sofas and cush-ions. There was even a snack of toast and jam. The house master hoisted a huge film reel onto the projector, and again the lights went down.

War and Peace, the screen said. Not Disney, then.

Harriet tried hard to follow the story. It didn't really make sense to her, but it was nice to watch people moving about on the screen. The landscape was pretty and reminded her of home.

A loo-ong time later, the reel was changed. The same people still moved about on the same screen.

And a loo-onng time after that, the reel was changed again. The same people still moved about on the same screen.

Eventually Harriet fell asleep.

When everyone came back in January, bragging about things they had done at home over the holidays, Harriet told them that she had seen a movie called *War and Peace.* And it was so long that it took *three* of the *biggest* film reels. And every single minute of it was just wonderful.

A few years ago, Harriet hunted the movie down. This time she stayed awake. And understood the story. It really *is* wonderful. Though still very long.

One year, after Christmas, Harriet found a thin plastic tray that had once lined a box of chocolates. In the plastic itself were the same fancy shapes and indentations that had once imprinted the chocolates. Harriet filled the little tray with water and set it on the narrow snowy sill just outside her window. She had to do it carefully

Harriet Snowe

so that the tray wouldn't fall and the counsellor wouldn't see it. The next morning she had fancy shaped ice cubes! She popped one out of the tray and sucked on it, pretending it was a chocolate. When the tray was empty, she filled it again. After a few weeks, she opened the window ledge to bring in a fresh batch – and the tray wasn't there. She bent over the ledge and looked down. The wind had blown it to the ground below. She couldn't retrieve it without getting caught and so she left it there.

It sure would be nice to give her dad a copy of that photo of the three of them on her first day of School. He so badly wanted them to get a good education, to go to college in the South and then come back. They all did. They wanted to please him, of course, but they understood that building a strong Nation was important. Her dad would like that photo.

He's in his eighties now, still healthy, still on the land as much as he can be. He's like the old traditional Cree from before, the ones who lived to be so old. Harriet's grandpa lived to be 105. His mom lived to 117. In those days, living past 115 wasn't unusual. Colonization changed that, of course, but you never know. It might happen again. People are healing.

She could try to steam it. Steam might loosen the glue and lift the tape from the picture... Oh but no. The steam would ruin the photo itself, and the photo is the treasure. It must be preserved. Even yellowed, it must be preserved.

Harriet turns to the stack of outgoing mail, checks the documentation one more time – hopefully she did it right – drops the packages into three big bags and closes them up.

Well of course there were bullies. What school doesn't have bullies?

Someday. Someday it'll be my turn to get you! Harriet thought, whenever a bully hurt her again.

Every evening, a train rumbled right close by the School and blew the loneliest whistle sound Harriet ever heard. That sound actually hurt. And right then, in the minutes the train was shaking the dorm, if you really listened closely, under the train sound, you could hear kids everywhere in the dorm crying, even the bullies. Other strange noises too, she could never make them out. The whistle made everyone lonely and homesick, she thought then, and hid her head under her blanket.

Harriet never did try to get back at the bullies. By the time she was old enough to be able to do something, she knew more about why some of the kids cried at night, about how difficult their lives were, about how lucky Harriet was.

Sometimes, when she looks back on her years in La Tuque, she's a little sad. She always understood, even then, that the things she didn't like had purpose. It was hard to hear, in the 2008 Government apology, that the purpose was to kill the Cree in her. It didn't work, but it was still a hard thing to hear.

Oh there's the delivery truck. Harriet runs to the door and opens it. Cold air blasts in, and just look at that sunshine sparkle up the snow!

"Aren't you the Meechum lady?" asks the driver.

"The postmaster has a cold," Harriet says. "I'm just helping out."

Together they carry bag after bag, box after box into the office. For a while they chat about holiday plans and the beautiful clear day, until it's time for the driver to leave and for Harriet to head back to the office and slowly, carefully register the boxes.

When Harriet got to high school age, she stayed in the Residential School dorm and walked to the public La Tuque high school.

There, she made some very good friends. One of them, Stacey, had a dark patch of skin on her white hand, and the patch was covered in thick hair. *Beaver*, Harriet thought when she first saw it. That girl didn't have many friends, which was strange because she was so kind, and it was also nice because she and Harriet became good friends. She invited Harriet to supper at her house, which was near the ski hill, so she could meet her parents and her grandmother. They served mashed potatoes! Mashed potatoes never ever appeared on the La Tuque tables – they were too expensive – and Harriet could hardly believe the luxury. She tried to be polite and just eat her share but really, she probably ate more mashed potatoes than she should have. Stacey's family didn't seem to mind.

It sure would be nice to find Stacey again. Harriet drove to the area around the ski hill once, trying to remember the way to their house, but too much had changed. She got there and nothing at all looked familiar.

Jennifer the bookworm was her high school friend too. She waited for Harriet after classes and they would walk together to the next class. She was creative. One Christmas she fastened, onto a paper clip, a wee Santa hat with a pompom on the end and gave it to Harriet to use as a bookmark. Harriet really loved that bookmark and teared up a little when she eventually lost it.

Funny the things you remember.

At home that evening, Harriet looks at the photo in the pink frame again. The only way she can think to make copies is to take a photo of the photo, tape and all. There's no safe way of separating the veneer from the story underneath it. She'll have to arrange it carefully so that there's no extra glare, and the tint will always be there, but at least she'll be able to share it.

Harriet sets the photo down and gets her camera.

Stories Heard Along the Way: Love and Marriage

An old woman in a remote community passed away leaving her husband alone.

"Guess ya can't go into the bush this year," their friends said to him. "Ya need a wife for the bush."

"I'm goin'," the old man said.

He knew of two widows in another town. He wrote and mailed two letters, both with the same offer of marriage, and sent a pilot to that town.

When the pilot arrived at the dock, two women and their bags awaited him – and both said they were going to marry the same man. "Thing is, I can take only one of you" the pilot said, "and, last I heard, he can take only one of you too."

The women chatted amongst themselves and decided to have the pilot snap a match in two. They each chose an end, and the woman with the shorter piece stayed behind.

Some names in Eeyou Istchee are so common that two people can have the same surname and not be related at all. In the '50s and '60s, a priest who performed marriages believed that two young people looking to marry were siblings because they had the same last name. The Elders assured him that they were in no way related and gave him the histories of both families going back many generations. Eventually, under pressure, he performed the ceremony but later, after he left Eeyou Istchee, he published a document that said a brother had married a sister.

A young Cree man wanted to marry a girl and needed the permission of her father who lived 300 kilometres away in the winter by snow-mobile and further in the summer by canoe and portage. The young man waited for winter, when he could safely cross the frozen lakes. He tied three cases of beer to the back of his snowmobile and left on a Friday night. He drove through the night, helping himself to a beer now and then to ward off the cold. By the time he arrived, he was down to two cases. He and his future father-in-law shared what was left, and on Sunday night, with permission to marry, he set out on the return journey. He arrived back in his home community in time for work on Monday morning, a little chilled but perfectly sober.

←

Dad: Better not go anywhere on Saturday.
Son: Okay. Why not?
Dad: We're going to Church.
Son: Why!? We never go to Church!
Dad: You're getting married.
(Traditional Cree marriages were arranged by parents.)

←

Heard at the funeral of an elderly woman in Eeyou Istchee:
"Well, she's gone now and we're sure gonna miss her. But we can give thanks that we've still got her husband. 'Course, his hair's gone, and his eyes are goin', and his hearing's shot, and his legs and heart are giving right out. But hey, we'll give thanks for what-ever part of him we still got left!"

That night, after lights out, they ate carrots in bed.

Artist: Tristan Shecapio-Blacksmith

Silvester Stalone

Silvester Stalone*

*Names and details have been changed to protect identities.

THE FIRST time Silvester wakened to find himself in an entirely new world, a new life that was not his, was in a hospital. He was taken there for tuberculosis treatment when he was three and, for about two years, he lived in that strange place, in a strange bed with cold silver bars on the sides and a crank that folded the mattress into an L. There he had a Cree friend, another boy from Eeyou Istchee. Eventually, after months and months, Silvester grew accustomed to the antiseptic smells, the nonsensical routines, the new language, the grating hospital noises broken up by long hours of silence.

The second world, the second life not his own, was stranger still. Again, he was in an enormous building – this one was red brick – and again, when he looked around for his parents, they were not there. He did find his brother. And his sister too, though she was on the other side of a barrier where Silvester couldn't see her. He was in Sault Ste. Marie, someone said, in a place called Shingwauk Indian Residential School.

Another thing was different. In the hospital, his friend had been the only other Cree kid. Here there were many Cree kids, crammed in like logs on a woodpile. They had all spent the summer outside and were browner than the two hospital boys. They said they were from Eeyou Istchee too but, strangely, not a one of them spoke Cree. If they did, adult men in robes came along and disciplined them with sticks or straps, implements of wood or leather, across their tender inner arms.

At supper that first night and again at breakfast and lunch the next day and every meal after that, Silvester and the other boys were given exactly fifteen minutes to eat. A tall man with rigid posture paced between the tables, tightly gripping a long wooden implement and making certain every child ate silently.

"He's Army," somebody whispered.

What was *Army*? And why was it here?

What world was this? Whose life had he fallen into?

"As-tu bien dormi?" a teacher asked Silvester one morning in French class.

"Oui, merci," Silvester answered automatically. French was the language of the hospital.

The eyes of the boys around him opened wide when they heard him speak.

"White trash," a Cree kid hissed at him.

What was *White trash*? Silvester didn't want to be rude so he smiled and nodded.

The other boy laughed openly. Many years later, Silvester realized that he had been insulted.

Other realizations, however, came more quickly. For instance, the night noises in this Shingwauk place were stranger still than those in hospital. Rhythmic creaking wood, sobs, gasps, sometimes muffled screams. It did not take many nights for Silvester to deduce that terrible things were happening in the beds of other children. Why they happened he couldn't rightly say, but all evidence pointed to some boys regularly being subjected to very great pain by robed men who pulled back their covers, stepped into their beds, and did secret things to their bodies.

Another realization came early. Despite the silent ordered meals, Silvester was not being properly fed. His stomach rumbled constantly and instilled in him a sense of great urgency. He needed food.

Silvester Stalone

Silvester began to take matters into his own hands. From time to time, Shingwauk students were allowed into town, an ordered row of brown kids in strange uniforms. On one such trip, in a store, he managed to sneak into his pocket a sack of candies and to slip unnoticed outside.

There stood his brother who detected immediately in Silvester's dropped chin and hunched shoulder that something had changed.

"Silvester. What did you do?"

Silvester led his brother around a corner and showed him the treasure in his pocket.

"I'll share them with you," he said. "But don't tell anyone else. I'm too hungry to share with everyone."

His brother's face tightened and paled.

"Are you kidding?" he said. "Getting caught will be so much worse than hunger."

"I won't get caught," Silvester insisted.

"Keep your candy. I want nothing to do with it," he said and walked away.

Secretly Silvester was glad.

He wasn't caught. He sucked and savoured every candy by himself. With each one, for a few minutes, he was a little less hungry.

It soon became apparent that other boys were in the same situation and were also taking matters into their own hands. Hungry older boys, for instance, ordered hungry younger boys to steal fruit for them from trees bordering the School. If they refused, or tried but didn't succeed, they would be beaten. Not with the teacher's implements but with the boys' closed fists. There was quite a bit of that sort of thing going on and Silvester did his best to avoid it.

One day, in the auditorium, as they were lining up for something, a bigger hungrier student curled his fist and slugged Silvester.

Silvester caught his breath, hesitated for a moment – in this strange world no one else looked out for him – and he punched right back. His knuckles dented the boy's nose. Later, he was disciplined with a wooden implement across his tender inner arms, but that particular boy never bothered him again.

There were a few weeks when no one was hungry because every single kid in the whole School was sick. In a crowded place like that, if one kid caught a virus, it took about two days for all kids to confine themselves to bed, coughing and vomiting and fevered.

Himself, he didn't like being sick, but it made for a change from being hungry.

As the months passed, Silvester made friends and grew accustomed to the strangeness, but the hunger problem only grew. Sometimes, he and his friends stole turnips from the School garden and ate them raw. Or they uprooted carrots, shook off the dirt and ripped off the tops, hid them under shirts to enter the School and then in their shoes when they slipped them off inside the door. They carried the shoes up to the dorm room and that night, after lights out, they ate carrots in bed.

Once they managed to sneak into the chicken enclosure beside the School and corner a clucking hen. One boy silenced it by snapping its neck like he would a goose, another filched matches from the School fireplace, and the whole group snuck into the bush.

They gathered brush and built a fire like they would have back home. They plucked the feathers and pulled out the long guts of the hen. They tore the flesh into equal pieces. And they cooked them on long sticks over the fire.

The wonder of that meal. The perfect char on the meat, the grease on their faces, the relief of chattering in Cree while they ate. The proof that they could fend for themselves. That night in bed, for the first time in this strange world, Silvester wasn't hungry at all.

Soon after, they tried for another chicken.

Silvester Stalone

This time, the principal saw them sneaking towards the coop and called them back, into his office. They were caught.

"Boys. You know you're not supposed to play there," he said calmly. "It's out of bounds."

"Yeah," they admitted. They knew the rule.

"You can choose your discipline," he said generously. "Either you get the strap now or you surrender your privileges for visiting town on the weekend."

The boys consulted one another and together chose the strap. Better to get it out of the way.

The principal nodded and solemnly opened his jacket. There, close to his body, where other men might carry a pen or a wallet, hung a supple leather strap, warm and ready for work across their tender inner arms.

It stung for sure.

Well, Silvester thought to himself, this is something I'm not supposed to do and I have to accept my punishment. Perhaps it was a bit much, though, just for being hungry.

Many years later, he would wonder – if they could grow vegetables and chickens there, couldn't they have grown *more?* Made a bigger garden? A bigger henhouse? So that the children could fall asleep thinking about something that wasn't food? Himself, had it fallen to him, he would have grown more food.

The first ten months in Shingwauk passed more slowly even than the two hospital years. Silvester was always taut, on highest alert, for he never knew what fresh grief awaited him.

Or what pleasure. He loved the classroom part of this world. Art and history especially. He could see, even then, that it would have use. That this learning would be important in whatever world would eventually be his.

If there were such a thing.

But he ached for love. For the comfort of a hug from someone who cared for him.

Eventually the tenth month ended, and Silvester boarded a plane home. He half expected to disembark in yet another strange world, but he needn't have worried. When the airplane door lowered, standing on the shore of Lake Mistassini were his parents.

He hadn't laid eyes on them in three of his six years.

Silvester treasured his parents' company. In the whole time he was with them, he never once went to bed hungry. The noises in the night were bush noises. Wind, owls, wolves, things that made sense. And the love. It was everywhere. If he wanted a hundred hugs a day he could have them, every one sincere and eagerly given. He could have lived in his mother's lap and she would welcome it. He stayed as close to her as he could.

Surely this was his world. He began to relax and settle into it.

Then, when the nights began to shorten, before the last of the summer's heat, his parents said he must return to Shingwauk. If he didn't, then they would not get their ammunition nor their winter rations nor their allowance.

In short, they said, they would starve.

It fell to a six-year-old child to provide, with his absence and his hunger, for his adult parents.

It was a strange world after all.

Back to School then. His mother dressed him nicely, in new clothes that fit perfectly, that she had bought for the occasion. But in the first minutes back in the red brick world, his clothes were taken away (to be burned, he later learned, because the robed men believed them to be infested). He was handed an ugly uniform instead.

Everything else was the same all over again. Hunger. Angry boys. Night noises. Viruses conquering the dorm. Wooden and leather disciplinary implements across tender inner arms.

One Saturday, five or ten boys walked to a corner store and spent some pennies on supplements to their meager diet. Chips, fruit, candy bars.

Silvester Stalone

They came out of the store, reaching into their bags – and there stood a group of well-fed White boys, fists balled and raised. Each one wore properly fitting shoes and clothes unique to him, not a uniform amongst them. Silvester deduced, from their raised fists, that they intended to prevent the Cree boys' return to School. In truth, he would have been happy never returning to Shingwauk, but he wasn't exactly dressed for a months-long trek to Eeyou Istchee. And there was no other place in Sault Ste. Marie for him to go.

Slowly, the White boys surrounded them. One pulled back his fist and slugged –

And then it was mayhem. Every Cree boy was punching down a White kid or two, whoever stood in his way of getting back to another crappy silent insufficient supper. Eventually they made it through, chips and fruit and candy bruised and broken and full of dust.

At the silent supper that night, Silvester noticed welts and shiners emerging on quite a few of them.

The following day, in the auditorium, the principal made an announcement.

"It has come to our attention that some boys from this very School picked a fight with town boys. *A fight!* Their parents have called to protest such maltreatment. We at Shingwauk are ashamed. Now. Raise your hands. Who among you so disrespected the good people of Sault Ste. Marie?"

Nobody raised their hands – but every student there smirked knowingly: of course they were the usual suspects. They were Cree.

About a month before Christmas, the principal pulled Silvester aside.

"Silvester, you know about Santa Claus and Christmas, yes?"

Silvester nodded.

"What would you like Santa Claus to bring you this year?"

Silvester thought for a moment. What he asked for wouldn't matter, he'd never actually get it, but the principal wanted to play a game and Silvester would play along.

He and his friends often played Cowboys and Indians. They'd never seen a real cowboy but knew plenty of Indians.

"A holster and six-shooter," he said.

On Christmas day, someone handed Silvester a package wrapped in shiny red paper. He peeled off the tape and opened it – and there lay a toy holster and six-shooter.

It was so confusing. You finally deduce that a world is out to get you, to label you the usual suspect, to make you pay for the hurt others have done – and you get a toy gun.

In the summers, Silvester went on the land with his family, and the day came when he did not have to return to Shingwauk to provide for them. Instead, under his father, he began to study the ways of the Cree. In-the-bush training demanded as much of him as classroom study had, often more, but never once in his years on the land did he experience implements of discipline across his tender inner arms. And the whole point of it was *not* to practise starvation, but to *avoid* it. It seemed a wiser approach.

In the bush, Silvester had, in abundance, time to think. He began to sort and order his memories and eventually arrived at some realizations.

First that this Cree world, this practice of living well in the bush, dependent on and caretaker of the land, belonged to him. It was his way, what his people had developed over millennia, and it felt good. It nurtured him. The classroom study into which he had been forced, even though he had enjoyed it, that was a foreigner thing. Being wrenched from home, placing his parents' survival on the shoulders of a child, that was also a foreigner thing.

Second, that the foreigners had such a terrible grip on Eeyou Istchee, they had shredded so many Cree ways and institutions, that their education had become necessary for a good life. Once, Silvester went with his father to buy rations. His job was to place the order in English.

Silvester Stalone

"Sugar and flour and powdered eggs," he said, "and – " He stopped. How could he ask for *pimii?* In his studies, the word had never come up.

"Lard, please," his father said, and smiled as Silvester's mouth dropped. Even his father, who spent nearly all his time on the land, had to speak some English.

Silvester took what further studies he could, went into mining and exploration for a while, and then into teaching. For a short while, he even took a Government job. It put a bad taste in his mouth to work for the people who created Shingwauk, and he moved on as quickly as he could.

Third, that his parents, whom Silvester had loved more than anyone, had suffered greatly to send him away.

Even so. The rations and ammunition they were able to purchase were not worth the high price a six-year-old had paid. Perhaps, had he not attended Shingwauk, they would have had to hunt with bow and arrow. Or to eat only animals. Perhaps they would have been hungry some of the time. But it might have been possible for them to live. Himself, had it fallen to him, he would have found a way to manage. That realization, with all its inner conflict, it stung for sure.

When Silvester looks back on those years now, he is less bewildered. In 2008, Stephen Harper admitted to the world what Cree kids had always known: that Shingwauk and other Schools like it existed to carry out cultural genocide, to remove Native ways of life from the planet and, like Silvester's beautiful new clothes, to scorch the earth of them.

Without a doubt, that explained a few things.

Stories Heard Along the Way: Left Behind

An Elder told this story to Shiikun:

When the Eeyou Istchee communities were developing, my kids were young. I had lotsa kids. I remember one time. It was summer, everyone was happy, sitting in circles, telling stories about bush life.

Suddenly someone came running. "Our kids are gonna be taken away!" he said.

"Why?" we asked.

He didn't know. The story went around. We tried to understand.

Then a White guy came up. "In two days, a bus will come to the end of the access road," he said. "Bring your children there. If you don't, you won't be able to buy winter supplies."

I didn't know what to believe. Why did they want our children?

Someone was making arrangements. Canoes were being lined up. We were just following orders. We didn't know what we were getting into.

On the day, we all piled into canoes and paddled to the beach at the end of the access road.

Yellow buses were there, lined up in a row, and Indian Agents were looking at clipboards and directing kids to this bus or that bus. Siblings were being separated and put on different buses.

"Where is my child going?" we asked. "When will she be back?"

They said nothing to us. They behaved as if we weren't there. They just took the kids from our arms and shoved them roughly into the buses. We stood on the beach and looked at the buses, full of our crying children. My kids, I could see through the window, were so scared. Nobody was talking. We were all just looking at our beautiful kids one more time. It was the worst thing I have ever felt.

And then the buses drove down the beach road and were gone. It happened so fast.

We paddled back to Mistissini. All the way back, nobody said a word.

As soon as we got into town, we all dug into our storage and pulled out bottles to wash and set the stills to work.

We drank for a whole week. We didn't talk to each other. We didn't pry to know what was happening in other families, nothing. We didn't know if we would ever see our kids again.

My kids never even came home at Christmas. On Christmas morning, my wife and I looked at each other, and together we got drunk again.

When you come upon the nest of young birds, the Elders say, don't disturb it. Don't even go near it. Nearby is a loving mother finding food for her young. If you touch her nest, she'll know her young have been traumatized and will be reluctant to return to them. She might think it kinder to let them die. Many storytellers talked about how the Indian Agents "disturbed the nests."

Sometimes, students returning from the Residential Schools were so unrecognizable that, when they had children of their own, their parents took custody of the children, taught them the ways of the land, and tried to restore a Cree line. Other parents chose not to pass delicate Cree knowledge on to those children who were especially traumatized. They taught survival knowledge and Cree history and language, so that their children could return safely to the land, but they did not always teach Cree medicine or spiritual knowledge. Rather, they preferred to let the sacred knowledge go back out onto the land where it could one day again be learned by future Cree generations.

"Mom," Rita said, yawning as she watched her stretch sinew across a snowshoe frame. "I'm gonna be a nurse when I grow up."

Artist: Jared Linton

Rita Gilpin

Rita Gilpin

WHIZZ!

All heads in the arena follow the hockey puck as it flies off the ice and over the plastic barrier. No one's hurt – it's just an early morning scrimmage and the stands are empty. From behind the goalpost, Rita watches as down on the ice the coach pulls another puck from his pocket and drops it. He whistles and play resumes.

Now Rita's grandson controls the puck. He's so fast, so smooth. He swoops and corners, his huge, padded body almost parallel to the ice. Someone manages to swipe the puck away from him and everyone skates to the opposite end.

Rita's been thinking lately about when she was young, before Eastmain had an arena.

The White people were playing with her life. To them, she was a puck, a cheap piece of rubber to slap and bash and score political goals. If she had been replaced by another little brown girl, they wouldn't have noticed.

But it was her life. The only life she had.

"Mom," Rita said, yawning as she watched her stretch sinew across a snowshoe frame. "I'm gonna be a nurse when I grow up."

Her mom didn't look up, but her lips widened in a smile.

"Rita, how many people do you think will miss their appointments because you'll be sleeping in?"

Rita watched her slip a knot perfectly into place. Her calloused, agile fingers made it look easy. Her mom had a point. Rita's bed was the best place to spend any morning.

"I'll figure it out," she said.

The next day she asked the teacher. Eastmain had twelve grades but just one teacher, so that's the one she asked.

"You need high marks to be nurse," she said. "And you'll have to go to college."

"Not a problem," Rita said. She was at the top of her class. And in ten more years she'd be ready to leave Eastmain.

A few weeks later, just before Rita started Grade Four, a red-faced visitor came by the tent and talked with her parents. Rita had to leave Eastmain very soon, he said. An Indian Residential School on the island of Fort George, far away, where the great Chisasibi River emptied into James Bay, was waiting for her. If she didn't go, he said, her parents would not get family allowance.

"It'll be okay," her dad said. "You need both Cree and school knowledge."

Yeah, Rita thought, *but can't it be Eastmain school knowledge?*

A few weeks later, as Rita stepped into the canoe that would ferry her to the airplane that would fly her to the School, her mom handed her a little grey suitcase that held her clothes and a bag of mixed candies.

"You can have one candy a week," her mom said.

From the front, the Ste.-Thérèse-de-L'Enfant-Jésus Indian Residential School building looked like a tall grey box set on the long end with another little box on top for the bell. In a straight

Rita Gilpin

line around the whole area, someone had pounded, right into the ground, hundreds of oversized matchsticks.

"It's called a *fence,*" a kid whispered to Rita. "Never cross it."

When Rita stepped inside the door, an adult guided her into line behind the other girls. Not long after that, all the girls had short haircuts. Then all the girls changed into brown clothing (Rita's outfit had a number sewn inside), their own clothing taken away.

Rita saw her packed grey suitcase, candies and all, leaving the room in the grip of an adult hand.

"My mother said I could have one candy a week," she explained politely in English to a tall lady nearby, pointing to her suitcase.

"Blenghh blenghh blenghh blenghh," the lady said.

And *hit* her!

Rita froze, a rabbit in a gunsight – no one had ever hit her before – but the lady walked away like it was nothing.

"You have to speak *French*," another girl whispered.

So this was French. It sounded like people were speaking from their noses. Rita wasn't even sure what sounds she was hearing.

But that didn't matter. Her first Ste.-Thérèse-de-L'Enfant-Jésus Indian Residential School lesson was about a "fence." Her second lesson was to look like every other Cree girl. Her third lesson was that if she didn't speak French as perfectly as the White people, someone hit her. Any kid who tried to help her got hit too.

Rita shut her mouth.

Had there ever, in the history of the world, been so many angry adults in one building? Rita got hurt all the time. If she spoke a word of Cree. If she spoke a word of English. If she was hungry and didn't wait until the clock said mealtime. If mealtime came and she didn't clean her plate because she wasn't hungry. If she wanted to do her homework right after School when the knowledge was still fresh in her head. If the after-supper-homework time came and she didn't do homework. If she wanted to wear her purple Sunday dress on Tuesday or her brown everyday tunic on Sunday. Everything made their anger boil over like an abandoned pot of stew. It never made sense and it never ended.

Once, just as Rita slipped off her moccasins for bed, a supervisor stomped in, shouting and pointing. Everyone was supposed to go downstairs. Rita slid her moccasins back on. Downstairs, the kids filed obediently into a long line in the playroom and waited.

The supervisor seemed calm now, a pious and superior smile on her face. "Blenghh blenghh blenghh," she said.

Rita stayed quiet. She did what other students did.

The supervisor got more and more upset. Her face grew red. She clearly wanted someone to answer her, but every student stayed quiet, so Rita did too. Eventually they all went back to bed.

Later, up in the dorm, after the lights were off, another girl explained: "Somebody climbed over the fence and played on the frozen creek. She wanted to know who it was."

Everyone was in trouble for something one person had done. And no one had said a word.

Usually, punishment meant being beaten with something. Most often it was a yardstick. But they had many ways to hurt kids. Sometimes Rita wasn't allowed to eat. Or, after eating a full meal, she would be made to eat a big bowl of something vile, like corn, which had a fermented-sickly-sweet taste that reminded her of marsh gas. With practice, she could manage it by pinching her nose, washing it down with great cups of water, and then holding her breath for twenty seconds to keep the vomit down until the urge passed. But if the only drink there was the white powdered "milk" drink that smelled like moose poo, if that was all she had to wash down "corn," Rita was in trouble.

The worst, though, was watching other kids be punished. Rita would rather be beaten bloody than to watch another kid go

Rita Gilpin

through a Ste.-Thérèse-de-L'Enfant-Jésus Indian Residential School beating. If she was ever lucky enough to grow up and have kids, she promised herself, they would never even see a beating.

And the praying.

First thing in the morning, Rita had to kneel by her bed on the icy dorm floor and pray nonsense syllables before getting dressed. And then to breakfast where she'd stand to pray nonsense syllables before sitting to eat. And then to class where she'd pray nonsense syllables before sitting to study. And at morning chapel. And at every class, every meal, and a bunch of times in between.

Maybe these people needed to pray so much because they were angry from their bad food. Maybe praying helped them cope.

Every day was a battle. To understand a little more, to make a French sound, to dodge whips and sticks and slaps. At the end of the year, the School said Rita had passed Grade Four. But she knew she couldn't have. She could barely count in French. They had fudged her grades to make their School look better.

And now she knew. She was nowhere near smart enough to be a nurse.

Rita leaves the boys to their practice, backs out of the arena parking lot, and heads for work, taking the long way around by the Church. For the longest time, she couldn't attend Church.

"Rita," her mom begged then. "If only to respect the Christians here, step into their Church."

"I can't, Mom. I need a break from their 'praying.' Maybe someday."

Her mom looked confused. "I do pray, Mom," she explained. "Just not like that. I pray to the Creator."

Eventually, Rita became the Director of Health and Social Services for Eastmain. Community leaders must support every-one's beliefs, it's their job, and Eastmain had some Christians in it. Rita had to go to Church at least sometimes.

It took a few months to work up the strength, but one Sunday she managed it.

The instant her shoe hit the tiled Church floor, her heart took off, beating faster than ever before.

She began to sweat, and worried that she would faint. A quick prayer to the Creator, a calculated lean against a wall – she calmed enough to hold it together.

"Rita Gilpin," the priest said. From the pulpit. With everyone watching. A pious and superior smile on his face.

"I'm so happy to see you here. Will you open your Bible and read aloud the passage for the offering?"

Her clients were in the room. She couldn't say no. And Rita was an adult in her own hometown. This man wouldn't dare hit her.

But her heart would not calm. He wielded what power he had and used her position as community leader to manipulate her into doing what he wanted. So little had changed.

Now, sitting in her truck and thinking about that day, Rita's heart races again. Thank goodness she doesn't have to go often.

After a service, she always spends some time on the land. She lets it work its healing ways in her. In all of life, there's nothing more reliable.

Young Rita was sick. Her bed was soaked from fever sweats. The Ste.-Thérèse-de-L'Enfant-Jésus adults laid hands on her forehead, mumbled amongst themselves, carried her to a small room in the Infirmary, and told her to sleep: *"Dormez."*

She didn't argue.

When she woke, she was absolutely alone. The building that usually percolated with the noise of kids and cooks and janitors was empty. Everyone had moved to the new building across the Schoolyard. They weren't coming back.

On the wall, the shadows stretched into giant nuns with yard-long ghost fingers brushing Rita's throat. The wind twisted through clapboard cracks and screamed like a thousand owls. Sometimes Rita heard footsteps and whisperings in the empty room.

For seven days, the only person Rita saw was the man who brought her food. Not even the Infirmary nurse – whose job Rita wasn't smart enough to have – came to visit.

For the seven days after that, a teacher came every day to give her School work.

For the next seven days, Rita stayed in the nuns' dormitory. She was in a separate room and never saw nuns (a good thing, for nuns weren't to be trusted), but it helped to hear human noises nearby. If she screamed someone would hear her. Even if they didn't do anything, they would hear.

After twenty-one everlasting days, she moved in with her friends again, this time in the new dorm.

Rita couldn't wait. Her parents, whom she hadn't seen in eight months, were coming! They had spent nearly all their money to fly up from Eastmain just to visit her, that's how much they loved her.

Rita was going to *tell.* It was her third year there and *awful* things were happening at School. She mustn't blame, her dad said. If she was there when bad things happened, then she was partly responsible. But even so, her parents should know.

The morning of their arrival, the principal-nun called Rita into her office.

Jiggling with excitement, Rita stood, still as she could, before the great wooden desk. The principal-nun sat behind it, still and solid, and made a teepee with her fingertips at her chin.

"You will see your parents this afternoon, Rita. For exactly one hour."

One *hour?* For all that money?

"I'm aware," she continued, "that there are, um, certain aspects of Ste.-Thérèse life that you might not, um, enjoy. You will not speak of these, um, aspects to your parents. Nor to anyone outside of this School. Ever. If even one word slips, we will hear. We will then punish you worse than you have ever been punished in your life. Also, we will punish your friends. And your brother over in the boys' dorm. You may go."

She waved her hand to dismiss Rita and turned to papers on her desk.

All Rita's excitement drained away. Her head dropped and she shuffled from the office. When it came to punishment, the principal-nun never exaggerated.

The visit with her parents that afternoon was the shortest hour of her life. They hugged her to their chests; she soaked up as much love as she could. But she couldn't relax. She wasn't safe. Someone was watching, someone was listening.

Rita's parents, however, had expected this. Later, in a hiding spot her brother told her about, Rita found treats they had left for her.

For four eternal aching years, Rita attended Ste.-Thérèse-de-L'Enfant-Jésus Indian Residential School.

Then the red-faced men sent her to the English day school in Eastmain.

Then back to the French Ste.-Thérèse-de-L'Enfant-Jésus Indian Residential School.

Then back to the English day school in Eastmain.

Back and forth, French and English, English and French. With each switch, she felt stupider.

One summer, at home on the land, Rita's mom was teaching her to clean a big sturgeon. She taught the traditional Cree way, going slowly and silently through the steps, expecting Rita to pay close attention and do it herself the next time.

But Rita couldn't follow.

She could watch her mom work, like she could watch a plane land, but she couldn't copy her. Rita's White teachers said the Cree way of life was stupid, and now she was too stupid even for that.

Rita Gilpin

Her mom, who loved her so much, saw Rita's wet face and confused look.

She began again, this time using words to explain to Rita, every step of the way, why you had to cut here and not there, pull there and not here.

With her sleeve, Rita wiped her cheeks, and then paid close attention.

The next time, she did it herself.

Rita was in a French School for the third time. She was used to the food now, if that's what they called it, but there was never enough of it. By the end of the year, she was emaciated.

In June, when the plane landed in Eastmain and she stepped onto her home shore with all the other kids, she scanned the crowd of parents until she found her father. He was looking for her too. When their eyes met, she saw his nostrils flare.

"Didn't they feed you *anything?*" he asked? "Welcome home, by the way. We love you."

That evening, in their tent, while her mom filled Rita's bowl again and again to get some weight on her, her dad sharpened his knife on a rock.

Whist, whist, whist. His arm went in an even circular motion.

Rita could tell he was thinking.

Whist, whist, whist.

Finally he spoke. "I don't like this. I thought the Schools would teach you to succeed in their world. But every time you come back, you look worse and you know less."

Rita ate silently.

Whist, whist, whist.

"No more School," he finally said. "I'm taking you on the land. Cree school."

Whist, whist, whist.

It was not the solution Rita had wanted. But, for a little while, she felt relieved.

Just after lunch, Rita runs from the clinic across to one of the trailer homes. When the door opens to her knock, she can see the kettle already going for tea.

Since becoming Director, she doesn't get to do many home visits herself but some cases are close to her heart. She tries to squeeze them in.

Both adults who live in this house are fighting depression. For the man, it's Residential School survivor trauma turned inwards. He's been working with the counsellor, talking about it. It's helping.

For the woman, it's post-partum depression, or PPD. You have to be careful with PPD: it's surprisingly powerful. Back when Rita was a new mom, she had it herself – she felt like she'd been hit by a train – but the traditional healer knowledge she got from her parents helped her through. Years later, Rita's daughter-in-law had it too and, in the end, the PPD was stronger than she was; she took her own life. On that day, Rita became mom to her grandson.

She looks around the house. Things are tidy and calm. She can hear the whirr-clunk of the washing machine. The baby looks healthy and gurgles like a well-loved infant. Even though both parents feel numb, they are going through the motions for the sake of the kid.

Rita asks some questions, talks about how she got through her own Residential School trauma, her own PPD, how both were like deep cuts that took a long time to heal – but they did heal.

It's a thoughtful, comfortable conversation.

Rita can sense, this home will be okay. They'll remember this as a difficult season but they'll get through. The kid will be safe and loved.

She waves goodbye and walks back to the clinic.

By the time Rita was twenty-one, she was married with two kids. In the breastfeeding years, her mom often came over with some goose wings, maybe a goose head, and a big saucepan – Rita's pots weren't big enough. She poured in water and a bit of oatmeal or

Rita Gilpin

something else to thicken it, boiled it up on Rita's stove, and made her drink it all right there because she wanted to take the saucepan home.

One thing bugged Rita, though. She loved being a mom, loved life on the land, loved her work as a traditional healer – but she had never finished her schooling. Even if nursing wasn't an option, she wanted to get more schooling.

So, when autumn came, Rita enrolled in a special program through her work at Cree Health that let her take four university courses a year while also working full time. At the same time, she finished up a few high school courses that she had missed in her years of going back and forth between the English and French Schools.

Like everything else in Eeyou Istchee, Eastmain school had changed. Now they taught Cree language classes. Once, a test asked her to name in Cree all the parts of a toboggan. Rita barely passed. She had spent too much time learning White languages.

But her Eastmain teacher didn't beat or starve or intimidate her. Instead, he encouraged and he taught and he mentored. It didn't take Rita long to catch up – and to pull again to the top of her class.

At work, they needed someone to do home visits. Rita applied. What a surprise that Social Work suited her better than nursing ever could have. Each case was different from the one before, each obstacle a new challenge. But always her clients taught her what she needed to know to look after them. They were her best teachers.

She began focussing on Social Work in her university classes. Every evening after work, after feeding her kids and tucking them into bed, she cleared the kitchen table, got out her books and studied. She loved it.

In between writing papers and exams, she had two more kids and took Social Work positions with more responsibility. For six years, she worked full-time, she took full-time classes, and, since her husband was often gone, she was a full-time single mom to four kids.

Her mom helped out quite a bit.

There was just one problem. One big secret.

Back when Rita was breastfeeding her first baby, drinking goose bone broth by the potful and figuring out how to finish her schooling, her husband muttered something, she didn't hear what – and then he *hit* her!

After that first time, it was just like Residential School. Rita got hit all the time. He abused her any way he could think of. Always always, she was afraid.

Worse, her promise to herself evaporated. On her kids' faces she saw the look that had once clenched hers: they would rather he beat them. Every time Rita thought back on the safe and loving home of her parents, she felt awful. Whatever this was, this life with a raging man, it wasn't the Cree way.

But Cree women didn't leave their husbands either. Besides – hadn't she brought the beatings on herself? What kind of mom would do that to her kids? What kind of social worker couldn't keep her own home safe? Why was Rita always so bad at everything?

Back and forth her mind jumped, snagging on contradictions like a sweater on rough bark.

In the tenth year of beatings, her husband began to talk. He whispered to Rita, in the voice of a child, about his own days in Residential School, about how hard they were, how badly he was treated.

"It's okay," Rita reassured him, "Cry. You're releasing pain."

The next day, he beat her again.

One cold day near the end of winter, Rita bundled up and walked over to her mom's. The wind off the bay was strong that day and she had to lean into it to stay upright.

Rita Gilpin

"Mom, I have to leave him," she said, and peeled back her sweater to reveal an oozing shoulder wound that she couldn't reach. "I'm having warning dreams. He's gonna kill me."

Her mom looked at the wound, got some supplies from the cupboard, and began gently to clean it. "Cree women don't leave their husbands, Rita," she said.

"Cree women look after their kids, Mom. What chance do mine have if they see their dad kill their mom?"

"Rita, you promised God. God will protect you."

"Mom," Rita said, "I love you. But your god is not coming through. Eleven years and it's getting worse. *I'm* responsible for my life. If I leave, it'll be *my* choice."

For a long time, her mom didn't say anything. She just worked on the wound, and pressed a warm poultice onto it, then washed her hands and sat down.

Rita waited.

"Promise me one thing," her mom finally said. "You don't go with another man. Not as long as your husband is alive."

"Okay," Rita said.

And she began to prepare to leave her husband.

A few weeks later, on the land for the spring goose hunt, some of the hunters in Rita's group were in a boat coming back from the hunt.

There was a heavy wind and, just as they approached shore, something strange happened in the water – and the boat flipped, dumping the men into the deep slush.

After the splashing cleared, people on shore saw one hand gripping the gunwale. One of them was alive and holding on. Someone ran for Rita, in her cabin with the camp radio.

Even before Rita saw the messenger, she heard "Rita! Accident!! Radio for help!"

Quickly Rita called – and then she grabbed the First Aid kit and sprinted to the shore.

"Chopper's on the way!" she said, breathless. "Who's hurt?"

Her mother-in-law was crying hard. Wailing.

"There's nothing we can do, Rita." Her voice lurched. "One of them held on for a minute – maybe him – but now they're all gone."

Everyone was looking at Rita.

Gradually, dully, she realized: her mother-in-law's son – Rita's husband, whom she was preparing to leave – was one of the dead. He had been a strong swimmer, but ice water takes you so quickly.

In the next weeks, divers recovered all the bodies except Rita's husband.

Seven months later, someone chased a fox away from its meal: a frozen body that had washed ashore. Body parts were missing, but the clothing identified him as Rita's husband. They buried what was left of him in the Eastmain cemetery.

And a while after that, Rita learned that, while her husband was abusing her, he had also been abusing an Eastmain child.

Rita wanted to climb into a snail shell and crawl away.

Rita's father was getting old.

One day, he said to her, "Rita, I'm so proud of you. Of all the schooling you're getting. You will use it for good things here in Eeyou Istchee. I have just one more thing to teach you before I go to the next world."

He must have changed his mind. He slipped into the next world without seeing Rita again.

She kept studying, finished a Bachelor's Degree in Social Work from University of Québec, and became the Director of Health and Social Services for all of Eastmain.

Back in her office, Rita finishes up the paperwork from her home visit. Then she reviews the latest reports from her Youth Protection workers. The team has been able to close almost all the

Youth Protection cases in Eastmain. The community, like all Eeyou Istchee communities, is really healing.

Hardships take you somewhere. Maybe that's what her dad wanted to tell her. That there is no justification for all the abuse she received, all the bad things that happened to her, but she has needed to understand every one of those bad things to do the work she now does.

Right at 5:00, Rita packs up and heads out the door. Her grandson has a game tonight and she has to get him his supper before that. In him, she has a second chance to parent. The first time around, so busy with studies and trying to manage a violent home, she didn't get it right. She's better at it this time. She appreciates it more. And he keeps her healthy.

It took a long time to get here, but her life is hers again.

On the land, food storage can be a complicated affair. In winter, the meat can safely freeze outside and the cooks can chop off as much as they need for the day. But around March, spring thaw sets in. At that point, Cree folks who are following traditional ways build a refrigerator. They chop a tree and saw it into pieces of even length, each about foot long, maybe a little more. Some of these they arrange in a small circle or square around the meat and others they lay on top for a roof. Then they shovel snow all over it and compact it. Finally, they gather the leaves and bark and twigs and sawdust from the chopped tree and pack a solid layer on top of the snow. Meat stays fresh inside the refrigerator for approximately two months, until about May. From May to October, they preserve meat by smoking it.

Back in the 1670s, a ship came from England every year and dropped anchor just off the coast where Eastmain River emptied into James Bay. The ship filled its holds with kegs of fish, mostly sturgeon, and returned to England. There, the swim bladders of the fish were dried and the gelatin extracted to make isinglass, a preservative.

When a spruce tree dies, the wood eventually rots, and the rotten wood can be ground into powder that can heal diaper rash and bed sores. It's also used to smoke moosehide into a burnished camel shade. Other trees, like jackpine or birch, are not used for smoking hide because the woodsmoke is black and the tree is gummy.

Homebrew, usually made from yeast and raisins and beans or peas, was sometimes made on Mondays and consumed on Saturdays. It was usually made in an open vat, so whatever fell in added to the flavour. But, often, with just five short days of fermentation, it didn't have much in the way of alcohol. It did, however, have more than enough action to be a most effective laxative, and inspired heated races to the outhouse.

←

Teepees, originally made of birch bark, come from along the Ontario coast and were introduced to the James Bay Cree of Québec later. The Québec James Bay Cree traditional lodging was a cabin built without nails. On the roof, baby moss (the kind of moss used as diapers for babies) was layered like shingles. Over time, the sheets of moss grew together. This kind of roof never leaked and lasted for fifteen to twenty years, sometimes more.

←

Out on the land, after a meal, if they run out of soap, traditional Cree cooks scoop some campfire ashes into the pot along with a bit of water and scrub. The ash mixes with the leftover fat in the pot and forms soap and sudses right up. Similarly, when doing laundry in the traditional way, they tie campfire ashes into a small cloth and drop that into the wash water. White ash is essentially lye and lye mixed with any kind of fat makes soap.

The morning sun had already melted the window frost and the view was clear.

Artist: Tristan Shecapio-Blacksmith

Thomas Chakapash

Thomas Chakapash

"TOM! WAKE up! It snowed!" Someone was whispering in Thomas's ear.

He jerked awake. On the ceiling, the morning light shone a little blue, the way it does when there's snow outside. He glanced down the row of bunk beds. Twenty-eight boys all still tucked in, but his friend Sam* was at the window. Thomas slid out from under the warm blanket – the floor was ice on his bare feet – and tiptoed to join him. Side by side, the boys stood on their toes and looked outside.

The morning sun had already melted the window frost and their view was clear. A thick layer of white sparkled over the grounds. It rested on fenceposts and spruce branches in smooth, round heaps. A set of rabbit tracks cut across the Schoolyard. Under the first snow of winter, even Ste.-Thérèse-de-l'Enfant-Jésus Indian Residential School yard looked beautiful.

After a while, the boys crawled back under their covers and slept until the morning call.

At breakfast, Thomas and Sam and all the other boys filed into the dining hall and took their places at the long wooden benches by the tables. One of the supervisors began to scoop out porridge. Another clapped his hands.

"*Écoutez!!*" he called. "Anyone who got out of bed before morning call today to look out the window, please step forward." His voice was calm and there was a serene smile on his face.

Thomas and Sam looked at each other and shrugged. It was against the rules to speak Cree, but there was no rule about looking at snow. No reason to be afraid. They stepped forward.

The supervisor reached behind himself to grab something and –

CRACK!!

He bashed a great big two-by-six wooden plank down on Thomas, twisting at the hip for extra force. Again and again the plank landed, mostly on Thomas's hands and arms. The shock of it took his breath away. Thomas clenched against the pain and refused to cry. After a while, welts on his skin began to rise. The supervisor got a little smile on his face then, took a deep breath – and turned the plank on Sam. The other boys looked at the floor. If they raised their eyes at a moment like this, they were likely to get it too.

Sometimes now, Thomas still feels the heat of those welts.

That's how it was at Ste.-Thérèse-de-l'Enfant-Jésus Indian Residential School in the early '70s, back when Thomas was about ten years old.

One day, not long after the Snow Incident, Thomas and Sam filed into the dining room with all the other boys and took their places at the supper table. The cook carried out the bins of food, the supervisor prayed over it, and then scooped it onto plates and distributed it. Once every boy had his plate and it was okay to eat, Thomas picked up his fork.

Something was strange. The dish was supposed to be hamburger and gravy but it smelled … different. It smelled *off.* Carefully, so the supervisor couldn't see him, he scraped some gravy to the side and leaned close to the plate to sniff – and then he saw. The meat was rotten. Even cooked, it was green, shiny, beginning to change into slime.

Thomas looked around. The other boys were sniffing and poking at their food too. Nobody said a word.

Thomas Chakapash

If Thomas ate the rotten meat, he would get sick from food poisoning. But if he complained or refused to eat it, he would be beaten, probably until he was sick, and then he couldn't eat anything at all for a couple of days; a day of no food was the usual punishment for not finishing your plate. Either way, he would be sick.

"*Juzt blug your doze and zwallow,*" Sam whispered, beside him.

Thomas took a deep breath and held it. Pretending to have a cold, he plugged his nose from the inside so that he couldn't taste or smell, he picked up his fork, stabbed it into the rot, and forced it all down in a few quick forkfuls. The bile began to climb the back of his throat so he grabbed his glass of water and chugged it all back.

And then he sat back and exhaled. He had done it. His plate was clean. Now he just had to wait for food poisoning to set in. A few hours, probably.

He looked around. Other boys were gagging. Everyone would be puking tonight. The dorm was gonna stink.

Suddenly it was all too much. Why should he have to wait to get sick just to avoid being beaten? Why should his friends have to gag? All anyone wanted was a good supper. What was wrong with that?

Thomas started to cry. Not just a few silent tears rolling down his face, but bawling really hard, so that it became hard to breathe.

Right away the supervisors were there. "*Thomas calme-toi!* What's wrong? You're okay! C'mon, calm down."

But he couldn't calm down and he couldn't explain, no matter how hard he tried, so the supervisors sent him back to the dorm. There, with no one watching, he began to hit stuff. A pillow. His mattress. A bunk bed. The wall. It felt good just to let it out.

Then he lay down and waited to be sick.

The next time Thomas saw his mom, he told her about how bad it was. About the food, about being beaten for looking at snow, all of it.

"Oh Thomas," she said, "It's okay. You're just homesick. They're taking good care of you. You're lucky to go to School!"

Thomas was stunned. She didn't believe him. She had always believed him. He thought he could tell her anything.

Things changed that day. He still loved being around her, still told her about things in his life, but that was the last time he told her everything.

That was the worst of it. Not to be believed by his own mom.

The most important rule at Ste.-Thérèse-de-l'Enfant-Jésus Catholic Indian Residential School was about language. No one was supposed to speak Cree. If you spoke Cree, breathed a single word of it, you'd be beaten. Sometimes, it seemed you could be beaten just for thinking Cree. What you were supposed to speak was French. But that's where it got tricky. None of the kids knew French to begin with and if you tried to speak French and you didn't get it right – well, you got in trouble for that too.

One night, Thomas's friend Bryan* had a bad dream. It was so scary that it made him wet his bed.

The next morning, the supervisor saw the wet sheets. He said nothing. He just picked up the plank, the same plank that had hit Thomas, and started to beat Bryan – but for some reason he forgot to stop. He beat and beat and beat him and, even after Bryan was on the floor, out cold from the pain, he kept on beating. The plank made one sound when it hit something hard like bone, and another sound when it hit something less rigid like an organ or muscle. Thomas wanted to cover his ears so that he couldn't hear, but if he did then he would be beaten too.

After a long while, the supervisor finally seemed to remember where he was and stopped beating. He looked around at everyone there with a rested, satisfied expression, as if he had just done his favourite thing. Another supervisor picked up limp Bryan and carried him to the Infirmary.

The next day Bryan wasn't at breakfast. Or at lunch. Or at supper.

Thomas Chakapash

Nor the day after that.

Nor the day after that.

Eventually, Thomas heard that Bryan was in hospital. And that he wouldn't be back in School. Ever.

The supervisor had beaten him mostly in the upper hip area, just where the kidneys sit. The beating had been so severe that both kidneys were pulverized right through the skin, as if someone had taken a meat tenderizer to them. They both had to be removed or Bryan would die of sepsis. For the rest of his life, he would have to be on dialysis and he could never live far from a hospital. Maybe eventually he could get a transplant but, even with transplanted kidneys, his life would be shortened.

It was the 1970s. The Schools were supposed to be getting better.

Everyone in Eeyou Istchee heard about it then and how bad it was at Ste.-Thérèse-de-l'Enfant Indian Residential School. The boys in the School, Thomas's parents, even the Chief of Fort George.

The school was on Fort George island which was Cree territory, so Chief, at least, could do something about it. He drove to the School and walked inside. By the time he left, the beating supervisor had been removed.

"See??" Thomas said to his parents. "See?? That's what I was trying to tell you. That's what it's like at Ste.-Thérèse-de-l'Enfant-Jésus Indian Residential School."

"Oh," his mom said. "Oh."

Thomas grew up and left the School behind. He became a police officer in the new town of Chisasibi when it was moved from the island of Fort George to mainland.

But he couldn't stop thinking about all the violence at Ste.-Thérèse-de-l'Enfant-Jésus Indian Residential School. In his dreams, the beatings happened again and again. Or sometimes, in the middle of the day, he would feel that plank bashing down on his arms though the School and plank didn't even exist anymore and the supervisor was long gone. Or he would hear a noise that reminded him of the plank colliding with Bryan – and all of a sudden he would see it in front of his eyes all over again. Not just a memory, but a full replay with sound and light and limp Bryan on the floor and everything.

Some of Thomas's old School friends took up drugs or drinking. Thomas knew why they did – the plank had landed on many of them – but drugs and booze never really fixed anything. Some of his family members had gone to Indian Residential School too and they had their own experiences to sort through, so Thomas didn't want to bother them with his. He sure didn't want to talk about those days with his kids. Not with anyone, really.

Mostly he kept his night terrors and flashbacks to himself.

His police work helped. It meant that, every single day, Thomas could go home after work and know that he had helped someone in his community that day. Sometimes only with little stuff, like getting safely to where they were going, but sometimes with bigger stuff too. That made him feel better. Later, he moved away from policing and found work in Mistissini in Public Health, helping his community in other ways.

Sometimes he went out on the land. As a kid, he had never been able to do that with his parents, but now he was grown and could go out by himself. He didn't have all the skills that some of his friends had, the ones who could live in traditional ways all year round, but he could go out for a few days and pitch a tent and feel what it was to be a Cree man on Cree land praying to the Cree Creator for healing and for understanding.

And it helped to speak Cree. To know that, even after all those punishments, even after all the efforts the White people had made to erase it, his language was healthy and alive. Even now, Thomas speaks three languages fluently – English, French, and Cree. His favourite is Cree.

Thomas Chakapash

Healing is a slow thing that takes effort. None of it was easy. Thomas had to choose to heal, and to behave in the ways of a healed man even when he didn't yet feel healed, again and again. It took a long time.

Eventually, the dreams and flashbacks stopped and Ste.-Thérèse-de-l'Enfant-Jésus Indian Residential School became nothing but a memory for him. A memory with grip and strength and tenacity, but just a memory nevertheless.

When the Indian Residential School Settlement process came through town, Thomas told his story. The lawyer listened carefully, wrote things down, and seemed to believe everything Thomas said. Thomas qualified for some compensation, but what mattered was that he had been believed.

A few years ago, Thomas stopped by his mom's house. She was old and he checked in on her whenever he could. She made him tea and they sat down at her kitchen table.

"Thomas, I'm so sorry," she said.

"For what, Mom?"

"I should have believed you. Back when you were a kid and you were so angry and you told me how things were at that School. I didn't want to believe you. I knew you were an honest kid, but – it's just – well, I went to Residential School too and – to think that the same stuff was happening to you and I couldn't do anything to help. I just – I didn't like to think things were still so bad. But I should have believed you."

She looked so sad.

Thomas took a sip of his tea. Then he reached across the table and laid a hand on her arm.

"It's okay, Mom. I'm working on it," he said. "I'll be okay."

And eventually he was.

* *"Sam" and "Bryan" are not their real names.*

Stories Heard Along the Way: Food

Until the mid-1960s, many Residential Schools operated farm facilities in which the children worked, usually for six half days a week, spending five half days in the classroom. Mohawk Institute, for instance, had several hundred chickens and a herd of cows. The eggs and cream and vegetables were sold while the students starved. The students received one egg a year, on Easter morning, and skim milk diluted with water. Children were so hungry they sometimes picked from the barrel that held scraps for the pigs.

Before airplanes flew up into Eeyou Istchee, mail was delivered along the coast in the summer months by boat and in the winter months by dogsled. The postmaster had to keep dog teams year 'round – and all of those dogs needed food and exercise and water. It was an expensive full-time job to look after them.

A Nation representative instructed an Eeyou Istchee restaurant to ship used cooking oil out of the community to the South, where it could be properly disposed of in a way that didn't damage the environment. A few weeks later, the representative went to a spot just outside of the community where geese often gathered. And there sat the big vats of used oil. They had indeed been shipped out of town. One kilometre out of town.

One of the Residential School teachers didn't really understand nutrition. She made a Cree girl swallow glass marbles for lunch.

←

In the Schools, starving children were sometimes bribed with food to bully or sexually abuse other kids while the clergy or staff watched.

←

One Ontario Residential School cook sold bread to starving students for ten cents a loaf. Students did odd jobs in the nearby community and then "bought" their meals from the cook.

←

In some Schools, while the children ate cold, meagre food, the staff sat in the same room and ate hearty, hot, fragrant meals. They were modelling correct table manners, they explained.

←

The first food an infant on the land ate was usually mashed fish, crushed by adult fingers. Parents packed the fish into a type of pouch made from a pike stomach and attached a nipple made from a goose quill. The baby sucked the liquefied fish out through the quill.

Sometimes, during a boring class, Leslie would think about that story. Her dad, a little boy bundled up, sitting on the back of a snowmobile, for all day and part of a night.

Artist: Tristan Shecapio-Blacksmith

Leslie Tomatuk

Leslie Tomatuk

DOWN THE gravel road and around two corners from Leslie's home stood Horden Hall, the biggest building in Moose Factory. It was four storeys high. Each storey had a long hallway running down the middle and four or five spacious rooms. It had been an Indian Residential School for a long time, so long that it had gone through nine different names, and all nine were versions of "Moose Factory" or "Bishop Horden." No one stayed in the dorms anymore, but the School still used the same classrooms they had always used. And the same barbed wire still curled atop the chain-link fence circling the grounds. Everyone in Moose Factory knew that place was haunted.

Leslie went to Horden Hall School. Sometimes, on the way to one of the classrooms, her class had to cut through a corridor that connected to the old dorms. When that happened, everybody, Leslie included, instantly stopped talking and began stepping silently like deer. Leslie never knew why. No one had asked them to be quiet. She didn't know what had happened there back when kids stayed in the dorms. She just knew that when she stepped into that place something wet and cold and creepy hung in the air. She didn't want even to breathe.

Sometimes Leslie asked her dad about it. What had happened back when he was a student and it was called Bishop Horden Memorial Indian Residential School? Why was it so creepy?

He brushed off the question. Or changed the subject. Or deflected with a joke. He didn't answer. Not once.

There were other things he wouldn't do. He wouldn't take her brothers hunting. And that was strange because, in a town of really good hunters, he was especially good at it. Their freezer always had game, their supper table curved under the weight of moose or goose or beaver, perfectly roasted. Sometimes he showed Leslie a thing or two about how to clean an animal, or about what to do with a hide, but he would not take his kids hunting.

"Take us," her brothers begged. "Show us how to do it."

"If you wanna know," he said, "learn it on your own."

And then he told them about the guys who went hunting and saw a sign that said "Bear Left" and so they went home. Everyone laughed – and the next time he went out hunting, he went alone.

And there was the Cree language. Leslie's dad wouldn't speak it to them.

"I'm Cree!" Leslie pleaded. "I wanna speak Cree. Teach me, pleeeeease?"

"Okay," he said. "Do you know the Cree word for 'bad hunter?'"

"What?"

"Vegetarian!" he said and smiled.

"Dad! Tell me!"

"I guess you'll have to study it yourself," he said.

It was like that with every Cree tradition. Leslie and her brothers would hear about it in town or at School but, whatever it was, it never happened at home. Their dad made sure of it.

And another thing. He wouldn't say, "I love you."

He did love her, she felt it, but from far away.

The person who didn't stay nearly far enough away was a Horden Hall janitor. When Leslie and her friends went into the bathroom at School, he nearly always followed them in.

Leslie Tomatuk

The girls went into the stalls to use the toilets, they came out and washed their hands in the big stone semi-circular sink, with a foot pedal and dozens of tiny streams of water curving out from the centre, and they smoothed their hair at the mirror. And through it all, the janitor leaned against the wall, watching. Sometimes openly leering.

Leslie felt danger wafting off of him.

"Are you actually a *girl?*" she taunted, ignoring the spark of fear on her neck. "Is that why you're in the *girls'* bathroom??"

He didn't say anything. He just smirked, like she and her Cree friends existed for him to have someone to ogle, and stayed where he was.

There was an old teacher, too – he had been there forever – and he stood at the front of the classroom, slid his hands down the front of his pants, gazed out at the students, and played with himself while his belly jiggled over his belt. It was revolting. Everyone knew. Everyone talked about it. Everyone was grossed out. Nobody did anything about it. Leslie couldn't understand why not.

Then she found out he was going to be her Grade Seven teacher.

She went straight to her Grade Six teacher.

"No *way!*" she shouted. "No way am I doing a whole year with Mr. Pocket-Pool. Don't you *dare* put me in his class!"

Surprisingly, he didn't. He put her in a different class. Probably because her mom was on the School Board. But her friends whose mothers weren't on the School Board had to sit in his class. They told Leslie all about it. Hands down his pants, rubbing himself, belly jiggling, staring right at them. Nothing changed.

Really, the teachers were careful around Leslie. They never openly mistreated her, even when she got mouthy. She could get away with stuff. Her friends, especially her Cree friends, got punished all the time. An angry teacher broke a ruler across the arm of the guy who sat beside Leslie. A girl near the front chewed gum and then had to wear the gum on her nose for the rest of the day. And the teachers were always yelling. These things were so ordinary Leslie didn't even bother telling her parents.

(But if her brothers pestered her over lunch at home, then Leslie telephoned the Moose Factory hospital: "May I speak to Anne Tomatuk, please? She's the Zone Director of Nurses." They put her through – they always put her through – and she whined, "Mo-om, they're *bugging* me!" And her mom stopped whatever she was doing and helped her kids work it out.)

Once, after Leslie was grown, she visited her dad's old home in Eastmain and asked her dad's older brother what he knew about Bishop Horden Memorial Indian Residential School.

"There was this once," he said. "I snowmobiled down to Moose Factory and brought your dad home to Eastmain for Christmas. I took along some of our mom's fresh bannock. When I gave it to him, he got so happy all of a sudden. 'It's just ban-nock,' I said. 'Nooooo,' he said. 'It's the world's *best* bannock. It means that now I get real food!' Then we bundled up and snow-mobiled home. Took about twelve hours, maybe a little more. After Christmas I took him back. I felt him crying against my back. He didn't wanna go."

Sometimes, at night or during a boring class, Leslie thought about that story. Her dad, a little boy bundled up, on the back of a snowmobile, arms wrapped around his older brother, for all day and part of a night. They would have followed the dog-team trail that hugged the shore of the bay and carried their fuel on a sled behind. At that time of year, winds would have blown horizontal across the huge expanse of James Bay and shot hard snow pellets into their faces.

How cold and long that ride must have been. And how won-derful that piece of fresh bannock that marked the beginning of food.

Leslie's dad was an orderly at the Moose Factory hospital. Every few weeks, he had four days off of work. And nearly every

Leslie Tomatuk

time it was the same. On the first day, he'd go somewhere in town and have a few drinks with his friends. In the middle of the night, about 3:00 AM, he brought the party home. It was always noisy, someone was always looking to rumble, and Leslie and her brothers and sister woke up from the racket and stared at the ceiling for the rest of the night.

A few times Leslie climbed out of bed and watched through the crack in the door. In the thin wire of light, she saw her dad – no matter how drunk – watching their bedroom door. Sometimes he took a chair and sat right beside.

Once, someone stumbled out of the bathroom next door and got too close to the kids' doorknob.

In a flash her dad was there.

"Hey Boy!" he said in a low even voice. "What're you doin'?"

And the man quickly stepped away.

The day after a party, Leslie and her brothers and sister always stumbled, half-asleep, to School. All day long, Leslie struggled to stay awake.

So many parties, so many half-awake School days. The way her dad couldn't say "I love you." The way he wouldn't talk about things. Leslie didn't really understand any of it.

But she mattered to him. She could feel it. With him she was safe.

Sometimes Leslie asked her mom about Bishop Horden Memorial Indian Residential School.

"Well, your dad got tuberculosis there," she said once. "He had to go to Toronto and have half a lung removed. That's why he has that scar across his back."

"Oh. But why is the place so creepy?"

"When you're older, I'll tell you," her mom promised.

And then one sleety messy windy day, when no one wanted to be outside, her mom made them cocoa and told Leslie this story.

Her mom was born in Toronto. When she grew up, she became a nurse and she worked at one of Toronto's big hospitals. There, she met and married Leslie's dad. He had moved to Toronto for tuberculosis treatment and had stayed and become a hospital orderly. He wanted to move North, and Leslie's mom was looking for a change from big-city nursing. She took a job in the small hospital in Moose Factory and the family moved there. Then a position as School nurse opened up at an Anglican School nearby. Scabies and lice, she thought, and minor scrapes. Probably quite a few colds. These were what School nurses treated, and that was fine by her. It was about as far away from big-city nursing as she could get.

Then children started showing up in the Infirmary—with war wounds. Deep injuries in places they should not even be touched.

Small children were being sexually assaulted. In many ways. All the time.

This was worse than anything she had seen in the big city.

She had to do something!

Bishop Horden Memorial Indian Residential School was Anglican. She had grown up in the Anglican Church. She understood it. Surely the Church authorities would want to know. Surely they would investigate, bring charges against the assailants, do right by small injured children.

She reported it in detail to the Church authorities.

A week passed. Then another.

One day, over the School intercom, she was summoned to the office. She walked in and folded her adult body into the chair that small children sat in when they were in trouble. Behind the big desk (what else had happened at that desk?) sat the head priest. He held in his hands a letter from the Church authorities. He read it aloud.

"Dear Mrs. Tomatuk," the letter said. "Your services are no longer required."

Across the desk, the priest handed Leslie's mom an envelope with her pay. And asked her to leave.

Leslie Tomatuk

She went back to work at the Moose Factory hospital. She and Leslie's dad thought about moving to Eastmain, where he was from, but, if they went, they would have to send their kids away to Indian Residential School. Where children had war wounds and her services were no longer required. But if they stayed in Moose Factory, then Leslie and her siblings could go to Horden Hall and sleep in their own beds. Kids attending Church Schools were safer sleeping in their own beds.

So the family stayed in Moose Factory.

Well.

That story explained a thing or two. No wonder the place was haunted.

Leslie never stopped thinking about Bishop Horden Memorial Indian Residential School. About what it meant.

It meant a haunted campus.

It meant a community of Crees who wouldn't speak Cree.

It meant a community of people who had always lived communally, where nothing belonged to a single person, who now had to figure out life under the confusing and unnatural boundaries of "mine" and "yours." Who now had to figure out when they should stand up for something and when it was safer just to stay quiet and let stuff happen.

It meant a dad with secrets.

It meant a place where kids lived away from their families. Most of Leslie's friends lived in group homes while their families stayed up in Eeyou Istchee.

It meant a town of no teenagers. Teenagers had to attend high school, and Horden Hall went only to Grade Eight. Leslie's sister left for Timmons at age thirteen. Except for visits, she never came back.

It meant that Leslie got bullied. *Wagon burner,* people hissed about her dad's family. *White and Proud* about her mom's.

But the worst, the worst, was what Bishop Horden Memorial Indian Residential School meant about Moose Factory. Whenever she told someone where she was from, they said, significantly, "Ohh Moose Factory." And then talked about someone they knew who had been horribly beaten or violated. Or even killed. Moose Factory was Leslie's *home*. It was where her family *lived*. But Bishop Horden Memorial Indian Residential School meant that Moose Factory was where Cree kids had been tortured for years. Generations. How does a town get past a history like that? How does it get to *normal*?

Maybe it would have helped if, back when they stopped using the dorms in the old Indian Residential School, they had at least sacked the teachers. But the teachers who had done those awful things were the same teachers in Leslie's School who didn't even try to hide their arousal. They stayed in Moose Factory, doing the same jobs on the same ground under a new roof. Leering at Cree children, pulling a salary and a pension. Leslie played with their kids.

They should have left, she thought. *They should have been made to leave.*

But then, who would replace them? Who would ever want to move to Moose Factory to teach in a new building still named Bishop Horden Hall?

Leslie married young. By the time she was twenty-four years old, she was working in Finance and had four kids. By then, some things in Moose Factory had changed. More of the roads were paved. More houses had been built. Mr. Pocket-Pool was finally in jail.

What had not changed was Leslie's dad. He was still so distant. He still wouldn't speak Cree. He still wouldn't take his kids hunting. He loved them, he would do anything to keep them safe, but he still couldn't hug them. He couldn't say "I love you."

Leslie wanted to respect whatever it was he couldn't say. For a long time, she didn't do anything.

One day – she was thirty years old – she had had enough. She drove over to her father's house, made a pot of tea, and waited for him to come from work. When he did, and got comfortable on his sofa, she went and sat beside him.

He looked at her with questions on his face.

"Dad," she said, "this has to change. I know you have reasons for all this distance, but you have to let it go. I'm not teaching my kids that this is how love works. You're going to have to start hugging them. You're going to have to start telling them that you love them because I know you do. And you're going to have to start hugging me in front of them. And now, we're gonna practise."

She leaned across the sofa with her arms open.

The look of terror that crossed his face. The fear she saw sparking at his neck.

He closed his eyes, stiffened like an icicle, straight macho shoulders – and allowed his grown daughter to wrap her arms around him in a long slow hug. After a while he even lifted a rigid hand to pat her back.

Something happened that day. Something eased. Not all at once – Leslie could sense his struggle – but the changes came faster than she had hoped.

Soon he was hugging Leslie and her kids all the time. Telling them how much he loved them. He even took his oldest grandson on the land for weeks at a time and taught him traditional Cree hunting knowledge. To all the grandkids, he became the best grandfather.

The one thing he could never do was to speak Cree to his family. Leslie let that one go.

One day, she ran into an old family friend who spoke Cree fluently but hadn't taught her kids either.

"Why didn't you teach your kids Cree?" Leslie asked.

"I wanted them to be safe," she answered. As if it were the most obvious thing in the world.

When Leslie turned thirty-one, she realized that, even though she had worked in Finance for nine years, she had hardly any education at all and was living the life of a much older woman.

She loved her family but didn't want to be married anymore – and asked her husband for a divorce.

Leslie took her kids and moved to Peterborough. She attended Trent University and studied Indigenous Studies. One of her professors said that, across Canada, Indigenous people were losing their language. *Have you been to Eeyou Istchee?* Leslie thought. *There it's so strong that they argue about which Cree language to use!* But then she remembered her dad and the old family friend. What it meant if even half the students of Indian Residential Schools in Canada had stopped speaking their language to keep their kids safe.

Leslie's dad had always said that, when he retired, he was going to move home to Eastmain. But, as he aged, the old tuberculosis flared and settled into his kidneys. It was one medical emergency after another. He got a kidney transplant, and that helped for a while. But he never moved back to Eastmain. To keep his kids safe, he spent his adult life in Moose Factory, the place of his love and his trauma, and he lived there until he passed away.

At his funeral, Leslie spoke with some of the older men who had gone to Bishop Horden Memorial Indian Residential School with him. They had heard him being beaten in the cloak room, they said. It was a U-shaped cubby where the coats hung and mostly absorbed the sounds of thwacks and thumps and shrieks. If you could hear a beating outside, right through the wall and through all those coats, you knew it was a bad one.

For a while Leslie worked in Corrections, then in Youth Protection, then in Victim Services. In each of these positions, the people she worked with were always healing. And what they were healing from was Indian Residential School. Places like Bishop Horden Memorial.

Her own cousin, even. They were at a family reunion, carrying food to the table.

"I was so angry at your family," she said to Leslie. "For so many years."

Leslie Tomatuk

"At us? Why?" Leslie asked.

"We were in that Residential School, that *dungeon*," she said. The spoon in her hand shook a little. "A nun came into our room at nights and took little girls back to her room and did – sex things. Every night I was terrified it would be my turn. And you – your family *lived* in Moose Factory. You could have had us over for Christmas. Or for one safe night. Or even just for supper. But you didn't even *visit* us. Not once."

"Oh wow," Leslie said. She set down the dish and looked at her cousin. "I didn't know you were there."

"Your dad knew," her cousin said.

Yeah, that sounds about right, Leslie thought. *Another one of his secrets.*

"I'm not mad now," her cousin continued. "I know it wasn't his fault."

Eventually, Leslie did what her father couldn't do and moved to his home community in Eastmain. She became a manager for Cree Health Board and came to understand the language. Not long ago, she had the chance to move back to Moose Factory, her own home, and so she did.

In 2021, the barbed wire around the old School finally came down.

Leslie still thinks, nearly every day, about what Indian Residential School means for her people. Partly what it means is that there are people and places that are still haunted.

Mostly what it means is that they are really good at healing.

Artist: Nathaniel Bosum

Note on Sources

Because of COVID-19-related restrictions during the work on this book, we were not always able to access physical archives for the sections of the book that lie outside of storytellers' experiences. In some cases, then, we have relied upon primary sources that could be accessed online and on published secondary sources. We are especially grateful to John Milloy's *A National Crime: The Canadian Government and the Residential School System 1879 to 1986,* to *Report of the Royal Commission on Aboriginal Peoples: October 1996,* (particularly *Volume One: Looking Forward, Looking Back),* and to the *National Centre for Truth and Reconciliation* website, www. nctr.ca.

Indian Residential Schools

AND

James Bay Cree Timeline

This timeline is a work in progress. As we acquire new information, we will update the timeline on www.resschoolrecovery.org

ACRONYMS

IRS	Indian Residential School
GC	Government of Canada
JB	James Bay
HBC	Hudson's Bay Company
RC	Roman Catholic Church
ANG	Anglican Church
BID	British Indian Department
DIA[ND]	Department of Indian Affairs [and Northern Development]

1400s to 1700s

1423   Pope Alexander VI issues Discovery Doctrine: in order for Christianity to "be everywhere increased," lands inhabited by non-Christians should be claimed by Christians.

1620s   Recollets introduce mission schools in Canada and struggle with runaways, student deaths, parental reluctance. None last long.

1633   After an Indigenous man asks French parents to beat him instead of their own misbehaving son, Jesuit Paul le Jeune notes: "Indian nations of these parts ... cannot punish a child." Anticipates "trouble ... in carrying out our plans of teaching the young!"

1668   British ketch *Nonsuch* drops anchor off Waskaganish coast. James Bay (JB) Cree find it. Cree-British fur trade begins. Hudson's Bay Company (HBC) is formed.

1755   Founding of British Indian Department (BID), a wing of British Army. Without command power, it needs Indigenous Nation consent for any projects.

1756-1763

Seven Years' War. Britain and France, competing on four continents for colonial lands/resources, both rely on Indigenous military alliances. Needing more, Britain sends missionaries among Nations. At end, Britain claims Canada. King George III issues Royal Proclamation that Nations are self-governing, "should not be molested or disturbed" in their lands, and, except for regions "ceded to, or purchased by" British Crown, own the land.

1775-1783

Britain, at war with Americans, again relies on Indigenous allies.

1800s

1812-1815

Britain, again at war with Americans, yet again relies on Indigenous allies.

1823   US Supreme Court Justice Marshall decides the Discovery Doctrine "gave European nations an absolute right to New World lands."

1830   Wars ended, Indigenous alliances no longer urgent. BID comes under civilian government control.

Sir George Murray, Secretary of State for British colonies, displaces 1763 Royal Proclamation for "more enlightened" path of "encouraging ... the progress of religious knowledge and education generally amongst the Indian tribes."

1831   Mohawk Institute, first Indian Residential School (IRS), Anglican (ANG), begins taking Indigenous students.

1838   Mount Elgin, first Methodist IRS, opens.

1840   Wikwemikong, first Roman Catholic (RC) IRS, opens.

1852   BID asks Nations to approve individual land ownership because Nation land ownership fosters "idleness." Nations reject the request – but embrace and allocate treaty payments for formal education.

1857-1858

Two reports (Bagot and Head Commissions) lead to *Act to Encourage the Gradual Civilization of the Indian Tribes in the Province* (1857)which redefines "civilization," formerly defined by self-sufficient communities, as assimilated individuals.

1861   Coqualeetza, first Presbyterian IRS, opens.

1867   Confederation gives Government of Canada (GC) power to
        legislate for "Indians, and lands reserved for the Indians."

1868   Federal oversight of IRS begins. GC backs 57 Indigenous-attended
        schools. Two, Mount Elgin and Mohawk Institute, are IRS.

1871   Numbered treaties begin. As requested by Nations, Treaty One
        "agrees to a school on each reserve ... whenever the Indians ...
        should desire it." Treaties Two-Eleven (1871-1921) have similar
        education clauses.

1873   Shingwauk IRS (ANG) opens, burns down six days later. Rebuilt.

1876-1884
        Under *Indian Acts* (1876, 1880) and *Indian Advancement Act*
        (1884), Indigenous self-government ends. GC now controls Nation
        elections, Nation resources, Nation funds, individual status and
        travel, etc. Some cultural traditions criminalized.

1879   17-year-old Duncan Campbell Scott becomes BID copy clerk.

        Nicholas Flood Davin finds American day schools failed because
        of "influence of the wigwam." Recommends Industrial boarding
        schools, where students spend half-days doing labour, half-days
        learning trades. Expecting high costs and Indigenous "great
        attendant distress," he recommends a four-school maximum and
        Church affiliation.

        Disregarding treaties, BID adopts new education model:
        A) Separate children from families ("the old unimprovable
        people");
        B) Use colonial curriculum to replace Indigenous culture;
        C) Integrate students into colonial society.
        Only A succeeds. Teaching quality is too low for B to succeed or C
        to be considered.

1880   BID becomes Department of Indian Affairs (DIA).

1880-1885
        Nations in the West protest CP Railway construction across their
        land. GC builds IRS strategically so "Indians regard ... [their
        children] as hostages" and will "hesitate" to resist.

1884-1823
> Industrial Schools era.
> Churches force rapid IRS expansion, building IRS quickly and cheaply without DIA knowledge, hiring illiterate teachers, then demanding payment from GC. While DIA opens 8 Industrial Schools, Churches open 59 more IRS without DIA permission.
>
> DIA complains about paying for unapproved IRS, about "being forced" by Churches "going wild," but prevents no further IRS-building. Instead, DIA budgets much less than Churches ask, too little for qualified teachers or for child welfare.
>
> Many reports of malnutrition, neglect. Churches blame low per capita (PC) rates (funds per student).
>
> For more PC money, Churches bribe families, kidnap children, and routinely admit visibly sick contagious children. They make revenue through student labour and sell farm goods raised by students who go hungry. They pressure DIA to make IRS mandatory.
>
> Church denominations cannot pay for IRS they have, but compete for more.
>
> Pre-1915, half the children in IRS die, mostly from preventable infectious diseases but also from abuse, neglect, dehydration, exposure, suicide, fire, drowning, etc.
>
> DIA complains about Church treatment of children, sets instructional and diet standards. After many abuse reports, DIA rules corporal punishment should be rare, and never scar or injure. IRS disregard and abuse at will.
>
> DIA does not enforce standards or address the continuing widespread problems.

1891   Metlakatla, first Non-Denominational IRS, opens.

1898   Another new education model is implemented: instead of joining colonial society, graduates go home to "elevate" their communities. Many grads are sick, infect home communities. Deaths skyrocket.

1900s to 1940s

1904   Transition away from Industrial School model announced.

1904   Indian agents advised to deny provisions to "unwilling parents" rather than directly kidnapping children.

1906   Protestant Churches agree it "might be a wise policy" to run fewer IRS but carry on as before.

        Bishop Horden Hall IRS (ANG) in Moose Factory opens.

        St. Anne's IRS (RC) in Fort Albany opens.

1907   St. John's IRS (ANG) in Chapleau opens.

        DC Scott's daughter dies of Scarlet Fever at boarding school in France.

        Chief medical officer Peter Bryce's Report on the Indian Schools: appalling conditions, alarming death rates in 35 IRS. Official SH Blake says DIA is "within unpleasant nearness to the charge of manslaughter." DIA dismisses report. Report is leaked to the press. Church and DIA officials try to discredit Bryce. RC Church complains about "vexatious requirements by physicians ... [making] unnecessary demands."

1909   Bryce reports on 13 more IRS with similar findings.

1911   New DIA contracts require teachers to speak the language they teach. RC bishops oppose it. DIA doesn't enforce.

1914   World War I begins. Funds diverted from IRS.

        Rather than addressing Bryce's report, DC Scott (now Deputy Superintendent General) pushes Bryce out of DIA and later eliminates medical inspector position altogether "for reasons of economy."

1918   World War I ends.

1919   Pressured by Churches, DC Scott finally concedes on paper and, under *Indian Act* (1920), makes IRS attendance compulsory for Indigenous children. Doesn't enforce.

1920   DIA controls parents enough to know that children going home for summer will return. Summer vacations begin.

        Alberni, first United Church of Canada IRS, opens.

1931   Rapid IRS expansion continues after Industrial era, along with disease, malnutrition, abuse. At this point, maximum number of IRS (80) operating.

1932   Because of the Depression, PC grants are cut.

        DC Scott retires. Immediately Churches, Indian agents, RCMP begin aggressively enforcing IRS attendance. Scott blames his decisions on "the law which I did not originate, and which I never tried to amend."

1933   St. Philip's IRS (ANG) opens in Fort George.

1934   Austin Airways opens in Timmins. Eventually, it begins service to Eeyou Istchee.

1937   Ste.-Thérèse-de-L'Enfant-Jésus IRS (RC) opens in tiny Fort George, in walking distance from St. Philip's IRS.

1939   World War II begins. Funds diverted from IRS.

1942   Doctors Moore and Tisdall (Pablum inventor) begin medical experiments on Indigenous people.

1944   DIA considers integration with students sleeping at home to "educate" parents.

1945   World War II ends.

1947   DC Scott dies: "I have never fought against anything nor worked for anything but just accepted and drifted from point to point."

        Whitehorse Baptist, first (and only) Baptist IRS, opens.

1947-1948
        JB Survey: vitamin and nutrition experimentation on Cree people in Attawapiskat and Waskaganish.

1948-1952
        Dr. Pett, whose work informs Canada Food Guide, conducts nutrition, malnutrition, and vitamin experiments in six IRS.

1948   Another new education model: shut down IRS; integrate Indigenous students into regular public day schools. Slowly, IRS begin closing.

1948   As they phase out, IRS become "a sort of foster home" for children considered "Welfare problem[s]."

St. John's IRS in Chapleau closes.

1950s to 1990s

1950   Korean War begins: funds again diverted from IRS.

1951   Half-day system abandoned in most schools. Standard curriculum introduced.

Amendments in *Indian Act* (1951) give Provincial Governments control over Indigenous Child Welfare, making way for Sixties Scoop.

1953   Korean War ends.

DIA: New rules limiting corporal punishment. Not enforced. Abuse continues.

1954   DIA takes over hiring/paying teachers. Education quality immediately improves.

1957   Reforms: PC grants end; DIA reimburses IRS "for actual expenditures within certain limitations."

DIA: New diet standards. Not enforced. Students still go hungry.

Late 1950s - late 1960s
To keep IRS running, Churches aggressively campaign against public school integration.

1958   Northern Hostels renamed "Halls" to avoid confusion with "hospital," "hotel," and "hostile," and because "Hall" has "homelike connotation."

1960s – 1980s
Sixties Scoop: another pathway to the goal of eradicating Indigenous cultures. Without Indigenous consent, welfare agencies "scoop" thousands of Indigenous children from their homes, from IRS, from hospitals into the Welfare system to be adopted by Settlers. Children lose names, language, and all family and community ties.

1960   GC quietly decriminalizes Indigenous traditions. Status Indians now able to vote.

1962   DIA: New corporal punishment rules. Not enforced. Abuse continues.

Poplar Hill, the first Mennonite IRS, opens.

1963   La Tuque IRS (ANG) opens.

1969   DIA formally ends partnership with Churches, secularizing IRS.
        Inadequate funding means abuse and hunger continue.

        DIA becomes Department of Indian Affairs and Northern
        Development (DIAND).

1970   Mohawk Institute IRS closes.

        Shingwauk IRS closes.

        JH Wiebe, Medical Services Branch director, while "acutely aware"
        genocide claims have begun, expands birth control without
        informed consent among Indigenous people to "reduce the
        incidence of unwanted children, of child neglect, abandonment,
        desertion, welfare dependency and child abuse."

1971   Without consulting the Cree in any way, the Province of Québec
        announces massive JB Hydroelectric Project. Fight begins to
        protect Eeyou Istchee.

        National Indian Brotherhood proposes Indian Control of Indian
        Education.

1972   DIAND accepts National Indian Brotherhood's proposal. Education
        gradually moves under Indigenous control.

1975   St. Philip's IRS closes. Fort George Hostels IRS opens.

        JB Northern Québec Agreement, first modern-day treaty, signed.

1976   St. Anne's IRS closes.

        Bishop Horden Hall IRS closes.

1978   Fort George Hostels IRS closes.

        La Tuque IRS closes.

1981   Ste.-Thérèse-de-L'Enfant-Jésus IRS closes.

1986   United Church of Canada (which merged with the Methodist
        Church in 1925) apologizes for "impos[ing] our civilization." In
        1998, apologizes specifically for "our church's involvement in the
        [IRS] system." Here begin decades of Churches minimizing and
        dodging responsibility for their participation in IRS.

1989-1990
        IRS abuse investigations. Ojibwe Chief Phil Fontaine speaks
        publicly about being abused at IRS. Many others follow.

1991   Emphasizing naïveté, good intentions, and larger imperialist
        "system," Missionary Oblates of Mary Immaculate, one RC branch,
        apologize for their part in IRS. Later, when asked to share IRS
        records, they don't.

1992   Through Aboriginal Rights Coalition, RC, ANG, and United
        Churches request acknowledgement that IRS responsibility is
        "shared with" GC.

1993   ANG Church apologizes for its role in IRS, partly blaming "a
        system." Later apologies (2019, 2022) take fuller responsibility.

1994   Presbyterian Church apologizes for its part, "with the encourage-
        ment and assistance" of GC, in IRS.

1995   Royal Commission on Aboriginal Peoples report calls for IRS public
        inquiry.

1997   The last IRS, Kivialliq Hall in Rankin Inlet, Nunavut, closes.

2000s

2006   IRS Settlement Agreement is approved by legal counsels for IRS
        students, Churches, key Indigenous organizations, and GC. RC
        Church, the world's largest non-governmental landowner, pays
        just a fraction. Treating other Churches differently, GC releases
        RC church from obligations.

2007   GC establishes the Truth and Reconciliation Commission.

2008   Stephen Harper apologizes on behalf of GC for IRS but obstructs
        access to key records and funds. Limits IRS definition so that
        many former students are excluded from settlements.

2010   Mennonite Church Canada resolves to "recognize and confess …
        complicity" in IRS. Later, while emphasizing "the national plan" of
        assimilation, one Mennonite ministry (Living Hope Native Ministries)
        apologizes to students of one IRS for inflicting physical, emotional,
        and "soul" pain, and for "not properly screen[ing]" staff.

2016   Emphasizing no "direct involve[ment]," (Americans founded the
        Baptist IRS), Canadian Baptists apologize.

2021   215 unmarked child graves confirmed at Kamloops IRS. Ground-
        penetrating radar searches begin at other IRS, and reveal many
        more unmarked graves.

        Canadian Council of Catholic Bishops apologizes for "participat[ing]
        in this system" and acknowledges abuses committed "by some of
        our Catholic community."

2022   Pope Francis acknowledges "physical, verbal, psychological, and
        spiritual" but not sexual abuse. Apologizes for "evil committed
        by so many Christians" but not on behalf of RC Church. Doesn't
        revoke Discovery Doctrine. Canadian Conference of Catholic
        Bishops uses event as fundraiser.

        Missionary Oblates of Mary Immaculate IRS records are opened to
        National Centre of Truth and Reconciliation.

At time of writing, thousands of IRS records remain closed.

Selected References

Abley, Mark. *Conversations with a Dead Man: The Legacy of Duncan Campbell Scott.* Douglas and MacIntyre, 2013.

"An Act to Encourage the Gradual Civilization of the Indian Tribes in This Province, and to Amend the Laws Respecting Indians." *Statutes of the Province of Canada, 1857.* https://signatoryindian. tripod.com/routingus-edtoenslavethesovereignindigenouspeoples/id10.html.

Adams, John Coldwell. "Duncan Campbell Scott (1862 – 1947)." *Confederation Voices: Seven Canadian Poets.* Canadian Poetry Press, 2007. https://web. archive.org/web/20120417104551/ http://www.canadianpoetry.ca/confederation/index.htm

Blacksmith, George. *Forgotten Footprints: Colonialism from a Cree Perspective: The Social and Psychological Impacts of Residential Schools on the James Bay Cree of Northern Québec.* Gordongroup, 2016.

Bryce, Peter H. "Report on the Indian Residential Schools of Manitoba and the North-West Territories." Ottawa, 1907. www.openhistoryseminar.com/ canadianhistory/chapter/document -1-bryce-1907/

The Canadian Encyclopedia. www.thecanadianencyclopedia.ca/en

"Doctrine of Discovery, 1493." https://www.gilderlehrman.org/history-resources/ spotlight-primary-source/doctrine-discovery-1493

Dossetor, John B. *Beyond the Hippocratic Oath: A Memoir on the Rise of Modern Medical Ethics.* University of Alberta Press, 2005.

DyckFehderau, Ruth. *The Sweet Bloods of Eeyou Istchee: Stories of Diabetes and the James Bay Cree.* Cree Board of Health and Social Services of James Bay, 2017.

Greer, Allan, ed. *The Jesuit Relations: Natives and Missionaries in Seventeenth-Century North America.* Bedford/St. Martin's Press, 2000.

Government of Canada. "British North America Act, 1867 – Enactment no.1." https://www.justice.gc.ca/eng/rp-pr/csj-sjc/constitution/lawreg-loireg/p1t11.html

Government of Canada. "The Indian Act, 1876," "The Indian Act, 1880," and "The Indian Advancement Act, 1884." *Consolidation of Indian Legislation: Volume II: Indian Acts and Amendements, 1868-1975.* Gail Hinge. R5-158-2-1978-eng v.2. https:// publications.gc.ca/site/eng/9.835895/publication.html

Government of Canada. Report of the Royal Commission on Aboriginal Peoples. October 1996. https://www.bac-lac.gc.ca/ eng/discover/aboriginal-heritage/royal-commission-aboriginal-peoples/Pages/final-report.aspx

Government of Canada. "Treaties, agreements and negotiations," and "Indian Residential Schools." Crown-Indigenous Relations and Northern Affairs Canada. www.rcaanc-cirnac.gc.ca/

Indian Residential Schools Settlement Official Court Website. https://www.residentialschoolsettlement.ca/

"The Indian Residential Schools Settlement Agreement, the Catholic Church, and the 2015 Court Case: Timeline." Indian Residential School History and Dialogue Centre: Collections. University of British Columbia. https://collections.irshdc.ubc.ca/ index.php/Gallery/342

Malone, Kelly Geraldine. "Very Profound: Hundreds of Residential School Photos Found in Rome Archives." *Terrace Standard,* 01 August 2022. https://www.terracestandard.com/news/very-profound-hundreds-of-residential-school-photos-found-in-rome-archives/

Miller, J.R. *Shingwauk's Vision: A History of Native Residential Schools.* University of Toronto Press, 1997.

Milloy, John S. *A National Crime: The Canadian Government and the Residential School System 1879 – 1986.* University of Manitoba Press, 1999.

Mosby, Ian. "Administering Colonial Science: Nutrition Research and Human Biomedical Experimentation in Aboriginal Communities and Residential Schools, 1942-1952." *Histoire sociale / Social History* XLVI.91 (May 2013): 145-172.

National Centre for Truth and Reconciliation. www.nctr.ca

"Residential Schools Resolution: Mennonite Church Canada Christian Witness Council." 31 June 2010. www.commonword.ca/ ResourceView/82/22161

Moses, Russell. "Russ Moses and the Mohawk Insitute Indian Residential School." *Beyond the Spectacle: Native North American Presence in Britain.* University of Kent. 14 July 2021. https://blogs.kent.ac.uk/bts/2021/07/14/russ-moses-and-the-mohawk-institute-indian-residential-school/

Shaheen-Hussein, Samir. *Fighting for a Hand to Hold: Confronting Medical Colonialism Against Indigenous Children in Canada.* McGill-Queen's University Press, 2020.

Stote, Karen. Open Letter to House of Commons Standing Committee on Health RE: Forced/Coerced Sterilization of Indigenous Women in Canada. 13 June 2019. www.ourcommons.ca

Turpel-Lafond (Aki-Kwe), Mary Ellen. "Background Note to the Collection of Materials on the Catholic Church and the Indian Residential School Settlement Agreement." December 7, 2021. https://collections.irshdc.ubc.ca/index.php/Detail/objects/11250

All websites accessed August 10-25, 2022.

Apologies

"Apology to Former Students of United Church Indian Residential Schools, and to Their Families and Communities (1998)"; "Anglican Church of Canada's Apology to Native People," 06 August 1993; "Read Archbishop Justin's apology to the Indigenous peoples of Canada," 02 May 2022; "The Confession of the Presbyterian Church as Adopted by the General Assembly, June 9th, 1994"; "The Missionary Oblate of Mary Immaculate: An Apology to the First Nations of Canada by the Oblate Conference of Canada," 1991; and "Read the full text of Pope Francis's speech and apology," 25 July 2022. Church Apologies for Indian Residential Schools. Christian Aboriginal Infrastructure Developments. https://caid.ca/church_apology.html

"The Apology." Canadian Baptist Ministries, 21 October 2016. https://baptist-atlantic.ca/news/indigenous-peoples-apology/

"An Apology for Spiritual Harm." Anglican Church of Canada, 12 July 2019. https://www.anglican.ca/news/an-apology-for-spiritual-harm/30024511/

"An Apology Statement To: the former Students of Poplar Hill Development School." Living Hope Native Ministries, 2022. https://lhnm.org/truth-and-reconciliation/

"Statement of Apology by the Catholic Bishops of Canada to the Indigenous Peoples of this Land." Canadian Conference of Catholic Bishops, 24 September 2021. https://www.cccb.ca/letter/ statement-of-apology-by-the-catholic-bishops-of-canada-to-the-indigenous-peoples-of-this-land/#_ftn2

Acknowledgements

This is a complicated and difficult community project that relies upon the support of a great many people. I'm grateful to all the storytellers, many of whom took significant personal risk to participate in this project and share their stories. I am honoured by your trust in me. Lexie, Riley, Nathaniel, Tristan, Jared, Payton, and Parker, your illustrations and alphabets breathed new life into this book. Thank you for your artwork! I'm grateful to Cameron Mosimann for his designs and general design expertise; to Natasia Mukash for her breathtaking artwork; to Nicole Ritzer who built the website and the story title font, and filled many gaps; to Dr. Kirsten Dyck who built the first 130+ page timeline that eventually became the timeline in this book; to Matthew Iserhoff for his audionarrative and delightful online companionship; to Morgan Kennedy for her diligent copyediting; to Lisa Quinn of Wilfrid Laurier UP for editing with grace and compassion; to accessible-design consultant Jocelyn Brown and the print-impaired readers who provided design feedback but prefer not to be named; to Clare Hitchens of WLUP for her marketing and her considerable patience with the lurches that are always part of this work. For wise and generous manuscript feedback, unending thanks to Joanna Campiou and longtime reader Daphne Read (I'm never at ease with a manuscript until she's read it). My heartfelt gratitude to Dr. Rosy Khurana, Helene Porada, and Catherine Godin for their health expertise; to Suzy Goodleaf who provided psychological advice for this project; to Charlotte Gilpin, Louise Etapp, Francine Moses, and other IRS survivor support workers who supported storytellers during this project; to Patrice Larivée, Rosy, and Catherine for opening their Northern homes to me during the work on this project, to the staff of Capissisit and Eneyaauhkaat Lodges and of Bella Loon Petawabano's BnB for warmth and shelter (and sometimes adventure) during long Northern stays, and to Bill and Lynn Cook in whose Sarasota home I stayed when I needed writing time. I can't even count how many times I was fed by Gabriel Doutreloux and Nicole, Jill Torrie, Rosy, Patrice, and the Eastmain MSDC ladies. Sheila's doughnuts deserve a chapter of their own. Thanks to Jacquie Voyageur, Charity Longchap, and all the folks in Mistissini Noah's Ark, in the Oujé-Bougoumou clinic, and in Eastmain clinic and MSDC whose offices and printers I've used over the years, and who have helped me figure my way through everything from local culture to Northern travel to CBHSSJB Finance.

Many Cree friends and colleagues willingly explained aspects of Cree culture to me, usually with a good deal of humour: Solomon Awashish, Orenda Loon, Jack Otter, Joey Saganash, Victor Gilpin, Matthew Loon, Johnny Neeposh, Bella Petawabano, Wally Rabbitskin, Jason Coonishish, Ena Weapenicappo, poet John Bosum, Nancy Voyageur, Louise Iserhoff-Blacksmith, Annie Bosum, Darlene Shecapio-Blacksmith, Tom Chakapash, to name a few. Joshua Loon, Irene Chu, and Weena Bosum helped me through so many quandaries, always knowing who to call, always willing to help out, never failing to make me feel welcome. Christopher Merriman and George Blacksmith taught me history and Marcela Henriquez taught me art. They teach me still but from the other side.

Thanks to Solomon and Nicole Awashish who, in the early stages, introduced me to storytellers and helped get this ball rolling, and to Bella Moses Petawabano who supported this project in both personal and official capacities; to Manikarnika Kanjilal with whom I talked through countless technical and emotional aspects of this work (and who helped with the Harriet pic), and to Christine Wiesenthal and Daphne in whose companionship I processed many Northern trips.

Above all, I'm grateful to Paul Linton and Lucy Trapper who supervised me during this project – which means that they removed obstacles and smoothed bumps, with kindness and wisdom, often under great duress, for years and years; and to David DyckFehderau (known as "DuckFeathers" in Eeyou Istchee) who volunteered hundreds of hours, who affected every part of this project from finding and contacting people to final design, who listened to this entire book being read aloud to him TWICE, who did the enormously difficult work of keeping me (relatively) sane. This project could never have happened without you.

In a project this long, I have surely forgotten someone. Whoever you are, please know that I'm grateful.

This is Ruth DyckFehderau's second collaboration with James Bay Cree storytellers and with Cree Board of Health and Social Services of James Bay. The first, *The Sweet Bloods of Eeyou Istchee: Stories of Diabetes and the James Bay Cree* (2017), won an International Book Award (2018), a Foreword INDIES award (2017), and an IPPY award (2018). *Sweet Bloods* is now in *Second Edition* (2020) and is being translated into Northern East Cree, Southern East Cree, Ojibwe, and French. In 2023, Ruth's novel *I (Athena)* was published by NeWest Press. She lives in Edmonton with her partner, sometimes teaches English Literature and Creative Writing at University of Alberta, and spends several months each year in Eeyou Istchee. She is hearing-impaired.

www.sweetbloods.org
www.resschoolrecovery.org
www.ruthdyckfehderau.com